DAILY LIFE IN
THE UNITED STATES, 1920–1939

The Greenwood Press "Daily Life Through History" Series

The Ancient Egyptians
  Bob Brier and Hoyt Hobbs

The Ancient Greeks
  Robert Garland

Ancient Mesopotamia
  Karen Rhea Nemet-Nejat

The Ancient Romans
  David Matz

The Aztecs: People of the Sun and
Earth
  Davíd Carrasco with Scott Sessions

Chaucer's England
  Jeffrey L. Singman and Will McLean

Civil War America
  *Dorothy Denneen Volo and
  James M. Volo*

Colonial New England
  Claudia Durst Johnson

18th-Century England
  Kirstin Olsen

Elizabethan England
  Jeffrey L. Singman

The Holocaust
  *Eve Nussbaum Soumerai and
  Carol D. Schulz*

The Inca Empire
  Michael A. Malpass

The Italian Renaissance
  *Elizabeth S. Cohen and
  Thomas V. Cohen*

Maya Civilization
  Robert J. Sharer

Medieval Europe
  Jeffrey L. Singman

The Nineteenth Century American
Frontier
  Mary Ellen Jones

The United States, 1940–1959: Shifting
Worlds
  Eugenia Kaledin

The United States, 1960–1990: Decades
of Discord
  Myron A. Marty

Victorian England
  Sally Mitchell

DAILY LIFE IN

THE UNITED STATES, 1920–1939

DECADES OF PROMISE AND PAIN

DAVID E. KYVIG

The Greenwood Press "Daily Life Through History" Series

GREENWOOD PRESS
Westport, Connecticut • London

Library of Congress Cataloging-in-Publication Data

Kyvig, David E.
    Daily life in the United States, 1920–1939 : decades of promise and pain / by
David E. Kyvig.
        p. cm.—(The Greenwood Press "Daily life through history" series,
ISSN 1080–4749)
    Includes bibliographical references and index.
    ISBN 0–313–29555–7 (alk. paper)
    1. United States—Social life and customs—1918–1945. 2. United States—Social
conditions—1918–1932. 3. United States—Social conditions—1933–1945. 4. Nineteen
twenties. 5. Nineteen thirties. I. Title. II. Series.
E169.K985   2002
973.91—dc21   2001023857

British Library Cataloguing in Publication Data is available.

Library of Congress Catalog Card Number: 2001023857
ISBN: 0–313–29555–7
ISSN: 1080–4749

First published in 2002

Greenwood Press, 88 Post Road West, Westport, CT 06881
An imprint of Greenwood Publishing Group, Inc.
www.greenwood.com

Printed in the United States of America

The paper used in this book complies with the
Permanent Paper Standard issued by the National
Information Standards Organization (Z39.48–1984).

10 9 8 7 6 5 4 3 2 1

Contents

Preface

Entering the twenty-first century, the people of the United States of America confronted various dilemmas. How should they deal with a diverse and growing population of uneven education, economic resources, and life experience? How should they manage their natural environment in the face of growing urban concentration and an economy organized around mass consumption of goods, many of them not essential and even more replaced before their useful life had been exhausted? How should they deal with a society accustomed to the near universal use of private automobiles? To what extent and in what fashion should there be controls on the nation's sexual conduct, access to the media of the day, and the personal use of "controlled substances," the latest euphemism for drugs and alcohol? How should inequities of income, nutrition, gender, race, and ethnicity be handled? How should the impact of new technology be managed, especially as it affects the ideas, tastes, and behavior of the society, in other words the nation's culture? What balances should be struck among individual, community, private business, and federal government responsibility for constructing a satisfactory life for the entire populace?

No easy answers to these pressing contemporary questions are at hand. Coming to terms with such issues requires, at first, an understanding of how such conditions initially arose. What were the circumstances of the American people before and during their emergence? Placing ourselves in the circumstances of those who confronted situations for the first time and who did not know how their choices and behaviors would shape the world today helps put current problems in perspective and perhaps encourages some humility about finding solutions. No better way exists to put ourselves in our predecessors' shoes than to examine carefully the day-to-day and year-to-year life of the mass of people who first confronted these aspects of modern existence.

This book attempts, insofar as is possible in one short volume, to examine what daily life was like for ordinary people in the 1920s and 1930s. It acknowledges that these people were not all alike and that their experiences varied considerably. It recognizes that distinctions in location, occupation, economic circumstance, race, ethnicity, gender, age, religious view, and cultural values differentiated their lives. Above all, its author is sensitive to the fact that in this space it is only possible to scratch the surface of a topic that should be explored in greater depth and detail. This book is offered in the hope that it will inspire some readers to further improve their historical understanding by investigating the topics addressed and others that could have been but were not included.

Historians have often focused their attention on dramatic situations and the leaders of those societies that coped with them. Crises of war and peace, changes of national leadership, momentous shifts in economic circumstances, extraordinary accomplishments, and singular events have naturally attracted the most notice. A bare bones outline of the 1920s and 1930s from such a perspective might appear as follows:

1920	National prohibition of alcoholic beverages begins
	Senate rejects U.S. membership in the League of Nations
	National woman suffrage amendment is ratified
	Republican Warren G. Harding defeats Democrat James A. Cox for president
1921	Washington Conference on international naval disarmament
1922	Sinclair Lewis publishes *Babbitt*
1923	President Harding dies in August; succeeded by Calvin Coolidge
1924	Republican Calvin Coolidge defeats Democrat John W. Davis and Progressive Robert LaFollette for president
1925	Trial of John Thomas Scopes for teaching evolution in Dayton, Tennessee
	F. Scott Fitzgerald publishes *The Great Gatsby*
1927	Great Mississippi River Flood
	Charles Lindbergh first to fly solo across the Atlantic
1928	Republican Herbert Hoover defeats Democrat Alfred E. Smith for president
1929	Stock Market crashes in October
1930	United States enters Great Depression
	Smoot-Hawley Tariff adopted

1931   Japan invades Manchuria

1932   Democrat Franklin D. Roosevelt defeats Republican Herbert Hoover for president

1933   Adolph Hitler is elected chancellor of Germany

Hundred Days Congress enacts Emergency Banking Act, Civilian Conservation Corps, Agricultural Adjustment Act, Tennessee Valley Authority, Home Owners' Refinancing Act, Federal Deposit Insurance Corporation, and National Industrial Recovery Act

Repeal of national prohibition

1934   Securities and Exchange Commission and Federal Communications Commission established

1935   Works Progress Administration, National Labor Relations Act, Social Security Act, and Rural Electrification Act adopted

1936   Democrat Franklin D. Roosevelt defeats Republican Alfred Landon for president

1937   Japan invades China

1938   Fair Labor Standards Act adopted, making common the forty-hour, five-day workweek

1939   German invasion of Poland precipitates World War II in Europe

It is no wonder that in considering this period historians have devoted their principal attention to the turmoil of the Great Depression and steps leading to World War II. Such developments unquestionably had a dramatic impact as well as far-reaching and long-lasting consequences for millions of lives.

While historians usually concentrate on important political, diplomatic, military, and economic developments of a past era, some acknowledge that such an approach presents an incomplete picture. A few find themselves drawn to examine the unusual occurrences, the eccentricities and frivolities, the human failings, and the pain and suffering of any era. The very first history of the 1920s to appear, Frederick Lewis Allen's *Only Yesterday*, published in 1931, did exactly that, forging a picture of the 1920s as a "lost weekend" of irresponsible excess by a cast of distinctive characters that left the Great Depression in its wake. Odd events are, of course, as much aspects of the human experience as are great depressions and world wars but neither individually or in combination do they represent the full story.

A comprehensive history of an era must go beyond the momentous and the distinctive to include the story of the unspectacular and routine everyday lives of ordinary people. Daily life for the mass of people in a society tends to get lost in the focus on rulers, religious and business leaders, generals, and other notable or flamboyant individuals. In order to grasp the full reality of any era, however, an investigator of the past must attempt the difficult task of understanding the routines of daily life for the many. Not only does such an undertaking illuminate the reality of most lives, it clarifies what makes so extraordinary the lives of the few who receive the lion's share of attention.

The decades between the two world wars of the first half of the twentieth century were both an important period for an evolving American nation and a time in which it was easy for historians to lose sight of the routines of life for the majority of people. At the outset, Frederick Lewis Allen and other historians of the era were drawn to focus on a relative handful of "jazz babies," stock market plungers, religious zealots, cultural celebrities, fallible politicians, and notorious bootleggers to create an image of "the Roaring Twenties." With the economic collapse that immediately followed, historians found it equally easy to construct a picture of unrelieved desperation during the Great Depression. Both portraits were, of course, too simple and one-sided, but historical myths, once created, are hard to dispel.

Serious historians, those not content to retell old stories but committed instead to digging deeper into the many surviving records of the 1920s and 1930s, have been gradually constructing a more well-rounded picture of the interwar years. For those who would like to pursue such questions a rich literature awaits, some of which is listed as For Further Reading at the end of this book. But these suggestions only scratch the surface. Fifteen years ago a group of graduate students and I compiled *New Day/New Deal: A Bibliography of the Great American Depression, 1929–1941* (1988), a bibliography of nearly 5,000 items that dealt with the second half of this period. Not only has the rich collection of studies of that period continued to grow, it has also been accompanied by a substantial shelf of works on the first decade after World War I. For anyone wishing to pursue an inquiry into the era between the world wars further or in different directions, much interesting reading awaits.

The dramatic developments in the United States during the so-called New Era of the 1920s and the Great Depression of the 1930s, about which so much has been written, occurred in the midst of a society that carried on its affairs day by day and year by year without much notice or comment. Those daily life aspects of the times are the focus of this book. In the pages that follow, the reader will not only discover that significant innovations were taking place in the way ordinary people handled their everyday affairs, but also that change was uneven and sometimes slow to be embraced. Readers need to appreciate differences between the experience of urban and rural life, among various regions of the country, among economic groups, and among races. Above all, the reader needs to recognize the fact that daily life was lived by individuals and that their experiences varied considerably, not always fitting neatly into the common pattern of the group of which they were a part.

An excellent way to understand clearly what common circumstances prevailed for the mass of Americans is to make use of the information gathered by the U.S. Bureau of the Census in the Fourteenth Census of 1920, the Fifteenth Census of 1930, and the Sixteenth Census of 1940. The census data compiled each decade on a wide variety of American characteristics provide a highly reliable picture of what the American people as a whole faced at any one moment as well as a useful index of the extent to which conditions changed from time to time. The alterations in daily life were not merely observable, but also quantifiable to those on the scene. The measures of progress in turn raised tangible prospects of further advancement. Census data may not at first seem as engaging to read as colorful individual stories, but they provide a realistic measure that an isolated example, however vivid, may not fully capture. Readers should be able to use census data to obtain a firm sense of the overall reality of the United States in the 1920s and 1930s. Census statistics will enable readers to perceive a story of change from decade to decade. The information will also allow those who wish to do so to make useful comparisons between a period a full lifetime ago and the contemporary realities of American life.

This book attempts, particularly in its opening and closing chapters, to stress that American daily life was carried out in communities of disparate character. People lived in a variety of circumstances in 1920. All were affected by some national developments, notably the arrival of national prohibition of alcoholic beverages and a federal declaration of women's right to vote, but factors of locality, ethnicity, and economic circumstances helped shape their lives in different ways. The variations in local condition were not erased by the changes of the next twenty years—the impact of automobiles, electricity, radio, and cinema; the evolving character of diet, fashion, health care, consumerism, courtship, family relations, education, religion, and leisure; the consequences of crime and disorder; the standardizing influences of culture; and the consequences of the economic collapse of the early 1930s. At the end of the era, Americans still lived in distinctive communities, six of which are examined in some detail. The appearance of conditions that raised the promise of a better life together with pain that beset people when those conditions were beyond reach generally characterized the United States in the 1920s and 1930s. It is important to remember, however, that the patterns of promise and pain were arranged in many different ways on the vast patchwork quilt of America. Differential experiences emerge as a central theme of this book as well as a source of fascination for anyone who tries to understand what daily life was like in the third and fourth decades of the twentieth century, decades when many of the structures, practices, and problems the nation still confronts began to emerge.

As does every author, I acquired a number of debts in the course of writing this book. I wish here to acknowledge the most substantial of them. It is the support of colleagues, students, friends, and family that makes the intensely individualistic work of writing a book such a rewarding experience. Authorship is in many respects along deferred gratification, but those who provide assistance and commentary along the way assure that not all of the satisfaction must wait until the book appears.

I first wish to acknowledge Barbara Rader and her colleagues Cynthia Harris, Heather Staines, and Emily Birch at Greenwood Press. Barbara tried to recruit me for this project, failed because I was in the midst of another undertaking, came back later when I was at greater liberty, and then waited, more or less patiently, while I produced the manuscript. Previous work with Cynthia and ongoing encouragement from her, Heather, and Emily kept me reasonably on track. I appreciate their faith that this book would eventually emerge.

Two of my finest graduate students at the University of Akron assisted me as they worked on their own Ph.D. dissertations. Howard Robinson provided insights into the life of the urban South, particularly its African American communities during the era of Jim Crow. Greg Stocke served as an able research assistant and provided especially shrewd observations on the nature of American culture. Both have shown me that they are capable of making significant contributions in their chosen fields of specialization.

My faculty colleagues at the University of Akron gave early encouragement to this project as they did to my other endeavors during my years there. My new colleagues at Northern Illinois University expressed interest in this work from the first moment they learned of it. Their support helped carry me over the finish line. The extraordinarily capable staff of media services at Northern Illinois University, colleagues to whom I have turned repeatedly and who have been unfailingly helpful and gracious, were a particular pleasure to work with. Finally, the staffs of the Prints and Photographs Division of the Library of Congress and the Still Pictures Division of the National Archives and Records Administration once again demonstrated why they are the best in the business.

My longtime friend and collaborator Myron "Mike" Marty, the Ann G. and Sigurd E. Anderson University Professor and Professor of History at Drake University, alternated between encouraging me and prodding me to complete this project. Mike is the author of *Daily Life in the United States, 1960–1990: Decades of Discord*. Both the example of his fine work and his reports of the satisfactions he experienced in doing it encouraged me to undertake this book. His example of energetic professionalism on another project on which we were collaborating kept me moving ahead on this manuscript. Finally, his thoughtful reading of the first full draft of the manuscript led to numerous and significant improvements.

Finally, my wife Christine Worobec, professor of history at Northern Illinois University, encouraged me directly and by the superb example of her own innovative, imaginative, and wise scholarship. Her interest in nineteenth-century Russian peasant life may seem far removed from the subject of this book, but she offers constant reminders of fresh ways of looking at the human condition in the past. When she took time from her hectic schedule to give the manuscript a final careful reading, she demonstrated anew that she is a superb manuscript critic who can call attention to matters that others, in particular the author, have overlooked. There is no one to whom I owe more.

Expressing my gratitude to those who have assisted me is not enough. I must also absolve them of responsibility for what follows. I did not always heed their suggestions or follow their advice. I made the final judgments and bear full responsibility for what appears in this book.

Edward Kyvig and Wilma Jessen Kyvig came of age and came together during the decades described in this book. Their lives, happier than many but more difficult than others, were indelibly stamped by their experiences and memories of those years. So, as a result, was mine. I therefore dedicate this book to my parents with love and respect for daily lives well lived.

1

The Circumstances of American Life in 1920

PROHIBITION

In 1920 residents of the United States found themselves surrounded by easily observable signs that they were entering a new era in their everyday lives. Less than three weeks into the new year, a constitutional amendment took effect that prohibited the manufacture, transportation, and sale of alcoholic beverages. Temperance enthusiasts staged mock funerals for "King Alcohol" while opponents offered a few sad eulogies for "John Barleycorn." The days when alcohol remained a normal, or at least legal, part of most American diets ended on January 16, presumably forever.

The Eighteenth Amendment brought the federal government into people's daily lives in a fashion never before experienced in peacetime. Significantly, national prohibition made it a crime to sell, but not to purchase or use alcoholic beverages, leaving many people with conflicted feelings about personal decisions on whether or not to drink. The resentment of many Americans toward national prohibition and the unhappiness of as many others with its ineffective enforcement would provoke debate about the dry law all across the country in the years to come. By decade's end, prohibition violators accounted for over one-third of the 12,000 inmates of federal prisons while a glut of prohibition cases overloaded the courts. Despite the turmoil over prohibition in practice, the new law seemed to be an unavoidable permanent reality of daily life in America. As one proud sponsor boasted, "There is as much chance

Women gathered to watch the governor of Kentucky sign documents certifying the state's ratification of the Nineteenth Amendment. Photo courtesy of the Library of Congress.

of repealing the Eighteenth Amendment as there is for a hummingbird to fly to the planet Mars with the Washington Monument tied to its tail!"[1]

WOMAN SUFFRAGE

A second profound transformation of American life by means of a constitutional amendment occurred only seven months after national prohibition took effect. On August 18, 1920, a tumultuous special session of the Tennessee legislature completed ratification of an amendment guaranteeing women the right to vote. While in recent years a number of states had granted suffrage to women, that fact scarcely reduced the Nineteenth Amendment's importance. The amendment not only gave the country's 30 million voting-age women a new political status, but also it conferred the opportunity to claim enhanced social standing and greater independence upon every female in the land.

MATERNAL HEALTH CARE

Eager to respond to women's new voting power, Congress moved quickly to improve conditions in the risky, fearsome, and uniquely female activity of child bearing. An appalling 250,000 infant deaths occurred in the United States each year. In the poorest families, one child in six died within a year of birth; while the rate stood at one in sixteen for wealthier families, it remained well above the rate in countries with maternal health care programs. The Sheppard-Towner Maternity- and Infancy-Protection Act of 1921 established the first modest federal health care program through small grants to states for maternity education. Social and political conservatives complained, however, that the Sheppard-Towner Act invaded family and state responsibilities. As Congress came to realize that women's votes would divide much as did men's, its enthusiasm for maternal health benefits faded, and it terminated the Sheppard-Towner Act in 1929. Yet despite its brief existence, this progressive reform underscored the potential of legal change and federal government action to influence daily life. Thanks no doubt to increased prosperity, improved diet, and the new widespread availability of pasteurized milk together with the Sheppard-Towner innovations, the U.S. infant death rate fell 17 percent during the 1920s.

FEDERAL GOVERNMENT INFLUENCE

These two reforms in the basic terms of U.S. government had both been long sought by politically active women and their many male allies who had, after all, cast the votes to establish prohibition and enfranchise women. No other government actions during the 1920s would have nearly as much immediate impact on the daily lives of ordinary citizens. However, in an era when the federal government generally remained distant from people's affairs, the effect of the two amendments would be felt by all. National prohibition and woman suffrage would alter both men's and women's views of the capacity of their national government to reorder their lives. As long as those lives appeared to be improving, as was generally the case throughout the 1920s, most Americans remained reluctant to encourage the government to intrude further. When the conditions of daily life changed dramatically in the 1930s, however, sharply revised thinking about government would follow. The circumstances of American daily life were both effect and cause of shifts in national policy through these two decades of prosperity and pain.

THE LEGACY OF WORLD WAR I

The establishment of national prohibition and woman suffrage at the very outset of the 1920s created a strong sense **Wartime** that the new decade marked a fresh beginning for American **Upheavals** society. The realization that an important episode in the nation's life had come to an end further enhanced that impression. World War I with its engagement of the entire society in support of an overseas military operation had concluded a little over a year earlier. The struggles at home to equip and feed the American Expeditionary Force, as the army sent to Europe was named, proved to be as absorbing and vital as the contest on the battlefield. Between 1914 and 1918, steel production doubled, farm exports tripled, and overall capital investment increased 25 percent. The flood of American equipment and munitions stiffened the allies and undermined the enemy's confidence. At the war's end, America stood poised to produce more than ever before.

Return to "Normalcy" Dismantling the war machine as rapidly as possible had been seen as necessary to bring an end to wartime's unprecedented government expenditures. Nearly half of the $6 billion in outstanding government contracts were abruptly canceled, costing many workers their jobs. Two million troops were quickly brought back from Europe and, together with many who had not gotten abroad, were mustered out of service to join the ranks of those seeking work. By the end of 1919, an army that once numbered four million was reduced to 130,000. In March 1920, the Senate's final rejection of U.S. membership in the new League of Nations, the international organization brought to life by President Woodrow Wilson at the Paris Peace Conference, seemed to lead people to believe that they were free of the prospect that their lives would again be disrupted by military service or civilian war work.

The new president elected in November 1920, Republican Warren Harding, promised a return to "normalcy," by which he seemed to mean that the federal government would reduce the domestic and international activities in which it had engaged during the war and not seek again to extend its influence abroad or at home. A government limited in scope and, except for mail delivery and prohibition enforcement, distant from the personal affairs of most citizens, would remain the pattern for the next decade. Almost nothing changed in the direction of government or the lives of ordinary people when Harding died in August 1923 and was replaced by Calvin Coolidge, or when Coolidge in turn retired after the 1928 election to be succeeded by yet another Republican, Herbert Hoover.

"Red Scare" American society in 1920 appeared on the verge of moving beyond the anxieties that had gripped the immediate postwar period. An unprecedented wave of labor strikes for higher wages in 1919, most notably a general strike of Seattle workers, nationwide strikes by steelworkers and coal miners, and a strike by the Boston police force, had produced widespread alarm. The American business community had generally resisted unionism until wartime circumstances induced a grudging acceptance. The conclusion of the war and a much expanded pool of potential workers terminated the temporary labor peace. A series of unexplained bombings in 1919 raised the question: might labor unrest signal the beginning of a Bolshevik uprising akin to Russia's two years earlier?

At first the reaction of mainstream America to perceived radicalism was extremely harsh. On the first anniversary of the November 1918 armistice, members of the American Legion, a newly formed World War I veterans organization, paraded past the Industrial Workers of the World (IWW) headquarters in Centralia, Washington. The confrontation led to gunfire, the death of four Legionnaires, and the subsequent castration and lynching of an IWW member by an angry mob. The Centralia "massacre" stirred second thoughts about the hysteria sweeping the country. By the end of 1919, the widespread failure of union-led strikes began to ease upper- and middle-class fears. Still, the momentum of the "Red Scare" led to the arrest and deportations of nearly a thousand alien radicals as well as the ejection of five duly elected Socialists from the New York state assembly and a Milwaukee Congressman from the U.S. House of Representatives. After the failure of predicted Bolshevik-style uprisings to materialize on May Day 1920, public anxiety about radical threats to the society appeared to evaporate rapidly.

Internal migration of large numbers of people during the war contributed to social tension. The northward **Social Tensions** migration of 500,000 southern African Americans to wartime jobs led to competition with working-class whites for scarce housing. Conflict increased once the number of jobs began to shrink. African Americans, their will strengthened by military and work experience, sought to hold on rather than step aside as white resentment rose. Racial riots broke out in Chicago in June 1919, in Washington, D.C., in July, and in a score of smaller cities as well. At least 120 people died, mainly in attacks by groups of young whites on blacks. The Chicago riot alone cost thirty-eight lives and hundreds of injuries. Meanwhile in the South, seventy-eight lynchings took place in 1919, thirty more than the year before, amid efforts to enforce "Jim Crow," the common term for law codes requiring rigid segregation and subordination of African Americans in schools, transportation, other public facilities as well as in social interaction with whites.

Concern about challenges to traditional social arrangements from labor unions, radicals, immigrants, and African Americans encouraged the founding and growth of various so-called nativist organizations. Among them were the American Legion and a fraternal society named after the Ku Klux Klan of the post–Civil War South. The revived Klan did not confine itself to the territory of the Confederacy or efforts to repress African Americans, but spread nationwide and sought also to restrict Jewish and Catholic immigrants and other perceived threats to the existing order. Notably, much of the membership of this new Klan was concentrated in areas with few African Americans, Jews, Catholics, or immigrants. In addition to the efforts of private groups to monitor what they regarded as dangerous elements of society, the Federal Bureau of Investigation, a federal agency whose rise had been stimulated by the 1919 Red Scare, began surveillance of groups thought to be "un-American." Daily life for nativists, rigid defenders of the power of long-present groups and traditional culture, became preoccupied by a sense of threat to their security and the need to keep close watch over immigrants, African Americans, Jews, young people who adopted unconventional dress and social practices, and even businessmen who adopted new practices that upset customary commercial arrangements. For those already on the fringes of American society, life became more precarious.

A sense of uncertainty lingered, at least in parts of society, because by 1920 the American economy had fallen into the depths of a postwar collapse. The demands of wartime had caused employment, capital investment, production, and prices to soar. When the war ended and the federal government immediately cut back its spending, overall economic activity went into a tailspin. Industrial and agricultural profits collapsed. Both military and civilian employment fell sharply, one reason that the strikes of 1919 so often failed and anxiety about immigration rose. During 1920 over 5 million workers were unemployed in a workforce of approximately 40 million. The most hopeful signs that economic recovery was not far ahead were declining prices and an apparently insatiable consumer appetite for automobiles.

THE AMERICAN PEOPLE IN 1920

Before the end of 1920 events large and small began signaling a new era just ahead in the nation's everyday culture. The first commercial radio broadcast opened a new age of home access to information and entertainment. The publication of Sinclair Lewis's *Main Street* ushered in a great era of literary creativity, one in which Lewis's disparagement of traditional American culture would be a recurring theme. More widely noticed at the moment, especially in the nation's largest city, was the New York Yankees baseball team's acquisition from the Boston Red Sox of George Herman "Babe" Ruth. Even Yankee fans could scarcely imagine what an impact Ruth would have on his new team, the game of baseball, or professional sports, indeed city life in general. Each of these developments loomed large among the many hints that the 1920s would become a decade in which Americans firmly embraced a new manner of living.

The 1920s would not, of course, represent a complete break with the manner in which people had lived their lives in the past. In most respects the new decade would witness the continuation of well-established patterns and developments long underway. Changes in the nature of everyday existence would take place bit by bit, often in ways that did not immediately attract much attention. Only long after the fact would significant alterations in people's overall normal circumstances become apparent. Furthermore, changes in the character of daily life would occur at different rates for Americans in various locations and situations. Many Americans would adopt new ideas, practices, technologies, and fashions reluctantly and selectively, if at all. Yet an awareness that shifts were taking place in the circumstances of everyday life would permeate society, influencing the outlook and behavior of those who resisted change as well as those who eagerly embraced it.

Attitudes toward alterations in the patterns of daily life, especially obvious and sharp changes such as national prohibition and woman suffrage, depended on the vantage point from which they were viewed. Rural America reacted differently than its urban counterpart. Prosperous citizens responded in a fashion unlike impoverished ones. Occupational, ethnic, religious, and regional distinctions also produced varying reactions, as did age and gender differences. In order to appreciate how inhabitants of the United States responded to the changes and continuities in their lives during this era, it is essential to understand something about who they were and how they were situated in 1920.

In January 1920 the federal government conducted a census, as required by the Constitution every ten years. **1920 Census** The Census Bureau found 106.5 million people living in the United States. By twenty-first-century standards, the population was small and strikingly young. Children under the age of fifteen accounted for 31.6 percent of the population and fifteen to twenty-four year olds another 19.6 percent. Not only was the median age just twenty-five, but two-thirds of the population was thirty-five or younger. Older Americans were relatively rare. Average life expectancy was just over fifty-six years for men, fifty-eight for women. Only 7.4 percent of the population was sixty or over, and a mere 4.6 percent had passed sixty-five. By way of comparison, the 2000 census found 281.4 million Americans and showed only 21.4 percent under fifteen, a median age of 35.3 years. Life expectancy had passed 77 years for males and 77 years for females, and 12.4 percent were over sixty-five.[2]

The American population in 1920 was also overwhelmingly white and native born. No less than 89.7 percent of the population was identified as white; that number included an undetermined but apparently small number of Hispanics of varied ancestry. The 1920 census identified 9.9 percent of Americans as black (African American), 0.23 percent as Native American, and 0.17 percent as Asian. Again, to compare, the 2000 census registered 75.1 percent of the population as white, 12.3 percent black, 0.9 percent Native American, and 3.6 percent Asian. Persons of Hispanic origin, within the white cohort but now identified, made up 12.5

percent of the population. Over the course of seventy years, the proportion of Americans who were white declined, while the black, Native American, Asian, and Hispanic populations grew well beyond 1920 levels.

Among those listed in the 1920 census as white, 18.4 percent of males and 15.4 of females were foreign born, while another 27.5 percent of males and 28.4 of females had one or more foreign-born parents. Thus almost 45 percent of the white population had either come to the United States themselves or were the children of immigrants. These figures compare with a 2000 population in which only 10.4 percent was foreign born. With immigration restriction about to take effect, never again would a foreign presence in an American census be as strong as it was in 1920. Nevertheless, in that year more than 83 percent of the white population and almost all nonwhite residents had been born and raised in the United States.

Family Households In 1920 most, but hardly all, Americans were members of family households. Just over 60 percent of people over the age of fifteen lived as married couples, while 36.9 percent of males and 29.4 percent of women remained unmarried. While most people preferred marriage, a significant portion failed to marry for one reason or another, a pattern shared by the societies of the United States and western Europe. In addition, 6 percent of men and 14.6 percent of women were widowed. Less than 1 percent listed their status as divorced. By 2000, married couples accounted for a smaller 51.7 percent of the total number of households. The proportion of widowers and widows had fallen as well. The most notable difference was that the percentage of people divorced and not remarried or living together without being married had risen substantially.

Income was distributed very unevenly among American households in 1920. A small elite fared very well and a significant middle class lived comfortably. Most Americans, however, lacked sufficient household income to live more than a modest and insecure existence. Between a third and two-fifths of the entire American population could be classified as poor even by the modest standards of the time. Rural incomes fell well below their urban counterparts, and southern incomes lagged behind those in the north. Good reason existed for considering wealthy Americans a privileged class.

Urban Population Increasing Census takers in 1920 confirmed a widespread perception that Americans were becoming increasingly concentrated in cities and were living under conditions very different from those in the traditional, agriculture-based, rural areas and small towns of an earlier era. For the first time in American history more than half of the population, over 54 million individuals according to the census, lived in places described as urban. The perception of a nation that had moved to the big city may have been exaggerated, however. Since the Census Bureau defined an urban place as any incorporated community of 2,500 or more residents, hardly all so-called urban dwellers found themselves in vast cities. In fact less than a third of their number, just under 16.5 million, congregated in the nation's three cities of more than a million and in nine others over 500,000. Almost 11 million found themselves in fifty-six cities of 100,000 to 500,000 each; over 17 million lived in 684 communities of 10,000 to 100,000; and 9 million resided in 1,970 towns of 2,500 to 10,000. Another 9 million lived in 12,855 villages of fewer than 2,500 each, while 42.5 million still lived outside any incorporated community.

The proportion of Americans living close to others had unquestionably swelled significantly in recent years. At the turn of the century only 40 percent of the population dwelt in urban areas. Fifty years earlier in 1850, a mere 15 percent of Americans lived in urban places. By 1920 the United States had barely reached the point where it could be termed a predominantly urban nation. The label would increasingly suit the country as the twentieth century wore on. By the 1980s over three out of four Americans could be found in urban areas.

In 1920, as earlier, the United States remained most densely settled in its northeast quadrant. Almost exactly half of the nation's 106 million people lived north of the Potomac and Ohio Rivers and east of the Mississippi, a region with an average population density of 141 people per square mile. In comparison, the states of the former Confederacy contained 27 million persons, a quarter of the nation's total, but dispersed at a density of less than 38 per square mile. The states of Missouri, California, and Texas contained the largest populations outside the northeast quadrant, but they had only 49, 22, and 18 people per square mile respectively, a stark contrast to the most urban northeastern states, Rhode Island, Massachusetts, and New Jersey, with 576, 492, and 419 residents per square mile; or even industrialized states with large expanses of farmland such as New York, Pennsylvania, Ohio, and Illinois with 217, 194, 141, and 116 people per square mile. The states of the mountain west and the northern Great Plains remained the most lightly settled. The Dakotas had a per square mile population density of less than 9, Idaho and Utah only 5, Montana 4, Wyoming 2, and Nevada less than 1.

Few Americans by 1920 lived as isolated an existence as had once characterized a large portion of the country's population. Increasingly convenient transportation and communication helped tie people together. It is as members of communities, varied types of communities to be sure, that Americans of 1920 can perhaps best be understood. The communities in which they lived or with which they associated determined the routines of daily life, set the standards of acceptable conduct, provided the restraints and assurances that bound people together, and in many respects shaped individual identity.

AMERICA'S VARIED COMMUNITIES

Those who lived in the most loosely connected communities were those who stayed closest to the land and engaged in the traditional economies of farming and ranching. They also appeared furthest removed from innovations affecting the larger society and most apprehensive about changes taking place in urban America. Nevertheless, many farmers and ranchers were alert to opportunities to ease their burdens and escape their isolation. In the 1920s they would be particularly attracted to new technologies and frustrated by their economic circumstances.

Rural Slump   Rural agricultural America in 1920 could look back on its era of greatest prosperity. During the 1910s and especially during World War I, urban growth, military needs, and food shortages in a Europe at war caused the market for agricultural products to boom. Farmers put more land into cultivation, bought more machinery, and borrowed money to do so. Once the war ended, however, the market for their crops and livestock began to shrink, land values started to decline, and the burden of debt weighed heavily upon them. The last year of any agricultural prosperity was 1920; thereafter farm income and land values would slide into a twenty-year depression and not emerge from that slump until World War II. Even in the relatively good year of 1920, over a half million of the nation's 6.5 million farms were sold, and others struggled to cope. Midwestern farm bankruptcies would quadruple in 1922 and double again in 1923.

The South   The postwar agricultural decline registered the slightest impact on the South, but only because its farmers were already the least prosperous in the country. The Civil War had devastated the South whose previous prosperity, comparable to the rest of the country, rested on forced labor. The defeated region's economy had not recovered, largely due to its inability to deal effectively with the end of slavery. By 1880 the South's per capita income had fallen to half the national average. Failure to participate in industrialization kept the region in that position during the next half century. A significant part of what C. Vann Woodward labeled *The Burden of Southern History* was the South's inability to afford "the good things that money buys, such as education, health, protection, and the many luxuries that go to make up the celebrated American Standard of Living."[3]

The disparity between agricultural patterns in the South and the rest of the country can be easily measured. Half of the nation's farms were located in the South. Two-thirds of the 2.5 million tenant farms, however,

Tenant farmer's cabin, Harmony, Georgia. Photo courtesy of the National Archives.

were in the South. Put another way, three out of four farmers outside the South owned land while in the South only half did so; the others were tenants renting the land they worked and facing the greatest economic obstacles to prospering from their efforts. In 1920, 56 percent of southern tenant farmers were white. At the least profitable end of the scale, however, where tenant farmers without financial resources had to pledge a share of the crop they expected to harvest for land rent and supplies, 59 percent were black. The value of the land and buildings of all American farms averaged $10,284, but on a sharecropper's farm the average was $2,633. While U.S. farms on the whole averaged 148 acres, tenant farms averaged only 108 acres and thus had a correspondingly reduced profit potential. Share-cropped farms were even worse off: they averaged only forty acres and were dismally poor. Outside the South, less than one percent (0.8 percent) of farmers were nonwhite, but in the South the proportion reached 29 percent. Nationally, about 64 percent of white farmers farmed their own land, while 75 percent of nonwhites were tenants. By every measure, southern agriculture, and particularly black southern agriculture, was exceptionally bleak.

Frustration or resignation at their own situation together
Farm Life with a sense of being left behind in a changing culture
Abandoned seized many rural dwellers, not only southerners, after
1920. Some viewed the different course that life seemed to
be taking for urban dwellers with envy, others with disgust; but few
remained unaware of what was happening. Overall growth of the rural
as well as urban population during the 1920s concealed the abandonment of farm life by many families. Nevertheless, farm households as a
percentage of the nation's total fell from 28 to 22 percent over the course
of the decade.

Residents of small town America remained close to
Small Town Life the countryside. Tied to the countryside as merchants,
mechanics, bankers, doctors, priests, and service pro-
viders for the agricultural producers, many shared their rural neighbors'
circumstances and views. Sinclair Lewis had grown up in such a small
town, Sauk Centre, Minnesota. It became the model for Gopher Prairie
in his novel *Main Street*, a fictionalized but quite realistic account of post–
World War I American life. The newcomer in town, doctor's wife Carol
Kennicott, found the residents friendly, generous, and willing to help
each other in times of trouble. At the same time, they were alert to all
their neighbors' activities, rigidly and narrowly traditional in their views
of acceptable social conduct, courtship, and female behavior, and quite
conservative in their ideas about innovation, authority, fashion, religion,
and education. Lewis alternated between sympathy and scorn for Gopher Prairie, finally conceding that if someone wanted to live comfortably in such a small town, they would be obliged to accept the social
code from which it was difficult to deviate unobserved and unpenalized.

The more than 17 million people who lived in hun-
Small and dreds of modest-sized cities of 10,000 to 100,000 found
Middle City Life themselves for the most part further removed from
rural life and more caught up in the social, cultural,
and technological changes that characterized the 1920s. Much the same
could be said of the 11 million residents of middle-sized cities of 100,000
to 500,000. In the early 1920s, when two social anthropologists from Columbia University wanted to study a typical contemporary American
community, one at the very center of the society they believed was taking
shape in the United States, they picked the middle-sized midwestern city
of Muncie, Indiana, population 35,000. Robert and Helen Lynd's book
about Muncie, which they called *Middletown*, provided as full and rich
a picture of American daily life in the 1920s as any created during the
era. The Lynds emphasized that Middletown was rapidly leaving behind
its nineteenth-century function as a commercial center for the surrounding countryside to become an industrial city. Manufacturing not only

increasingly defined the city's economy, it also divided the population into two classes: laborers and managers, each with a different daily pattern and style of life. Unlike the fictional small town of Gopher Prairie, Middletown was large enough for people to exercise some social independence, though on the whole they stayed within the bounds of either working-class or middle-class norms.[4]

Big cities represented the most notable departure from the patterns of an earlier day. The growth of large cities   **Big City Life** was a recent development, made possible by the invention of new technologies and stimulated by demand for their production. In the first U.S. census in 1790 only two cities exceeded 20,000; New York was the largest at 33,000. By 1850, New York had reached a half million but no other city exceeded 250,000. A dozen cities had passed the half-million mark by 1920 with New York, Chicago, and Philadelphia each over a million. New York City with 5.6 million residents had a population almost one and a half times that of the entire nation 130 years earlier.

The vast dimensions of America's great and growing cities rendered the daily lives of individuals within them quite different from rural or small town life. A city's size itself conferred anonymity on its residents. Individuals could decide with whom to associate and how to behave. With all the congestion, tumult, hustle and bustle of the modern metropolis, no community overseers could keep track of, much less reward or punish, people's behavior. City dwellers could hardly avoid noticing new developments on the urban scene; they could then choose for themselves whether or not to embrace them. Personal preference and economic circumstance had much more influence on such decisions than community approval or disapproval. With the pressure of an observant community gone, so too was public awareness and support. The reassurances of a small town in a time of uncertainty or distress, the guidance, comfort, and charity offered individuals in need were at best haphazard and for the most part absent in the anonymous city.

The bulk of recent immigrants to the United States could be found in big cities in 1920. Often immigrants   **Immigration's** did not travel beyond the city of debarkation. Conse-   **Effect on Cities** quently, great arrival ports such as Boston, Philadelphia, and, above all, New York had huge immigrant populations. Smaller nearby cities, such as Fall River, Massachusetts; Providence, Rhode Island; and Newark, Patterson, and Camden, New Jersey, served as convenient alternatives. In other cases, immigrants would travel on to other cities where a cluster of countrymen already resided and there was the promise of employment. Buffalo, Pittsburgh, Cleveland, and Detroit each bulged with recent arrivals, and Chicago alone had three quarters of a million foreign-born residents. With high concentrations of foreign-language speaking immigrant residents, American cities sounded, looked, and in other ways seemed very different from smaller communities with largely English speaking, native-born populations.

Various immigrant nationalities tended to gather in their own distinct neighborhoods within big cities. In the Italian North End of Boston or South Side of Philadelphia, Portuguese neighborhoods in Fall River, Jewish Lower East Side of New York, Slavic and Serbian enclaves of Pittsburgh and Cleveland, Polish section of Chicago, or dozens of similar ethnic clusters across the urban landscape, new arrivals could find familiar languages, foods, social rituals, churches, and other comforts. No wonder they inclined to settle in such communities and retain as much of the culture of their homeland as possible, rather than integrate themselves into the unfamiliar customs of the new land. No wonder either that they seemed strange and exotic, if not frightening, to old-stock Americans residing in, visiting, or hearing about the cities.

Minority Communities

Even more set apart and isolated were minority communities. Despite the migration of a half-million African Americans to northern cities during World War I, 85 percent of the African American minority still lived in the former slave states of the old South. There they found themselves extraordinarily isolated. Their meager economic circumstances alone did not set them apart from the many poor white farmers. However, their political disenfranchisement and their legal segregation through so-called Jim Crow laws cast them into a situation of abject and thoroughgoing powerlessness. Jim Crow virtually excluded African Americans from voting and required them to use separate, usually inferior schools, rest rooms, drinking fountains, transportation facilities, and even Bibles when swearing oaths in court. No wonder that even the most disadvantaged whites looked down upon African Americans trapped in such a situation and regarded them as innately inferior. Likewise, no wonder that the distinctive abilities and qualities of individual African Americans were overlooked. Those African Americans who had escaped to the North during World War I enjoyed somewhat better economic circumstances, but there again they found themselves segregated socially in residential ghettos and disparaged for living in circumstances they could scarcely avoid.

Smaller minority populations were found elsewhere in the country. Hispanics lived primarily in the Southwest and Asians on the west coast. These groups found themselves in similar situations to that of African Americans: socially isolated, politically powerless, and economically disadvantaged. In the Rocky Mountain West, a religious minority, members of the Church of Jesus Christ of Latter-day Saints, or Mormons, were just as isolated, though generally more prosperous and in control of local government and schools.

COMMUNITY RESPONSE TO CONSTITUTIONAL CHANGE

While every individual experienced the 1920s in his or her own way, those in similar circumstances shared much in common. The same held true for communities, with each different type of community within American society, whether rural, small town, big city, old-stock, new immigrant, or racial minority, encountering a distinctive reality. The peculiar nature of a community shaped its views of the rest of society. This was particularly evident in the manner each dealt with such innovations as national prohibition and woman suffrage. Each community responded in its own fashion, demonstrating that approaches to matters of daily life varied considerably.

Rural America viewed alcohol as primarily a problem of urban life where drinking took place in saloons. There, ru- **Prohibition** ral dwellers believed, saloon keepers encouraged drinking **Compliance** to excess, workers spent wages that should have been going to support their families, political machines influenced voters, prostitutes and gamblers plied their trades, and immigrants gathered to discuss the homeland, speak their native languages, and carry on old customs that slowed their progress toward becoming good Americans. These negative images help explain why the largest, most influential prohibitionist organization called itself the Anti-Saloon League of America.

The Volstead Act encouraged rural dwellers to view their own continued drinking as legal and harmless. The law prohibited manufactured beverages containing more than .5 percent alcohol, a standard that outlawed not only distilled spirits but even low-powered beer, the staples of working-class saloons. At the same time, the Volstead Act outlawed naturally fermented cider and wine only if proven intoxicating, which was in fact a much higher standard and one rarely if ever policed. Indeed, California grape juice or concentrate was shipped legally with U.S. Department of Agriculture labels indicating that, if allowed to sit and ferment for sixty days, it would become wine of 12 percent alcohol content. As a result, the California wine grape industry grew by 400 percent during the 1920s, reinforcing the rural view that the government did not consider homemade fruit-based beverages to violate prohibition.

Inhabitants of villages, towns, and smaller cities across the country generally observed alcoholic beverage prohibition, though, as elsewhere, there were exceptions, especially as the decade wore on. These middle-sized communities contained the bulk of Women's Christian Temperance Union and Anti-Saloon League members. Also concentrated there were many of the one-third to two-fifths of American adults who had not used alcohol before prohibition and a substantial number of those who gave up drinking when liquor became illegal. A nationwide survey by social workers in 1926 reported that, outside of a few large metropolitan areas, prohibition was largely effective. In Lima, Ohio; Sioux Falls, South Dakota; Boise, Idaho; and Tacoma, Washington, little evidence of drinking was to be seen. Community opinion, the subtle social pressure in places where individual behavior was easy to observe, appeared to be a stronger influence in achieving this result than police enforcement of the law.

Prohibition Ambivalence In somewhat larger cities prohibition violation reportedly occurred more frequently, although the law met with general compliance. In Middletown, the Lynds noted, the example and influence of a core of industrial and civic leaders discouraged drinking by the business class, while the closing of legal saloons reduced it among the working class. Sinclair Lewis, whose *Main Street* (1920) appeared too early in the decade to address prohibition, subsequently turned his attention from Gopher Prairie to the fictional middle-sized midwestern city of Zenith, the setting for both *Babbitt* (1922) and *Elmer Gantry* (1927). In Zenith, respectable middle-class people occasionally drank. Businessman George Babbitt regarded prohibition as good for the working class but surreptitiously bought gin from a bootlegger in the poorer section of town in order to fix cocktails for his dinner guests. Lewis showed some sympathy for Babbitt's mixed feelings and his awkward, infrequent transgression of the dry law, but none whatsoever for Protestant evangelist Gantry, an active prohibitionist characterized as a complete moral hypocrite.

Prohibition Defiance Prohibition violation occurred most frequently in large cities from San Francisco to New Orleans to New York. In big cities, the native-born middle classes tended to drink less than either the wealthy or the working class. Among the reasons for this pattern was the high cost of alcoholic beverages during prohibition. Whiskey or beer could be, and often was, obtained legally with a physician's prescription declaring it necessary for medicinal purposes, but that required a visit to the doctor as well as the pharmacy where it was sold. The alternatives were to buy illegally manufactured or smuggled liquor or make your own. At $.80 for a quart of beer (up 600 percent since 1916) or $5.90 for a quart of gin (up 520 percent) by 1928, the cost of domestically produced beverages was more than the average family income of $2,600 per year could frequently absorb. Imported liquor, such as Canadian or Scotch whiskey or French wine, was better quality but much more expensive. Those who were wealthy or could produce their own liquor were best able to afford it. Thus, not surprisingly, drinking was most common among the upper classes and immigrant groups.

Immigrant communities did not generally consider drinking a crime regardless of what U.S. law declared. Most came from cultures that took alcoholic beverages for granted as a normal part of everyday life. Home brewing and wine making were common traditions. Distilling any form of sugar into neutral spirits and then adding flavoring agents required less skill and soon spread in popularity. Hardware stores did a brisk business legally selling small inexpensive home stills. The most common and simple practice was to fill a bottle half full with neutral spirits, add a few drops of glycerin and juniper berry juice, and top up with water. Since the preferred style of bottle was too tall to fill under a sink tap, the process was usually carried out in a bathtub, hence the term "bathtub gin."

Those who made alcoholic beverages at home found it difficult to accept that what was allowable for personal use became illegal when collected and sold. State and local officials and the small force of federal prohibition agents found it impossible with the available resources to police small-scale but widespread alcoholic beverage production. Instead they concentrated their attention on commercial bootleggers and outlaw saloons, variously referred to as blind pigs, gin joints, or speakeasies.

Bootlegging, the business of obtaining, transporting, and selling illegal liquor, was a perilous but lucrative business **Bootlegging** in the 1920s since a substantial number of people, especially in big cities, were prepared to ignore the prohibition law. Young, ambitious men, who because of their immigrant background found it difficult to obtain jobs or advancement in legal occupations, saw opportunity, profit, and no disgrace in bootlegging. Italian, Polish, and Jewish men in their twenties dominated bootlegging, often establishing and managing large and complex organizations to carry on the business. Competition among bootleggers was fierce and often violent, not surprising considering that the lucrative trade completely lacked the government regulation or protection enjoyed by legitimate enterprises. While bootleggers fought and sometimes even killed each other, customers remained almost entirely untouched. They received the care and consideration essential in any successful retail business, particularly one dependent on repeat purchasers. As the most successful of the bootleggers, Chicago's Al Capone (the New York–born son of Italian immigrants who was only thirty-two years old when finally sent to prison in 1931 for income tax evasion after a decade in the business) observed, "I'm a public benefactor. . . . You can't cure thirst by law. . . . Some call it bootlegging. Some call it racketeering. I call it a business. They say I violate the prohibition law. Who doesn't?"[5]

While African Americans in urban areas shared the prohibition experience of other city dwellers, the large **Prohibition and** number situated in the rural South confronted different **African** circumstances. White southerners, including those with **Americans** little desire to give up drinking themselves, supported prohibition to take liquor away from African Americans. The social control whites exercised over blacks in all respects, together with the pervasive poverty of the African American community, insured that prohibition effectively reduced access to alcohol for at least this one segment of the population.

Alcohol Consumption

Consumption of alcohol in the United States during the years of national prohibition, 1920 through 1933, remains difficult to determine. Any illegal activity is hard to measure, and prohibition violation was no exception. The evidence is strong, however, that more Americans observed the law than did not and that total alcohol consumption fell by more than 60 percent. Per capita consumption in 1911–1915, the last years before state and federal laws began significantly to affect drinking, amounted to 2.56 gallons of pure alcohol for every American above the age of fifteen, though obviously some drank nothing at all and others drank much more. This was actually consumed as 2.09 gallons of distilled spirits (45 percent alcohol), 0.79 gallons of wine (18 percent alcohol), and 29.53 gallons of beer (5 percent alcohol) per capita. In 1934, the year after prohibition ended, per capita consumption measured 0.97 gallons of alcohol consumed as 0.64 gallons of spirits, 0.36 gallons of wine, and 13.58 gallons of beer, suggesting that drinking alcohol had become a much less widespread practice during prohibition. During the same years, milk and Coca-Cola consumption almost tripled. Although alcoholic beverage consumption increased during the 1930s, three more decades would pass before liquor consumption again reached pre–World War I levels.[6] Clearly national prohibition influenced the drinking patterns of a generation of Americans.

Prohibition Repeal

Despite the actual decline in alcohol consumption, an image of widespread drinking prevailed during the 1920s. The substantial amount that did continue was concentrated in cities where it was most visible. Bootleggers and speakeasies had to advertise, carefully to be sure, in order to attract customers. Bootlegging violence, not to mention police arrests of bootleggers and confiscation of liquor, gained a lot of media attention. Magazines and movies implied that a great deal of drinking was taking place, especially within the upper classes of society. As an overall impression emerged by the early 1930s that prohibition had not worked well, it became increasingly unpopular. Congress modified the Volstead Act in April 1933 to allow the manufacture and sale of weak beer. By December, despite the difficulty of changing the Constitution and the predictions of prohibitionists, the Eighteenth Amendment was repealed and, except in several states that retained state prohibition, Americans resumed legal drinking.

Effects of Woman Suffrage

The Nineteenth Amendment, like the Eighteenth, affected various communities differently. At first women did not exercise their new right to vote in the same proportion to their overall numbers as did men, but this stemmed particularly from low turnout in certain types of communities. Immigrant women, used to leaving political matters to men, rarely cast a ballot until Al Smith, a son of immigrants and opponent of prohibition, gained the Democratic presidential nomination in 1928. Southern black women, still disenfranchised because of race even after the removal of gender restrictions, voted least often of all.

Rural women, tightly bound to traditional domestic roles which demanded that they manage a household, rear children, and assist a husband at planting or harvest time, voted more often but apparently along the same lines as their husbands. Quickest to take advantage in large numbers of the right to vote and exercise independent political judgment were better educated middle-class urban women, especially the increasing number employed outside of the home. But as politicians discovered that the Nineteenth Amendment did not generate a huge new block of female voters who behaved in distinctly different ways from their male counterparts, their interest in women's issues speedily declined. The Sheppard-Towner Act and efforts to restrict child labor gave way by the mid-1920s to general indifference to proposals for legislation affecting women's daily lives. The Nineteenth Amendment may have enhanced women's general image, but it was far from clear that it elevated their individual circumstances.

Circumstance and Identity

Changes in the Constitution and national government touched the lives of ordinary people throughout the United States in a variety of ways. However, the busy and complicated daily lives of most Americans were shaped to a much greater degree by the circumstances of their activities as workers, consumers, students, audiences, and members of social communities. Examining the country in the 1920s in these terms and keeping in mind that a variety of distinctive communities made up the United States, it is possible to best understand the nature of daily life for Americans during that decade.

NOTES

1. Quoted in Charles Merz, *The Dry Decade* (Garden City, N.Y.: Doubleday, Doran, 1931), 297.

2. These statistics as well as others throughout this book, unless otherwise noted, come from U.S. Bureau of the Census, *Historical Statistics of the United States, Colonial Times to 1957* (Washington, D.C.: GPO, 1960).

3. C. Vann Woodward, *The Burden of Southern History* (Baton Rouge: Louisiana State University Press, 1960), 17.

4. Robert S. Lynd and Helen Merrill Lynd, *Middletown: A Study in Modern American Culture* (New York: Harcourt, Brace and World, 1929).

5. Quoted in John Kobler, *Capone: The Life and World of Al Capone* (New York: G. P. Putnam's Sons, 1971), 313–14.

6. These statistics, along with a much fuller discussion of American alcohol use, can be found in Mark Edward Lender and James Kirby Martin, *Drinking in America: A History* (New York: Free Press, 1982), especially 196–97.

2

Automobiles and the Construction of Daily Life

MORE MOTOR VEHICLES HIT THE ROADS

Gasoline-powered, internal combustion engine-propelled vehicles had been around for more than a quarter century by the start of the 1920s, but not until that decade did they become a central factor in the everyday lives of ordinary Americans. Mass production, together with innovations in design, engineering, manufacture, and sales, brought a new or used car, truck, or tractor within the reach of most people. In 1920, barely one household in three possessed a car, though this represented a dramatic increase from one in thirteen at the outset of World War I. Automobile ownership tripled during the 1920s, and by decade's end, four families out of five owned one. By 1929 almost 27 million cars were on the road, in the driveway or parking lot, at the gas station or repair shop, or, increasingly, stuck in traffic. Meanwhile truck and tractor registration tripled as well to 3,550,000 trucks and 840,000 farm tractors. Outside the impoverished South, car, truck, and tractor ownership was fairly widespread and evenly distributed. According to a 1927 survey, 54 percent of families in cities over 100,000 owned a car, while 60 percent did in towns under 1,000; farmers were even more likely to have a car or truck. In less than a decade, motor vehicle ownership had gone from being unusual to being commonplace, and American daily life was thereby transformed.

Used car lot, 1938, Lancaster, Ohio. Photo courtesy of the Library of Congress.

THE AUTOMOBILE INDUSTRY

By the mid-1920s one of eight U.S. workers was somehow involved in the production, sales, service, and fueling of automobiles. The auto business, the biggest American industry, was reshaping the nature of employment and the economy. The automobile significantly changed the way people worked, conducted their business, shopped for necessities and desires, and spent leisure time. The automobile was undoubtedly the most notable of various new technologies that gained popularity in the 1920s. Radios and electrical home appliances such as vacuum cleaners and washing machines were others. The widespread adoption of the automobile and these other devices altered the manner in which people conducted their daily affairs, involved large numbers of people in their manufacture, sales, and maintenance, and established new assumptions about what individuals and families must possess and use in order to carry on a normal and satisfactory life.

THE RISE OF THE AUTOMOBILE

The idea of self-propelled carriages had long fascinated American inventors, not to mention the carriage-using wealthy classes. Given the problems of highly polluting horse-drawn vehicles, especially in congested urban areas, a cleaner-running automobile had great appeal. In 1900 in New York City alone, 15,000 horses dropped dead on the streets, while those that lived deposited 2.5 million pounds of manure and 60,000 gallons of urine on the streets every day. The most obvious alternative transportation systems, above or below ground cable, steam, or electric powered trolleys and trains, required large capital investments and could only be envisioned in densely populated areas.

At the outset, automobiles were not built with the masses in mind. As early as 1895, over 300 individuals and companies were constructing experimental automobiles, mainly one-of-a-kind, large, expensive, motorized buggies for wealthy hobbyists who could afford a chauffeur/mechanic. **Early Automobiles** In 1901, Ransom Olds of Lansing, Michigan, began producing a car for the middle class, but even at a mere 40 percent of the average price of that year's automobiles, the $650 curved-dash Oldsmobile still cost more than an average American worker's annual income. In 1906, another Michigan automaker, Detroit's Henry Ford, began building a reliable four-cylinder, 15-horsepower, middle-class car, the $600 Model N. Ford was deluged with orders and was soon producing 100 Model N's per day. Then in 1908 Ford announced,

I will build a motor car for the great multitude. It will be large enough for the family but small enough for the individual to run and care for. It will be constructed of the best materials by the best men to be hired, after the simplest designs that modern engineering can devise. But it will be so low in price that no man making a good salary will be unable to own one—and enjoy with his family the blessings of hours of pleasure in God's great open spaces.[1]

An unprecedented ten thousand of Ford's new car, the 20-horsepower Model T, sold in the next year at $825. To reach the mass audience he sought, Ford quickly began seeking ways to reduce the Model T's price.

Henry Ford sought to simplify and speed production to reduce prices and make the Model T affordable to more people. He announced in 1909 that customers could buy a **Tin Lizzie** Model T in any color they wanted, as long as they wanted black. By having only one color, Ford could reduce inventory and supply costs as well as cut production time and cost because black paint dried fastest.

Ford's greatest innovation was the replacement of individual construction crews with the moving assembly line. By subdividing the task of assembly, bringing parts to the assemblers, delivering them waist high so as to reduce wasted motion, and speeding up the chain-driven line whenever possible, Ford dramatically reduced the time and cost of manufacturing. By 1914, the price of a Model T had fallen to $490.

The Model T's simplicity and sturdiness were major aspects of its appeal. Designed and built for durability as well as easy maintenance and repair by its owner, the Model T was reliable and comparatively inexpensive to operate. Once purchased, it would not involve significant additional expense, except for fuel, for a long time, and for nearly two decades its appearance changed but little. The Model T's hand-cranked starter and awkward planetary transmission were no more difficult to deal with than the mechanisms on most cars, at least in the 1910s. Its high axles and road clearance enabled it to travel the rough and rutted dirt roads that, outside main thoroughfares in major cities, had to be regularly traversed; and when, as often happened, a driver found himself stuck in mud, the light-weight Model T could be easily extracted. The popularity of Ford's "Tin Lizzie," as the Model T came to be called, helped to account for the jump in the number of automobiles from fewer than a half million in 1910 to 2.5 million in 1915 to 9 million by 1920.

GM At the same time that Henry Ford was promoting the Model T, another Detroit businessman, William C. Durant, was creating the General Motors Company. The impetuous if brilliant Durant, much more a speculator and salesman than an engineer like Ford, built or bought up numerous auto manufacturing companies, including Buick, Ransom Olds' Oldsmobile, Cadillac, and Chevrolet, as well as parts makers such as Fisher Body and Charles Kettering's electric starter and battery company. He also acquired numerous companies that soon proved worthless, such as firms making the two-cylinder Elmore and the Cartercar and, worst of all, the Heany Lamp Company whose incandescent headlight patent turned out to be fraudulent. Durant fought a long battle for control of General Motors (GM) with the bankers who financed his acquisitions. He ultimately lost out to minority stockholders from the Dupont Company who used their enormous World War I munitions profits to buy a controlling 28 percent of GM common stock. By November 1920 when Durant was forced out of General Motors, he had, however, assembled a huge, sprawling company poised to take advantage of the rapidly growing market for automobiles.

REDEFINING THE AUTO MARKET

Consumer Credit While Henry Ford had opened the mass market for automobiles, General Motors expanded and reshaped that market during the 1920s. The first and most influential GM innovation was its introduction of consumer credit. Prior to the 1910s purchasing an automobile required immediate cash payment. Banks declined to lend money without secure collateral, immovable property they could seize if the loan were not repaid, certainly not a vehicle that could be driven away. No wonder that at first only people with substantial reserves of cash on hand could afford automobiles. In the 1910s a few banks, finance companies, and independent auto dealers experimented with time purchase plans. However, not until General Motors and Dupont, awash in World War I profits, established the General Motors Acceptance Corporation in 1919, did a manufacturer itself finance credit buying of automobiles. Within two years, 50 percent of automobile buyers were entering into credit purchase agreements; by 1926 the figure reached three-fourths.

Credit buying not only dramatically enlarged the population that could afford the initial cost of an automobile, it also altered their buying habits. Henry Ford sought to attract customers with a low-price product, one simple and durable enough to last a very long time. The Model T's unchanging appearance and longevity were a great part of its appeal, as was its price, reduced to $310 by 1921. However, the availability of credit from other manufacturers and dealers made it much easier for a car buyer to get behind the wheel of a more expensive car with conveniences (such as electric starters) that the Model T lacked. When the added cost represented only a small difference in a monthly loan payment, buyer preference for more powerful, better equipped cars began to supersede desire for the lowest priced and longest-lasting vehicle.

Credit purchasing also facilitated the growth of a market in lower-priced used cars. Not having to pay the full amount at the outset reduced customer resistance to buying a new car and, likewise, their incentive to hold onto an old one as long as possible. The partially paid-for automobile became more and more often the down payment for a newer or better model. Dealers soon had lots full of traded-in used cars where even people of modest income might find a car they could afford.

General Motors, with its range of models from the low-price Chevrolet to the mid-range Oldsmobile to the up-scale Buick and luxurious Cadillac, benefited from these market changes. Recognizing that gaps existed in its lineup but not **Marketing Strategies** wanting to make the large investment to develop an entirely new automobile, GM combined parts from a Chevrolet and an Oldsmobile with a new six-cylinder engine to create an intermediate-priced Pontiac. The same new approach to the idea of interchangeable parts produced the LaSalle midway between the Buick and Cadillac. Now when any GM car owner desired to trade up to a somewhat better car, there would be another General Motors model to buy.

Innovations such as hydraulic brakes and the closed car stimulated automobile sales in the 1920s. Two-wheel mechanical brakes, the original automobile stopping mechanisms, were not very effective or safe. They required a strong arm to operate and lots of stopping room; since they wore unevenly, they could pull a car sharply to one side or the other. Foot-operated hydraulic four-wheel brakes began to appear in 1922, making driving both safer and easier, especially for women and young people. The Model T and all but the most expensive other early cars were open; at best passengers were protected by a canvas top and side curtains or transparent fabric windows. General Motors was first to see that people who were becoming dependent on their cars in all sorts of weather would pay extra for a closed car with roll-up windows. In 1919 only 10 percent of the cars on the road were closed, but by 1927 the proportion had reached 83 percent.

Since new technology did not emerge every year to provide a fresh incentive for the purchase of a new car, other means had to be found to entice customers. Once again, General Motors led the way. Redesigning a car's fenders or dashboard proved neither difficult nor expensive but provided a means of distinguishing each year's model from that of the year before. Dupont developed new fast-drying, hard-finish Duco lacquer paints so that a variety of colors could be offered to compete with Henry Ford's basic black. Such cosmetic changes rendered a car old-fashioned and out of style before it had worn out. Creating the impression of out-of-date products, "planned obsolescence" as the process came to be called, became the strategy of General Motors and other manufacturers.

Advertising Advertising campaigns to call attention to new models and features sought to persuade automobile owners that to be up-to-date they should trade in and trade up. Stimulating sales through advertising became a major activity of the automobile industry. Advertising was entering a new stage in which large, eye-catching illustrated ads, use of brand names, and subtle psychological appeals replaced the prosaic announcement of product availability that characterized an earlier era. Advertisers paid increasing attention to new studies of human psychology and devoted considerable effort to sending subtle messages that simply owning this or that car would bestow upon its owner social status, power, or sex appeal. Readers of newspapers and magazines were bombarded by big display ads with cleverly crafted texts and pictures of cars with, depending upon their type, smiling families enjoying them or attractive young women draped across a fender.

Ford's Model A Henry Ford resisted the new approach to the auto business as long as he could. He tried to keep the Model T an inexpensive car "built to last forever." He made no effort to provide credit. In the Tin Lizzie's waning days, Ford offered closed cars and colors other than black, but he hung onto mechanical brakes (and would do so until 1939). The Model T continued to sell well, reaching 2 million units in 1925. But sales declined to 1.5 million in 1926. Finally, early in 1927, Henry Ford announced that he was closing his factories and would reopen when he had a new car to sell. From May until November, Ford assembly lines remained idle while the replacement for the Model T was designed and the factories retooled. At least 300,000 of the new Model A were sold before the first one appeared, so high was public confidence in Henry Ford. The four-cylinder, 40-horsepower, closed-body Model A quickly became the country's most popular car, but the unplanned production shutdown and changeover proved enormously costly to Ford, his laid-off workers, and his dealers. During the Ford shutdown, General Motors with its full line of cars seized the overall sales leadership. Ford even faced a challenge for second place from Walter Chrysler's newly established company, which was putting together its own rival line of Plymouth, Dodge, Chrysler, and DeSoto.

Although by 1929 there were still 44 companies making automobiles in the United States, 80 percent of all cars **Automobility** were produced by Ford, Chrysler, and GM. General Motors in particular had defined automobility for Americans: easy access to cars in a wide price range which could be paid for while they were being driven, cars where improvements in technology and design mattered more than cost, cars intentionally outmoded before outworn. The annual model change, rather than the 19-year production record of the Model T, set the pattern for the automobile industry.

RESHAPING FACTORY WORK

The spreading use of new mass market commodities such as the automobile and the techniques developed for their **New Jobs** production and distribution altered the country's economic life. The means by which Americans earned their daily bread shifted perceptibly during the 1920s. While the overall labor force grew from 41.6 to 48.9 million workers during the decade, the number of workers engaged in the traditional pursuits of agriculture, forestry, fishing, and mining fell slightly (from 12.6 to 11.9 million). Meanwhile, even as the methods of production changed and output per worker grew, the number of persons engaged in manufacturing held steady (10.988 to 10.99 million). A huge increase in so-called white-collar work contrasted sharply to the stable number of workers producing food and commodities. The workforce engaged in sales (from 2.1 to 3.1 million), service (1.9 to 2.8 million), clerical (3.4 to 4.3 million), managerial (2.8 to 3.6 million), and professional and technical work (2.3 to 3.3 million) grew rapidly, for the most part a direct reflection of opportunities and needs presented by new commodities.

Automobiles in particular transformed patterns of work for millions of Americans. The use of automobiles, **Mass Produced** together with that of their close relatives, tractors and **Efficiency** trucks, created or markedly changed many jobs. The nature of work was perhaps most nontraditional for those who came to be employed in the auto industry itself. In addition, however, the auto industry set the pattern for other manufacturing enterprises that mass produced consumer goods based on new technologies. One of Billy Durant's acquisitions for General Motors, for instance, had been a little company that at the time had only 42 customers for its electric refrigerators. Durant, deciding that refrigerators could be built like automobiles since both consisted of cases containing motors, renamed the company Frigidaire and put it in a position to adopt the GM system of advertising, credit sales, and production. While established industries such as steel and textiles, food processing, mining, and lumbering changed but little, lessons learned in automobile and other manufacturing influenced still other large-scale employment, such as office work. The fruits of mass production also altered farm and housework.

Henry Ford led the way in the creation of vast factories, but he soon had many imitators. Beginning in 1910, Ford gathered the previously scattered and subcontracted manufacture of parts for the Model T into one huge plant at Highland Park, Michigan. He brought together thousands of machine tools to fabricate the myriad parts required for even as simple a car as the Model T. The machines, closely spaced on the factory floor, functioned at set speeds and set the pace for the workers who tended them. Ford's metal-cutting machines made possible what few manufacturers had previously achieved: the production of parts so nearly alike that they could be used interchangeably. Then, rather than adjust each part to fit, a much more rapid process of assembly became possible.

Within three years of moving into his Highland Park plant, Ford discovered that, whereas one worker at a bench took twenty minutes to build a magneto, a team of workers each doing a single task, then handing the unit along, could assemble the same devices at a much faster rate. By moving each unit along with a chain-driven line and refining the process still further, Ford soon had magnetos being produced at the rate of one per worker every five minutes. The use of the same techniques reduced the time required to assemble an engine from ten hours to six.

Increased Wages for Assembly Line Stress
Operating a constantly recycling metal-stamping machine or working on a steadily moving assembly line did not require great strength, skill, or even training. In fact, Ford workers were themselves very much interchangeable parts. Most jobs did, however, involve constant, rapid, repetitive labor, performed hour after hour with only a fifteen-minute lunch and bathroom break in the middle of a shift while the line was briefly stopped. Such work was tedious and boring, yet as processes were refined and the pace of production speeded up, increas-

ingly stress-filled. Workers used to a less-feverish pace and a greater sense of individual accomplishment found it difficult to take and at first often quit.

In order to secure dependable workers to operate his machines and staff his assembly lines, Henry Ford found it necessary to depart from conventional hiring practices. He offered jobs to those most likely to appreciate them, those whom most employers avoided: African Americans, Mexicans, ex-convicts, and people with disabilities. He also challenged the standard practice of paying wages so low that industrial workers and their families could barely subsist. To attract capable workers and avoid the high cost of frequent turnover, Ford began in 1914 to offer wages of $5 a day for a work week of forty hours after six months of probationary employment. Compared to the prevailing standards of $2 to $3 a day and a forty-eight-hour or longer workweek, the offer drew workers to Ford's assembly line and kept them there despite the strain.

The wife of one Highland Park worker revealed some of the costs and benefits of the Ford labor system to the average worker in a 1914 letter to her husband's employer:

The chain system you have is a slave driver! My God! Mr. Ford. My husband has come home and thrown himself down and won't eat his supper—so done out! Can't it be remedied? . . . That $5 a day is a blessing—a bigger one than you know but oh they earn it.

The Ford labor system forced other employers to boost wages as well in order to compete successfully for workers. In 1919 Ford upped the ante further by raising wages to $6 a day. Even at that level, Ford wages fell below the auto industry average during the 1920s. The increase in industrial wages put funds for the purchase of cars and other consumer goods in the pockets of a larger population. Not coincidentally, beginning in the mid-1910s, the sales of automobiles, Model Ts especially, grew at a faster rate.

The manufacturing of other new large-volume consumer goods, vacuum cleaners, washing machines, **Industrial System** radios, and low-pressure balloon automobile tires, to name only the most common, employed fabrication and assembly line innovations similar to those of the automobile industry. Likewise, attention was constantly paid to ways in which the production process could be made more rapid, efficient, and inexpensive. In all varieties of manufacturing, a premium was placed on quick, nimble movements done over and over. Young men under thirty-five years of age were, therefore, the most highly sought industrial workers. Once they began slowing down, however, their days were numbered. In Muncie, Indiana, where auto parts manufacturing was a large source of employment, few factory workers held onto their positions far into their forties; and once laid off, they found it very difficult, if not impossible, to find another factory job.

Not all factory work was unskilled labor. Even in the mass production auto plants, roughly 30 percent of the workforce practiced skilled trades. Painters, upholsterers, carpenters, welders, and mechanics were all needed, and especially with the advent of the annual model change, tool and die makers were in constant demand. Skilled workers usually enjoyed more varied tasks, normally received higher wages, and almost always held their jobs longer. They, too, however, labored under the unrelenting pressure to work quickly and efficiently that characterized the industrial system.

Difficult Time for Unions

When workers responded to the stresses of factory work by trying to form labor unions, they faced unwavering opposition from management unwilling to negotiate over restrictions on its ability to set wages, much less determine working conditions. During the war, federal government pressure had led to some acceptance of unionization, especially among the skilled trades, but once the war was over, government support quickly faded and business resistance again stiffened. The failed steelworkers strike of 1919 marked the beginning of an extended period of ineffectuality and declining membership for American unions, especially in mass production industries, that would not be reversed until the depths of the depression of the 1930s. Unionism did not die altogether. The American Federation of Labor's skilled trade unions managed for the most part to hold their own during the 1920s. Meanwhile, more progressive companies, recognizing the benefits of a less-disgruntled work force, created their own employee associations, advisory councils, or management-controlled "company unions." They also established personnel departments to begin making various efforts at reforming hiring practices, improving health and safety conditions, and providing recreational opportunities for employees. These efforts, whether enlightened or merely the result of calculated self-interest, were intended to reduce employee turnover, a chronic problem, and convince workers that independent labor unions were unnecessary. As long as the economy prospered so that employers could provide relatively full employment and steady or even slightly increased wages, they were able to keep unionism at bay among the blue-collar work force.

WHITE-COLLAR WORK

The volume of white-collar work expanded dramatically as the manufacturing, distribution, sales, and service of consumer goods increased. The evolution of the retail store and business office paralleled, indeed in some respects even preceded, the transformation of the factory. Both experienced the mass employment of interchangeable low skilled workers carrying out subdivided tasks. Not coincidentally, the time clocks to monitor the arrival and departure of masses of employees that became increasingly common in factories began to appear as well in large offices and retail stores.

Retail sales work had begun to change in the late nine-   **Retail Sales**
teenth century as large department stores began to domi-
nate the urban commercial scene. Department stores relied
on volume sales stirred by lower prices as well as greater selection of goods and services to compete successfully with specialty stores. By the early twentieth century, chain stores, multiple retail emporiums under centralized management, brought the same economies of scale to smaller cities and towns. Determined to cut costs, department and chain stores relied far more on the eye-catching display of goods than on the sales staff's knowledge of products and customer needs. Sales work came to require few substantial skills; instead it became primarily a matter of gracious treatment and gentle encouragement of customers who examined products for themselves and then the processing of sales transactions. Except in the case of male-oriented markets, such as the automobile business, sales work was increasingly dominated by women. Supervision, however, remained overwhelmingly in male hands. Men were assumed to be full-time workers in the wage economy who could be depended upon, while women were thought of as temporary workers likely to depart for home and family when they had earned a little "pin money." These gender stereotypes reinforced a preference for hiring men, a custom of paying women less, and a casualness about dismissing women first when business declined.

The management of larger numbers of workers, the pro-
duction and distribution of an increasing volume of goods,   **Office Work**
and the provision of a wider range of services required a
notable expansion of office work. Much like mass production manufacturing, office work came to be organized and subdivided in the interest of efficiency. Old-style rolltop desks with many drawers and pigeonholes for storing various items were replaced in most larger, more modern offices by flat top desks and centralized files. The introduction of the typewriter in the 1870s, its gradual improvement, and its widespread adoption after pools of trained female typists became available (male clerks aspiring to advance could not be expected to learn such a dead-end skill as typing) led to the adoption of standardized forms and a growing concern with the flow of paperwork. Office work was subdivided, and employees came to do one job only, whether it was typing, operating the telephone switchboard, maintaining personnel records, processing accounts receivable or payable, or distributing the office

New York City traffic jam, 1939. Photo courtesy of the Library of Congress.

mail. These changes presumably improved paperwork management and cut costs. They definitely increased the monotony of office work and reduced each worker's sense of privacy and individuality.

OUTSIDE THE FACTORY AND OFFICE

Mobility Motorized transportation reshaped work patterns beyond the factories where vehicles were made and the offices where commerce was managed. Physicians were often the first to acquire automobiles in smaller towns and rural communities. The ability to make house calls more quickly and over a wider area improved the extent and effectiveness of their service. Access to professional medical care, thanks to the automobile, significantly reduced a rural dweller's sense of isolation.

Accepted professionals such as doctors and lawyers were not the only beneficiaries of the automobile. The new 1920s trade of bootlegging made a great deal of use of motor vehicles to transport supplies of liquor quickly and surreptitiously. The mobility of bootleggers proved to be one of the major reasons they were so hard to suppress. Other lawbreakers also saw the potential of the automobile. One notable result was a sharp increase in small-town bank robberies. Police and prohibition agents responded by adopting automobiles themselves. Police work changed with the new obligation and ability to move quickly. As with other occupations adopting the automobile, mobility replaced, for better or worse, connection and confinement to a limited space that could be reached on foot or with a horse.

Trucks eventually had a major impact on work patterns but won approval more slowly than automobiles. The construction   **Trucks** of large trucks, mainly by specialty manufacturers not geared to mass production, developed gradually. As late as 1914, fewer than 25,000 trucks a year were being built. World War I greatly stimulated truck production, and by 1920 1.1 million were registered. That number tripled during the 1920s and affected all varieties of work involving the cartage of goods and materials.

A notable development was the emergence of a variant of the automobile: the small pickup truck. The origins of the pickup truck are cloudy, but no doubt grew more out of early auto manufacturing rather than the heavy truck business. At first someone wanting a light cargo-carrying vehicle simply bought an automobile chassis (consisting of frame, engine, drive train, and steering), then added whatever sort of cab and cargo hold they chose. Trucks were assembled by their owners, specialty suppliers, farm wagon makers, and village blacksmiths. Henry Ford, noting how many Model Ts were being turned into light trucks, began to make pickup cargo beds in 1924 as items to be installed by dealers. Then in 1925, Ford began to offer a fully assembled pickup truck. It was named the Model T Roadster Pick-Up because of its convertible top. In his initial year of production Ford sold 33,795 of this first mass-produced factory-built pickup. Chevrolet soon entered the pickup truck business and quickly took the sales lead. Ford responded by offering the first pickup with a V8 engine in 1932.

The value of trucks to supplement and even replace rail transportation was proven in World War I. Thereafter, trucks, and especially the pickup truck, came to be widely used in city, town, and countryside. Trucks served a variety of purposes, and small trucks proved especially useful to merchants, trade and service workers, and farmers. By speeding and easing travel and the delivery of goods, trucks reduced the isolation and increased the productivity of farmers and other rural workers. Likewise, they allowed small-town dwellers wider contact or even relocation to larger communities. Switching from horse and wagon to a truck reduced distances between work sites and increased the appeal of moving to a regional commercial and service center. Large towns like Muncie, Indiana, grew, not only because people were leaving the farm but also because they were abandoning smaller towns nearby.

FARMING WITH TRACTORS

Prior to World War I, almost all American farmers depended upon their own muscles and those of horses or mules to carry out the strenuous labor of preparing fields and producing crops. The previous half century had seen tremendous improvement in devices for plowing, cultivating, and harvesting, but the power to operate such equipment came mainly from harnessed teams of animals, though after the 1880s it came increasingly from heavy, ungainly steam engines. Indeed, Henry Ford first encountered a self-propelled vehicle when, as a twelve-year-old, he saw a steam-powered tractor on a road near Detroit; it made such a profound impression upon him that more than 45 years later he could still describe it in detail. Not only was young Ford fascinated with machinery, but also he, like many of his generation, was convinced that farming involved "too much hard labour."[2]

Gasoline-engine powered tractors began appearing just after the turn of the twentieth century, but their great size and weight as well as their huge **Increased Appeal** turning radius made them unsuitable for all but large Great Plains wheat farms. In the 1910s smaller, better-designed gasoline tractors that shared more and more technology with automobiles began to emerge. World War I, which produced farm labor shortages as well as heightened demand for food supplies, increased the appeal of tractors overnight.

In 1917, Henry Ford began mass production of the Fordson tractor. By 1920, he had built 100,000 Fordsons, twice as many as the total number of tractors in use in the United States when production began. William Durant bought the Samson Sieve Grip Tractor Company so that General Motors could compete with Ford. Although Samson proved to be one of Durant's missteps and GM soon withdrew from the tractor business, International Harvester, the largest such company, John Deere, and other farm equipment manufacturers remained in competition with Ford. Mass production and frequent price cutting brought tractors within reach of more and more farmers. By the end of the 1920s, tractor ownership more than tripled to nearly one million, although a farm was still four times as likely to have an automobile and just as likely to have a truck as possess a tractor.

Farm machinery exhibit, 1939, Marshalltown, Iowa. Photo courtesy of the Library of Congress.

During the 1920s, International Harvester forged ahead in tractor sales by heeding farmers' needs and providing a full line of compatible plows, cultivators, and other equipment. Especially important, Harvester developed the tall, narrow, tight-turning Farmall, the first successful tractor for cultivating and harvesting row crops such as corn and cotton, and introduced a power take-off to run other machinery directly from the tractor. Meanwhile, Henry Ford proved unwilling to listen to customers and alter the short chassis Fordson design to correct its deadly tendency to tip over backward. Ford lost ground to his competitors and eventually gave up tractor manufacturing in 1928.

The farm family that acquired a tractor experienced a transformation of its working life. Traditionally every member of a family, except for very young children, participated in agricultural work, especially in the planting **Farmwork Transformed** and harvest season. A "hired man," or sometimes more than one, was commonly added to the farm's labor force because of the strenuous and time-consuming tasks that needed to be accomplished quickly as soon as it was possible to get into the fields in the spring and, later, once a crop had ripened. Plowing, cultivating, and harvesting had all been eased by the many improvements in farm machinery, but still had to be carried out using animals pulling the equipment at one to two miles per hour. The amount of work that could be accomplished in a day was further limited by the sheer physical stamina of animals and farmers.

A tractor that could pull farm equipment at a steady, tireless five miles an hour dramatically increased the productivity of each farmer who used one. The number of long tiring hours spent in the fields was either reduced or used to tend many more acres. During the often-brief peak harvest season, a tractor did not need to be rested or have its workday curtailed to avoid excessive fatigue, further raising productivity. Between 1920 and 1940 the hours of labor required to produce one hundred bushels of wheat fell from 87 to 47, one hundred bushels of corn from 113 to 83, and a bale of cotton from 269 to 191.

Not only did tractors render fieldwork less strenuous and time consuming, but they also eliminated the necessity to deal with horses or mules. Working behind horses meant, one Iowa farm boy ruefully observed, spending all day "in the direct line of fire of all discharged solids, liquids, and gasses, usually disposed of in enormous quantities." When fieldwork was done for the day, there was no need to spend more time, an estimated 250 hours a year on average, caring for the draft animals. A tractor farmer's output rose even further when a quarter of a farm's acreage did not have to be set aside to grow feed for the draft animals, but could be turned to cash crops. Half of the increase in farm produce for human consumption between the world wars came from acres previously used to feed horses. The farmer could then specialize in a few market crops rather than divide attention among a wider variety of crops and tasks. At first, however, many farmers kept their horses after buying a tractor and so did not enjoy the full time and economic rewards of mechanization. Nevertheless, agricultural production per acre and man-hour increased, helping account for the farm surpluses that made success as a farmer difficult throughout the 1920s and 1930s.

No Benefits for Small Farms Small acreage tenant farms and sharecroppers, concentrated in the South, lacked the annual volume of production, not to mention the cash resources, to be able to afford or justify the cost of a tractor and its fuel. Remaining dependent on horses, or more often mules in the South, they were obliged to continue the more physically demanding and time-consuming practices of traditional agriculture. Not surprisingly, they fell further behind in an economic competition where they already trailed. As a result, they also lagged in the social changes that were affecting farmers in other regions of the nation.

Mechanized Farming Tractor farmers rapidly came to depend less on the help of family members or other workers in the fields. Farm wives saw their labor shift more to housework and to the keeping of the increasingly elaborate records required by bankers providing credit for the purchase of farm machinery. Young people were in a position to devote more time to education. The full-time hired man began to disappear as three-quarters of a million fewer workers were engaged in paid farm labor in 1940 than twenty years earlier. Migrant harvest workers satisfied the need, if any, of tractor farms for extra labor.

Buying a tractor offered the prospect of a more modern lifestyle, but also a new set of burdens. The tractor industrialized the farm. A mechanized farm required more capital and better records keeping. Rather than brute strength and stubborn persistence, the farmer now needed mechanical and financial skills as well as agricultural knowledge. Business negotiations, credit anxiety, and management tasks replaced drudgery in the fields. Many small farmers, especially those closest to towns and cities, gradually shifted to part-time farming and part-time off-farm wage work to sustain their machinery payments as well as support their family.

Mechanized farming also brought a greater risk of injury. Limbs and lives could be lost operating a tractor or a harvester. Furthermore, long-term negative effects were certain for regular tractor users. A tractor's constant vibration and noise produced steady jolting of the spine and severe stress on the inner ear. Back trouble and hearing loss became widespread among longtime tractor operators. While a tractor may have liberated the farmer's family from the fields, at the same time it often meant a longer workday, sometimes one stretching to sixteen or eighteen hours, for the operator himself since, unlike teams of horses, tractors did not tire.

THE IMPACT OF AUTOMOBILITY

Tractors, trucks, and automobiles altered daily life in the 1920s in an extraordinary variety of ways. Motorized vehicles reshaped the landscape as well as altered business, education, and social life. No wonder that automobile makers, and particularly the best-known individual among them, Henry Ford, came to be regarded as the most influential figures of the age. Humorist Will Rogers repeatedly declared that Ford had influenced more lives than any man alive. "Mr. Ford," he wrote, "It will take a hundred years to tell whether you have helped us or hurt us, but you certainly didn't leave us like you found us."[3]

The economic influence of the automobile only began with its purchase. Its operation created another vast industry. **Oil and** Large numbers of workers gained employment in the gaso- **Petroleum** line and oil business. Petroleum had been pumped from the ground, refined, and used for heat, light, and lubrication since the mid-nineteenth century, but gasoline, the lightest of petroleum's distillates, had few uses before the arrival of the automobile. Not until 1905 was there enough of a market for gasoline that the first roadside station was built primarily to dispense it. Gasoline remained so inexpensive that even the frugal Henry Ford chose to sacrifice fuel efficiency to achieve greater power when he designed the Model T. Subsequently, his competitors were even less concerned about conserving gasoline.

In the second decade of the twentieth century John D. Rockefeller's Standard Oil and other large oil companies began opening gasoline stations to meet the growing demand for automotive fuel. By the early 1920s, the discovery and development of vast new oil fields in Louisiana, Oklahoma, and Texas reduced gasoline prices even further despite rapidly expanding demand. The oil boom in the Southwest created a dominant new industry in the region, one that created thousands upon thousands of jobs at drilling rigs, wells, refineries, and pipelines. The oil industry also generated wealth previously unknown in the region.

Roads and Highways   Before gas engine vehicles, the American transportation system was limited. One could go anywhere on foot, horseback, or by wagon, but even on established roads the pace was slow and off them slower still. River and canal boats and coastal ships were somewhat faster, but limited to waterways. Railroads provided the most rapid means for traveling any distance in the interior; however, despite their 260,000 miles of track by 1920 (not counting multiple lines and yards), railroads only covered particular routes. Until automobiles and trucks came into use, only main urban thoroughfares were thought to merit hard-surfaced roads; the expense could not be justified for routes lightly traveled and then by slow-moving, horse-drawn vehicles. In fact as late as 1900, only 200 miles of paved roads existed outside of cities.

As motor vehicle usage grew, so too did desire for better roads. When the Model T first appeared in 1908, only about 6 percent of the nation's roads had gravel or hard surfaces. The rest, rutted dirt roads that turned to mud when it rained, were better suited to horse-drawn vehicles than automobiles. The same year the first mile of concrete roadway was built in Wayne County, Michigan. Hard surface roads were popular but expensive, so construction, considered a state and local responsibility, proceeded slowly. The World War I need to move supplies and soldiers rapidly over long distances and across state lines made it evident that a satisfactory and standardized road system was vital to national security and appropriate for the federal government to support. Congress in 1916 appropriated $75 million to pay 10 percent of the cost of rural road construction to help isolated farmers get crops to market.

Highway Subsidies   The war, which strained the rail system and demonstrated the potential of trucks, made clear the value of a network of highways linking cities together. In 1921 a new, much larger federal act subsidizing state highway construction stirred a boom in road building. A number of states, urged on by auto and tire manufacturers, cement producers, and other business interests, cooperated to build the first completely hard surfaced coast-to-coast road, initially labeled the Lincoln Highway. By the time this two-lane road from New York City to San Francisco was finished, it had become part of a federal highway numbering system that gave it the prosaic denomination U.S. 30. By the end of the decade, nearly 700,000 miles of U.S. roads (over one-fifth of all roads) were hard surfaced. But since road building remained for the most part a state and local duty, improvements were slow and uneven, especially in rural states where the combination of distances and limited resources presented formidable challenges. By the end of the 1920s, $2.5 billion a year was being spent on roads, but especially in the South and West a great deal remained to be done.

Highway construction increased in the 1930s with the federal government paying more of the cost as a means of stimulating economic recovery. The 1940 opening of the first high-speed, limited-access highway, the Pasadena Freeway in Los Angeles, foreshadowed the further growth of the nation's highways. World War II would again stimulate highway construction as a national security measure, this time with Congress absorbing 75 percent of the cost.

The growing legion of automobile drivers desiring better roads meant that for once there was little resistance to a new tax to finance a government program. Taxes were imposed on gasoline sales, first by states and then by the federal government, to support road construction and maintenance. Even with a tax added, gasoline still remained a very low-cost commodity. In 1919, Colorado, New Mexico, and Oregon became the first states to impose a gas tax for road construction; by 1925, forty-four states and the District of Columbia levied gas taxes, and by 1929, every state did so. In 1921, property taxes and general funds still paid most of road construction costs, but 25 percent did come from auto registration fees. By 1929, gas taxes were the main source of revenues (and the sole source in 21 states).

As roads improved and traffic moved faster, gasoline stations and the growing number of other roadside businesses felt the need to catch the motorist's eye. Large signs were erected to advertise a nearby gas station. Simple images and symbols that could be grasped in an instant became commonplace. In 1925, a shaving cream manufacturer began using a series of small roadside signs, each with a line of rhyming jingle and the final line naming the product. For instance:

> Within this vale
>> Of toil and sin
>>> Your head grows bald
>>>> But not your chin.
>>>>> Use Burma Shave.

"World's Highest Standard of Living," West Virginia, 1937.
Photo courtesy of the Library of Congress.

These signs attracted, almost demanded, the motorist's and passenger's attention, and made Burma Shave an immediate commercial success. By the 1940s there would be 7,000 different jingles lining the nation's highways. Within two decades, roadside advertising had become well established. Large billboards and bizarre roadside architecture, gasoline stations in the shape of an oil well or Dutch windmill, became common on the American landscape.

Driving Risks Due only in small part to the distractions along the roadway, driving or riding in an automobile was, by the standards of a later day, quite dangerous in the early twentieth century. As of 1921, twenty-four automobile deaths were being recorded per 100 million miles traveled. This represents a ghastly level of carnage compared to the 1995 death rate of 1.7 deaths per the same distance traveled. Poor roads, inexperienced drivers, and automobiles which were increasingly powerful but not designed to protect passengers in case of an accident all contributed to the high death and injury toll.

Speed limits, 1939, Waco, Texas. Photo courtesy of the Library of Congress.

In order to restrain speed and reckless driving, as well as finance highway policing and road construction, states began to require motor vehicle registration and licensing. New York was the first to license vehicles in 1901. Thirty-six states did so by 1910, but not until 1921 did every state adopt some form of motor vehicle registration law. States were more reluctant to test the competency of drivers. By 1909, only twelve states and the District of Columbia required all drivers to be licensed, while seven additional states required professional chauffeurs to obtain licenses. Most of these relatively vigilant states allowed drivers licenses to be obtained by mail. Not until the 1930s would drivers' examinations prior to licensing become widespread.

Whatever the risk, Americans took to the roads with enthusiasm in the 1920s. A federal agency, the Office of Public Roads, estimated that altogether American motor vehicles traveled 55 billion miles in 1921. Within the next decade, the figure increased almost 400 percent to 206 billion miles. Automobiles made it possible for drivers to live conveniently a greater distance from their workplace. Thus for those who could afford it, the shift from city to suburb accelerated. Between 1920 and 1930, for instance, Baltimore's population grew 9.7 percent, while that of the surrounding suburbs rose 52 percent. Houses in the suburbs were set on larger lots than those in the city, allowing gardens and yards for playing children. Each suburb tended to draw people of similar ethnic background and economic status, producing much less diversified societies than in the city left behind.

Impact on Education   While the automobile encouraged city dwellers to disperse, its close relative, the bus, was bringing rural people together. By 1926 some 27,000 school buses were in service, allowing the replacement of rural one-room schools to which students walked with schools large enough to offer a much more varied, high-quality education, especially at the high school level. The school bus became a crucial instrument of educational improvement. Between 1914 and 1929 the high school population nearly tripled to the point that half of all high school age persons were enrolled. Many high schools, as a result, introduced vocational training programs for the increasing number of students uninterested in or unequipped for the traditional academic course. With more and more young people spending more and more time there, schools also took on new social functions through extracurricular activities and athletics.

Pleasure Driving   While driving for work, school, business, shopping, or other serious purposes remained of foremost importance, driving for pleasure increased, much as Henry Ford had predicted it would in 1908. Sunday drives became an alternative to church attendance and helped to undermine Sunday business-closing blue laws. Couples embraced automobiles as an alternative to the family parlor or front porch so that courtship could take place away from parental supervision. In Middletown, Robert and Helen Lynd reported, disputes over use of the car frequently divided parents and teenagers. Driving vacations became popular, and visits to national parks and historic sites skyrocketed. Hotels were needed to accommodate automobile travelers, and new facilities with ample parking close to the guest rooms began in the mid-1920s to be called "motels." In an enormous variety of ways, then, the automobile influenced the daily lives of ordinary Americans.

NOTES

1. Quoted in Roger Burlingame, *Henry Ford* (New York: Knopf, 1954), 62.

2. Quoted in Robert C. Williams, *Fordson, Farmall, Poppin' Johnny: A History of the Farm Tractor and Its Impact on America* (Urbana: University of Illinois Press, 1987), 12.

3. Quoted in Michael E. Parrish, *Anxious Decades: America in Prosperity and Depression, 1920–1941* (New York: W. W. Norton, 1992), 39.

3

Electricity and the Conditions of Daily Life

Electric current, generated and controlled for human use, was not a new phenomenon by the 1920s, but, as with the automobile, in that decade it first came to be used by a multitude of people. In the 1920s, electricity started to influence the daily lives of Americans far more than it ever had before. Whereas in previous decades electric current had begun to provide large-scale power for urban street lighting, public transit, elevators, and substantial machinery, post–World War I society experienced the introduction of more and more applications suited to the personal lives of individuals and available to a mass market. Furthermore, while automobiles served to bring residents of town and countryside closer together during the 1920s, electricity and its applications managed further to distinguish everyday life in electrified urban America from that in the largely electricity-less countryside. A small minority of urban dwellers remained without electricity, but the vast majority enjoyed its benefits; the opposite was true in rural America.

LIFE WITHOUT ELECTRICITY

Electrified life not only had a different look than pre-electric life, it also had a different rhythm, feel, and **Pre-electric Life** even aroma. Outside the domain of electricity, where natural sunlight, wood and coal fires, candles, and in recent decades kerosene and natural gas were the available light sources, there was, according to David E. Nye in *Electrifying America, 1880–1940*, "less light at night, and people tended to cluster around what little there was. The night outside was darker than the city's dark."[1] Artificial light produced from wood, coal, candle, or petroleum was dim, smoky, sooty, and smelly. Its grime and odor permeated a home; even strenuous regular cleaning could not eliminate these residues. Light from fossil fuels was also expensive, therefore necessarily used sparingly. For the most part, people lived lives illuminated by the sun, with the rigid limitations and seasonal variations that it imposed.

The pre-electric environment lacked elements that subsequently have come to be taken so much for granted as to disappear from conscious notice. Nye calls attention to simple features of life without electricity: "The farmhouse had a lower noise level, and not just because there was no television; it had no humming refrigerator, no flushing toilet, no whirring appliance motors. Things did not make noises; the only sound came from people, animals, and natural forces, like the wind."[2] Even before examining specific functions of electricity, one ought to consider the fundamentally different look, sound, and feel of the electric and electrified environment.

REARRANGING TIME

Redesigning Daily Life   Bright light able to banish the night's darkness and lengthen the day was the earliest and in many ways most significant consequence of electrification, if scarcely its only result. Electric lighting enabled its possessors effectively and economically to make greater use of pre-dawn, twilight, and evening hours. Thus it literally empowered them to redesign the basic schedule of their daily existence.

With electricity people could begin to arrange their days as they (or at least someone) chose. Electric lighting made it possible to live conveniently by the clock rather than constrained by the patterns of sunrise and sunset. By 1924 in Muncie, Robert and Helen Lynd found that middle- and upper-class business and professional men, the group with the greatest ability to determine their own schedules, did not begin their workday until 7:45 A.M., 8, 8:30, or even 9 A.M., but mostly commonly 8:30 A.M. Their daily schedules stood in marked and deliberate contrast to the 70 percent of the labor force that belonged to the working class. The latter group normally started its workday between 6:15 and 7:30, chiefly at 7:00 A.M. Farmers who began their day's labor before 6:00 A.M. presented an even sharper contrast to the business and professional class.

Gender differences in daily schedules were also noticeable. In Muncie, working-class women began their day's labor even earlier than their husbands, with 40 percent up by 5 A.M., 75 percent by 5:30, and over 90 percent by 6 A.M. A majority of business-class housewives did not arise until 7 A.M. or after. In every case, electrification helped determine the day's routine.

The shift of daily schedules and the expansion of the productive hours of those with access to electricity were profoundly important. Growing industries and bureaucracies were able to manipulate their operations. Outside of the work environment, electrified society gained more opportunity to devote time to nonproductive, pleasurable pursuits. Nothing more rapidly and notably differentiated urban from rural life.

AN EMERGING PUBLIC UTILITY

By 1920, electricity under human control had been available for more than forty years, with Thomas Edison's invention of the incandescent light bulb in 1879 marking the beginning of its substantial practical usage. Edison and his laboratory assistants quickly thereafter developed lamp sockets, household wiring, and generators to make electric lighting systems functional, if at first very expensive. In 1882, Edison began offering home electric generators. In New York City in the same year, he also opened the first central generating station to provide power over utility lines. Within two years, 500 homes and several thousand businesses were using electric lights. Also during the 1880s direct current arc lamp street lights began to compete with older coal gas-powered lighting systems in modernizing towns and cities. Electrically driven streetcars, industrial machinery, and elevators for new high-rise buildings started to appear as well.

The nature of work, particularly in the industrial sector, was dramatically affected by electricity. As late as 1905, less **Electricity** than 10 percent of all motive power nationally was electri- **in Industry** cal, but thereafter usage grew so rapidly that by 1930 the figure reached 80 percent. Electricity could drive small motors, reducing the need for elaborate systems of drive shafts, gears, and belts linking every factory mechanism to the central power source. Electric current could propel assembly lines for Henry Ford's automobiles and many other mass-produced goods. Electricity could coordinate a series of machines with automatic feeding devices and moving belts, and it could also regulate other systems of production with temperature gauges, flow meters, shut-off devices, and other control mechanisms.

The effects of electrification, from better lighted, cleaner, and safer factories, to increased output, to changes in the nature of work, could be momentous. For instance, Muncie's Ball Brothers Glass Manufacturing Company adopted electrical bottle-blowing machines to turn out as many glass jars with eight workers as could have previously been made by 210 skilled glass blowers and their assistants. Likewise, electric trucks, mixers, and cranes sharply reduced the need for unskilled heavy labor.

Although electrification displaced many workers, it did not reduce employment. Instead it fostered new enterprises and created demand for different sorts of labor, for the most part semiskilled, clerical, or service work. Together with better organization of production in redesigned factories, electrification helped account for the great surge in productivity per American worker in the 1920s and 1930s.

Electricity in Homes   Domestic use of electricity was for the most part at first devoted to lighting. Otherwise applications inclined less to practical uses than to novel and ostentatious displays of wealth. In New York City, Mrs. Cornelius Vanderbilt, for example, would greet visitors to her home in a dress covered with tiny electric lights. Fortunately, electric doorbells to announce the arrival of visitors became much more common than electrified fashions. Electric lights on Christmas trees proved popular as early as 1882. By the 1890s, children's toys, such as electrically powered model trains for boys and lighted doll houses for girls, were applying the new technology as well as defining gender roles. The gradual introduction of alternating current to replace direct current in the 1890s allowed the transmission of electricity over longer distances and thus a greater diversity of uses.

Natural Gas   Gas had earlier begun the reform of domestic lighting. Gas manufactured from coal, available since the first decade of the nineteenth century, had been supplanted after mid-century by petroleum-based kerosene and in the early twentieth century by natural gas. Piped delivery became commonplace within cities. For quite some time gas and electric utility systems waged a direct and often fierce competition. Both electricity and natural gas were viewed as expensive and novel in the early twentieth century, but their advantages over wood, coal, and kerosene were widely recognized. The relative inflexibility of gas pipes, the more limited applications of the fuel, and the dangers associated with leakage put natural gas at a disadvantage in the contest. As a result, the gas industry began concentrating its efforts on the improvement of gas cooking stoves, water heaters, and hot air furnaces. Gas ranges with easy-to-clean enameled surfaces and effective thermostats were introduced with great success. By 1930, nearly half of all American homes cooked with gas, a quarter used coal or wood, a fifth used oil, and less than 3 percent employed electricity. Meanwhile, the percentage of gas used for illumination fell from 75 at the turn of the century to 21 by 1919.

Nationally standardized transmission of electric current (alternating current delivered to households at 120 volts) by 1910 and significant reductions in the price of electricity in the early twentieth century further affected the competition. Standardization created a national market and encouraged the mass production of electrical products. In the decade before World War I, salesmen for electric utilities peddled electric irons, toasters, hair-curlers, and other appliances based on the electric resistance heating coil to households already signed up for electric lighting. By the end of the war, electricity, the more versatile of the two commodities, had pulled ahead of gas. Except for water and home heating and cooking purposes, electric current would maintain its lead.

The introduction of home lighting substantially altered domestic life. Industry and street railway use of electricity peaked during the day, encouraging power suppliers to seek off-hours customers. Electric utilities naturally sought to encourage residential use of electricity. Meanwhile the spread of transmission lines for industrial and transportation purposes made residential connections less expensive. After 1910 falling prices helped home electrification to spread rapidly beyond the small proportion of homes, mainly residences of the urban wealthy class, which had enjoyed it for some time.

RESHAPING THE HOME

American home design was transformed as architects and builders came to appreciate the possibilities of electricity. Late-nineteenth-century gas-equipped Victorian homes tended to be dark and divided into many rooms. Gas burned oxygen, produced odors and soot, and required gas jets which could ignite fires or, if snuffed out, release poisonous fumes and cause explosions. Gas-fueled houses were most functional, appealing, and safe if individual rooms could be shut off for airing out and minimizing drafts. Interiors decorated in deep reds, blues, greens, and browns were preferred for their capacity to conceal soot.

Around the turn of the century, a few architects, the best known of whom today is Frank Lloyd Wright, began to recognize the superior properties of electricity and take advantage of its adaptability and relative safety. They started designing houses with open interior plans in which living rooms, dining rooms, and kitchens flowed together. The only isolated and private spaces in these designs were bedrooms and bathrooms, the latter newly developed as piped water and sanitary waste disposal sewers made it practical and appealing to consolidate in one room sinks, toilets, and bathtubs previously placed in different locations inside and outside the house. Houses illuminated by electricity could have more numerous and flexible light sources, thus more freedom in furniture arrangement. Also, since electric lights did not produce soot, electrified homes could also have lighter-colored carpets, walls, and ceilings, making their interiors much brighter than before.

Open Interior Plans

Electric wiring, together with indoor plumbing, added substantially to the cost of house construction. To keep housing prices stable while adding these new technologies, builders proved eager to cut costs elsewhere

Can be built on a lot 30 feet wide

FIRST FLOOR PLAN

SECOND FLOOR PLAN

Page 48

THIS popular style of architecture provides for the greatest amount of comfort in a two-story six-room house. The simplicity of the exterior, together with the fact that there is no waste space, makes the Gladstone a high grade house at a low price.

Shingles on the roof, dormer and porch can be stained either bungalow brown or moss green to harmonize with the painted cypress siding. Porch is 8 feet wide by 24 feet long. Foundation for porch can be built of brick or similar material, with a concrete cap serving to support the twin columns. If screened or glazed the porch will make a comfortable room in season. The house is 24 feet wide by 24 feet 7 inches long.

FIRST FLOOR

The Living Room. Entering the house from the porch you pass through a bevel plate glass door. You will be charmed with the living room, which is 11 feet 5 inches wide by 16 feet 5 inches long. Here ample space is provided for piano, library table, davenport and other furniture. Full length plate glass mirror door opens into a clothes closet equipped with wardrobe pole and shelf. From the end of this room a stairway leads to the second floor. Living room is well lighted and cross ventilated by three windows.

The Dining Room. A cased opening between living room and dining room makes them available as one very large room when entertaining. Dining room is 11 feet 5 inches wide by 13 feet 7 inches long, and contains space to seat the family and friends. An abundance of sunshine and air is secured by the double window in front and a window at the side.

The Kitchen. The kitchen is directly off the dining room and has a swinging door. A table may be placed beneath the double window. The location provides for cupboard, table, sink and range, reduces steps and saves time. Air and light come from three windows.

The pantry with shelves and space for refrigerator, opens from the kitchen. Here steps lead to grade entry opening to yard and to basement.

SECOND FLOOR

The Bedrooms. Three bedrooms and bath are entered from hall on second floor. Ample sunshine and air are furnished the front bedrooms through double windows and one side window in each room. The rear bedroom has two windows. A clothes closet with wardrobe rod and shelf is provided for each bedroom.

The Bathroom. All plumbing is on one wall, affording installation economy. Wise use of space is demonstrated by a linen closet in this room.

The Basement. Basement under entire house is lighted by four hinge sash. Room for furnace, laundry and storage.

Height of Ceilings. Basement, 7 feet from concrete floor to joists. Main floor, 9 feet 2 inches from floor to ceiling. Second floor, 8 feet 8 inches from floor to ceiling.

For Our Easy Payment Plan See Page 144

Honor Bilt

The Gladstone

No. P3222 "Already Cut" and Fitted

$2,029.00

What Our Price Includes

At the price quoted we will furnish all the material to build this six-room house, consisting of:

Lumber; Lath;
Roofing, Best Grade Clear Red Cedar Shingles;
Siding, Clear Cypress or Clear Red Cedar, Bevel;
Framing Lumber, No. 1 Quality Douglas Fir or Pacific Coast Hemlock;
Flooring, Clear Douglas Fir or Pacific Coast Hemlock;
Porch Flooring, Clear Edge Grain Fir;
Porch Ceiling, Clear Douglas Fir or Pacific Coast Hemlock;
Finishing Lumber;
High Grade Millwork (see pages 110 and 111);
Interior Doors, Two Vertical Panel Design of Douglas Fir;
Trim, Beautiful Grain Douglas Fir or Yellow Pine;
Windows of California Clear White Pine;
Medicine Case;
40-Lb. Building Paper; Sash Weights;
Eaves Troughs; Down Spout;
Chicago Design Hardware (see page 132);
Paint for Three Coats Outside Trim and Siding;
Shellac and Varnish for Interior Trim and Doors.

Complete Plans and Specifications.

Built on concrete foundation and excavated under entire house.

We guarantee enough material to build this house. Price does not include cement, brick or plaster.

See description of "Honor Bilt" Houses on pages 12 and 13.

OPTIONS

Sheet Plaster and Plaster Finish, to take the place of wood lath, $208.00 extra. See page 109.

Oriental Asphalt Shingles, guaranteed 17 years, instead of wood shingles for roof, $29.00 extra.

Oak Doors, Trim and Floors in living room and dining room, also Oak Stairs, Maple Floors in kitchen and bathroom, $162.00 extra.

Storm Doors and Windows, $74.00 extra.

Screen Doors and Windows, galvanized wire, $49.00 extra.

For Prices of Plumbing, Heating, Wiring, Electric Fixtures and Shades see pages 130-131.

See Interior Views of The Gladstone Home on opposite Page

The Gladstone, one of dozens of houses that could be ordered from Sears, Roebuck and Co. All materials needed for construction, from pre-cut lumber and nails to a doorbell, would be shipped by rail to the customer for construction on his own lot. From the Sears, Roebuck and Co. 1926 Modern Home catalogue. Reprinted by arrangement with Sears, Roebuck and Co. and protected under copyright. No duplication is permitted.

The GLADSTONE INTERIORS

Above—The dining room atmosphere is cordial and vivid.

Center—Living room where one may entertain his friends confident of their hearty approval.

All of the furnishings shown in these interiors were selected from the pages of our big General Catalog, "The Thrift Book of a Nation."

Above—Sunshine floods this example of modern kitchen efficiency.

At left—The simple beauty of the bedroom tells its own story.

"Happiness abides with folks who recognize the value of a good home for themselves and their children."

—CHARLOTTE DEXTER

P602   See Description of The Gladstone Home on opposite Page   Page 49

Gladstone Interiors. Sears, Roebuck and Co. sold through its catalogue everything needed to decorate and furnish one of its "mail order" homes, including paint and wallpaper, draperies, carpets, linoleum, furniture, and appliances. From the Sears, Roebuck and Co. 1926 Modern Home catalogue. Reprinted by arrangement with Sears, Roebuck and Co. and protected under copyright. No duplication is permitted.

by reducing the size and number of rooms. Early-twentieth-century house plans started to eliminate formal front parlors, merging them with the family sitting room to create a single living room, often opening directly into a dining room. Large entrance halls were reduced in size or even eliminated. As Gwendolyn Wright pointed out in *Building the Dream*, "By 1910 it was rare to have single-purpose rooms such as libraries, pantries, sewing rooms, and spare bedrooms, which had comprised the Victorians' sense of uniqueness and complex domestic life. In a moderately priced two-story house there were usually only three downstairs rooms: living room, dining room, and kitchen."[3] Even kitchens began to shrink in size, allegedly to save housewives' steps but no doubt also to reduce construction costs.

The Bungalow

The most widespread manifestation of the new minimalist approach to house design was the bungalow, which first appeared in California at the start of the twentieth century and spread rapidly eastward. Small, simple, informal, efficient, and intended to be sparsely furnished, the bungalow was quickly proclaimed to be a new standard of sensible and thrifty family living. Between 1900 and 1920, nearly 7.5 million new urban dwellings were added to a turn of the century total of 10 million. In the 1920s, another 5.7 million were occupied. Thus by 1930 a majority of urban homes had been built within the past thirty years. During that period changes in house design had the result of reducing the amount of privacy within homes and drawing residents into an increasingly electrified common realm.

ELECTRIFYING DOMESTIC LIFE

Small Manufacturers

The major manufacturers of electrical equipment, General Electric and Westinghouse, were initially oriented toward providing industrial power, streetcars, and street lighting. Accustomed to dealing with a relatively small number of large-scale customers, they were not prepared to respond immediately when residential wiring began to increase and the potential market for small-scale devices other than lights started to expand. Instead, small manufacturers, ill-equipped to build heavy machinery but well-suited to produce home appliances, led the way into the domestic market. James Reichart of Muncie started the Excel Electric Company in his basement and soon was shipping electric toasters, cookers, and popcorn makers throughout the nation. George Hughes of Fargo, North Dakota, developed an electric range in 1904 and six years later established the Hughes Electric Heating Company in Chicago. The Hotpoint Electric Company of Ontario, California, manufactured electric irons and other small appliances. But even as these enterprises prospered, the total number of electrified residences and thus the market for domestic appliances remained tiny The market was so small before World War I that major consumer goods distributors such as Sears & Roebuck hardly bothered to give it attention in their mail-order catalogues.

The growth of electricity use was in part a result of education. Between 1900 and 1920, school buildings had been **Education** widely equipped with electric lights, gas heat, and better **Promotes** ventilation. After 1920 higher standards were set for illumi- **Electricity** nation of schools. These were implemented in the course of new construction. Home economics curricula, increasingly popular in the 1920s, preached a doctrine of greater domestic cleanliness, more varied diets, and the greater sophistication of a life with modern devices. As students learned about lighting, heating, cleaning, and cooking with electricity, they gained new ways of thinking about desirable domestic arrangements even if they were not in a position to put those ideas into effect immediately.

One of the less apparent but most profound consequences of domestic electric lighting was the encouragement of reading at home. Increased reading broadened knowledge, stirred new interests, and created a more sophisticated society, especially away from centers of culture, which in turn increased demand for electricity. Persons who had trouble reading by dim fire- or candlelight, and especially young children who could not be left alone to regulate gas lights, could easily and safely read by electric light. Partly for this reason, the Muncie, Indiana, public library loaned out eight times as many books per inhabitant in 1925 as it had in 1890. The cartoon symbol of a light bulb being switched on over someone's head as they achieved new insight was firmly grounded in reality.

After lights, electric irons were usually the first acquisitions for newly wired homes. The electric iron became pop- **Electrified** ular because it did not require its user to stand next to a hot **Home** stove; not only the ironer but also the entire home could be **Appliances** kept cooler in warm weather. For similar reasons, electric fans, using small Westinghouse-developed motors, also achieved early success. Early efforts of individual homeowners to attach small motors to foot treadles or hand cranks were supplanted in the 1910s by the introduction of one-piece electric sewing and washing machines. Fans were attached to mechanical carpet sweepers to create the first electric vacuum cleaner, the only home appliance other than the iron to gain wide distribution before the end of World War I.

When the number of wired houses began to increase rapidly after 1918, the market for home appliances expanded just as quickly At that point General Electric bought several promising small appliance companies, including Hughes and Hotpoint, and began devoting its considerable technological skill and financial resources to the developing market. Improved design and mass production of washing machines, sewing machines, and vacuum cleaners reduced their cost and increased their sales. The attachment of small motors to egg beaters and food grinders created highly popular kitchen products: electric mixers and blenders. Home appliances went from being expensive and unreliable toys for the rich to more moderately priced, dependable, and useful tools for a mass of middle-class Americans.

While electric power enhanced various devices, it did not immediately turn them into the home appliances of the late twentieth century. The electric washing machine, for instance, was at first a far more simple device than it would eventually become. A motor powered the agitation of water, detergent, and soiled items and drove the wringer into which wet items had to be inserted by hand. The physical drudgery of hauling and heating water as well as scrubbing and wringing clothes was reduced, but time-consuming and somewhat strenuous human involvement in the laundry process continued. More modern washing machines, which could spin-dry as well as agitate, did not appear until the end of the 1930s.

Early versions of some electrical home appliances existed by the 1920s but were far too expensive for widespread use. Electric refrigerators were both costly and undependable at first, leading most households to continue relying instead on either underground storage or iceboxes, insulated chests cooled by a block of ice. A 1921 survey of thirteen hundred electrified Philadelphia homes found that while most had irons and vacuum cleaners, and upper-class homes usually had an electric coffee percolator and washing machine, virtually none had an electric refrigerator. During the 1930s mass production and price cutting made electric refrigerators practical to a wide market for the first time; by the eve of World War II, half of all Americans homes possessed them. Electric ranges, dishwashers, and clothes dryers had similar histories, but did not gain popularity until after the war.

Appliances and Women's Work

The advent of electrical home appliances altered the work routines of most married women in cities and towns large enough to be electrified. Prior to the introduction of such devices into the home, women spent a great deal of time and vast amounts of energy on house cleaning, laundry, and food preparation. Upper-class women might employ servants while poor women had less space to tend but often no running water to ease their burdens. Nevertheless, the tasks consigned to women were much the same for every household.

Especially in houses not equipped with natural gas furnaces or electric lighting, the battle against dirt and soot was a constant and arduous one. Lamps had to be cleaned every few days at the least; surfaces had to be dusted and floors scrubbed almost as often; windows required frequent

Kenmore® electric washing machine ad with depression price reductions. From the Sears, Roebuck and Co. Fall 1931 catalogue. Reprinted by arrangement with Sears, Roebuck and Co. and protected under copyright. No duplication is permitted.

Harmony, Georgia, woman with her new electric refrigerator but not yet ready to give up the old icebox. Photo courtesy of the National Archives.

washing; carpets had to be swept regularly and once a season hauled out of doors to be hung up and beaten. Laundry involved perhaps the most strenuous frequent labor: hauling and heating water, scrubbing items by hand, and ironing nearly every piece. Most fabrics were cotton, woolen, or linen; easy-care synthetics and blends lay in the distant future. The acquisition and preparation of food consumed substantial time and effort as well. Observed Ruth Schwartz Cohen in *More Work for Mother*, "Some women, determined to keep their homes as orderly and healthful as they could make them, exhausted themselves at the task; while large numbers of others—perhaps less optimistic, perhaps less brave, perhaps more realistic—just gave up and rarely attempted it."[4]

Appliances Raise Expectations   Home appliances altered the nature of women's work by the 1920s but scarcely eliminated it. Instead, expectations of domestic cleanliness rose higher at the very time that house servants virtually disappeared due to immigration restriction and the increased availability of higher-wage factory and office work. A massive growth in advertising for new-style bathroom fixtures, home appliances, and cleaning products spread the impression that people, their clothing, and their homes should be cleaner than ever before. Electric appliances allowed middle-class women to cope with demands for cleaner homes and wardrobes without servants, although the hours they devoted to housework did not shrink. Three studies in the 1920s showed that women spent between fifty-one and sixty hours a week on housework.

Significantly, the domestic workload had not shrunk a half century later. The increased availability of electric appliances appears, instead, to have caused expectations regarding domestic conditions to rise. Better and more varied meals, cleaner houses, larger and more frequently laundered wardrobes all came to be accepted as normal. During the 1920s and 1930s, the burden of these expectations shifted ever more to women. The fuel and water hauling and carpet beating tasks often assigned to men and the laundry done by servants or commercial laundries disappeared. Meanwhile women's electrically assisted chores simply, and conversely, expanded. In fact, as the acquisition of appliances became more and more a defining feature of middle-class life, some women found it necessary to begin working for wages outside the home in order for their family to have the financial resources to hold onto middle-class status. This added responsibility seldom reduced the burden of housework.

Various indices show that the use of electricity doubled during the 1920s and tripled by the end of the 1930s. By **Rural Areas** 1920, 47 percent of urban dwellings had been wired to re- **Left Behind** ceive and employ electricity, but only 1.6 percent of farm dwellings were so equipped. A decade later, 85 percent of urban dwellings had been electrified but the same could be said of only 10 percent of farm dwellings. Perhaps never in the nation's history was the distinction between urban and rural lifestyles so clear-cut. The political tension between town and country that manifested itself in the 1920s was no doubt in part rooted in rural resentment at being left behind technologically and culturally as well as differences of viewpoint about alcoholic beverages, religion, and other matters.

UNWIRED FARMS

Some farms, beginning around World War I, generated electric power for themselves. The cheapest method of doing this was a water-driven generator, which led a few farmers to construct small dams on their property. Windmills were more commonly used as generators. Other farms used a gasoline- or kerosene-driven engine to power a generator intermittently and charge a set of batteries. Each of these solutions was expensive and therefore accessible to only the wealthiest farmers. By the late 1920s, only 600,000 of 6.5 million farms had electricity, half self-generated, half transmitted from utility companies or interurban lines.

The 600,000 were concentrated in the Northeast and Far West. With farmers expected to bear the cost of building transmission lines at as much as $2,000 per mile, a sum greater than the average farm's annual income, it is not surprising that in those regions such as the South, where farms were least profitable, and the Great Plains, where farms were most spread out, electrification was least common.

Rural people, particularly women, understood from magazine advertisements and mail-order catalogues what they were missing by not being connected to electric lines. For instance, without an electric pump they had to haul water into the house from a well or stream, a tiring task in itself, and then heat it for bathing, cleaning, or laundry. In addition, the risk of fire in houses and barns was always much greater with wood or coal stoves and kerosene lamps than with electric lights. No wonder one Tennessee farmer declared that, after religious faith, "the next greatest thing is to have electricity in your house."[5]

The REA By 1940 the proportion of urban dwellings with electricity had grown to 91 percent. Rural electrification had doubled during the previous three years as a result of the federal government's Rural Electrification Administration (REA). However that only meant that a third of rural dwellings were wired. Admirers of REA asserted that when, and only when electric wires stretched everywhere would there be a truly *United* States. The gulf between rural and urban circumstances had begun to close, but not until after World War II would rural electrification become commonplace.

AN AGE OF MASS ELECTRIFICATION

Overall, the number of American homes making use of electricity increased remarkably during the years between the two world wars. The total number of dwelling units increased from just over 24 million in 1920 to just under 35 million by 1940. Almost all of this enormous increase occurred in urban areas. In that much expanded number of dwellings, the percentage equipped with electric power grew from 34.7 percent in 1920 to 78.7 percent by 1940.

Electricity a Necessity Americans considered the acquisition of electricity to be more important than obtaining other domestic conveniences. No doubt this had to do with the wide variety of things that electricity could do besides providing clean and inexpensive home lighting. In Muncie, for instance, by 1934 only 4 percent of families lacked electricity while 55 percent lacked central heating, 37 percent had no bathtubs, 34 percent had only cold running water, 18 percent still used outdoor privies, and 13 percent had no running water at all. Electricity had become a necessity before central heating, hot running water, and indoor toilets.[6]

Birney, Montana, woman on the telephone, 1939. Photo courtesy of the Library of Congress.

While electricity had come to be regarded as essential, other technologies remained nonessential conveniences. For instance, in Muncie between the prosperous year of 1926 and the depression year of 1936, the number of houses equipped with telephones declined despite a one-third growth in city population. Even at the end of World War II, fewer than half of all U.S. houses had telephones while electricity was becoming nearly universal.

Some forms of electric usage did shrink during the years between the wars. Electric streetcars and interurban light railways gradually disappeared as the use of automobiles and buses increased. In Muncie, for example, streetcars disappeared in 1931, but interurbans lasted a decade longer. The Great Depression reduced ridership but made higher fares unthinkable. Economic circumstances more than technological inadequacy accounts for the decline of electrified public transportation.

For the most part however, the employment of electric power in American domestic life soared. The average amount of electricity used within each wired home more than doubled, expanding from 339 kilowatt hours in 1920 to 952 by 1940. Total power usage by wired residential units went from a total of 3,190 million kilowatt hours (mkwh) in 1920 to 11,018 mkwh in 1930 to 24,068 mkwh in 1940. These indeed were the decades during which American domestic life became electrified.

NOTES

1. David E. Nye, *Electrifying America: Social Meanings of a New Technology, 1880–1940* (Cambridge: MIT Press, 1990), xiii.
2. Ibid.
3. Gwendolyn Wright, *Building the Dream: A Social History of Housing in America* (New York: Pantheon, 1981), 171.
4. Ruth Schwartz Cohen, *More Work for Mother: Women and Household Technology* (New York: Oxford University Press, 1977), 163.
5. Nye, *Electrifying America*, 304.
6. Robert S. Lynd and Helen Merrill Lynd, *Middletown in Transition: A Study in Cultural Conflicts* (New York: Harcourt, Brace and World, 1937), 195.

4

Radio and the Connecting of Daily Lives

The new electrically powered technologies with perhaps the greatest impact on the daily lives of ordinary Americans in the 1920s and 1930s were radio and sound motion pictures. Interestingly enough, they represented instances in which the presence or absence of electrical wiring did not force a wedge between city and countryside. Battery-operated radios in particular, but also movie projectors driven by electric generators, made it possible for rural and small town Americans to experience the same striking sounds and, occasionally, sights as city dwellers. Town and country could share experiences impossible to obtain in their own immediate cultural environment. Thus far more than any previous systems of communication, radio and the movies drew Americans together into a new and common culture

RADIO LINKS THE NATION

Radio became enormously popular in a very short period of time. It soon linked rural and urban America together in a common listening experience. In the two decades after the first commercial radio broadcast in November 1920, nearly 41 million radios were manufactured in the United States, considerably more than one for every household in the nation. For the first time in the nation's history, one could realistically talk of a national audience for a political, sports, or other event. People across the country could simultaneously hear exactly the same thing, whether it was a presidential speech, a musical performance, an adver-

tisement for a commercial product, or an eyewitness description of a
World Series baseball game. A nationwide community of people sharing
the same experience at the same moment was first formed.

THE ORIGINS OF RADIO

Marconi's Invention
Italian Guglielmo Marconi had discovered how to transmit
telegraphic code through the air in 1896, initiating a scientific scramble to advance wireless communication. Marconi
first demonstrated his wireless telegraph in the United
States in October 1899, sending to shore reports on the America's Cup
yacht races in New York harbor. With a variety of inventors working on
aspects of the problem, less than a decade later Americans achieved wireless transmission of voices and music, the first crude radio. In 1909, a
primitive radio station began broadcasting every Wednesday evening
from the San Jose, California, College of Engineering. Messages sent and
received in the dots and dashes of Morse telegraph code remained the
common medium, however, having quickly become commercially important.

Wireless messages from the sinking S.S. *Titanic* in 1912 underscored
the value of ship-to-shore communication and increased enthusiasm for
Marconi's invention. By 1913 advances in vacuum tube technology effectively amplified wireless telegraph and radio signals, marking a great
improvement over existing transmitters and widely used crystal receivers. Soon several thousand amateur radio operators began demonstrating
that interest in this new medium of communication existed beyond na-
val, military, journalistic, and business circles. They talked, sang, made
speeches, gave time signals and weather reports, played phonograph
records, and read poetry for other amateurs. In 1915 a voice message
transmitted from Arlington, Virginia, was picked up in both Paris and
Pearl Harbor, Hawaii. In 1916 a network of amateur operators was able
to relay a message from Davenport, Iowa, to New York City in only two
and a half hours, using a series of intermediate receivers and transmitters. A year later they sent a message from Los Angeles to New York
and obtained a reply in less than two hours.

De Forest's Vacuum Tube
In 1915, Lee De Forest, using the vacuum tube equipment
he had developed during the previous decade, began broadcasting phonograph music and lectures in New York. By
regularly replicating a feat he had first accomplished in
1910 with a very limited broadcast of tenor Enrico Caruso
from the Metropolitan Opera, he hoped to expand the market for the
devices his company produced. In 1916 De Forest broadcast the Harvard-
Yale football game and even presidential election results. De Forest's
broadcasts (including the incorrect report that President Woodrow Wilson had been defeated for reelection) could be picked up within a 200

mile radius of New York by listeners using vacuum tube sets or home-made crystal sets and earphones.

In late 1916 a young visionary at the Marconi Wireless Tele-graph Company in New York, David Sarnoff, proposed as **Sarnoff's** "entirely feasible" a rethinking of uses for the rapidly devel- **Vision** oping technology. Rather than focus on sending private mes-sages from point to point to compete with the telegraph and telephone, he urged the broadcast transmission of music, lectures, news, and sports over several channels to "radio music boxes" which combined receivers and loud speakers. Sarnoff envisioned a "household utility" for urban and, perhaps most usefully, rural homes.

World War I, however, redirected radio development for the time being by centralizing control and development in **WWI and** government hands. Speedy and secure military and dip- **Armstrong's** lomatic communication took priority for the moment. The **Circuit** war shaped the evolution of radio by, among other things, standardizing the many competing technological systems. Also, wartime desire to intercept German communications inspired Edwin Armstrong's 1918 invention of the superheterodyne circuit, an effective tuning device for electromagnetic signals that remains to this day the central element in radio and television transmission at precise and differentiated fre-quencies.

In the fall of 1919, the Radio Corporation of America (RCA) was formed with government encouragement and the support of **RCA** the General Electric Corporation (the outgrowth of Thomas Edi-son's early enterprise) to take over the interests of the American Marconi Wireless Telegraph Company and avoid continued postwar government control of wireless communication. Although focused at first on ship-to-shore and international wireless telegraphy, the new company's leaders did allow Sarnoff to explore his idea of broadcasting to radio music boxes. By July 1920, the potential for conflict with the American Tele-phone and Telegraph Company (AT&T) over patent rights and compet-ing systems for transmitting signals to American homes was resolved. RCA simply gave a million shares of its stock (about 10 percent) to AT&T, and the two firms agreed, with government approval, to coop-erate rather than compete. RCA found itself in a powerful position to determine the nature of broadcasting.

BROADCASTING BEGINS

Meanwhile General Electric's principal rival, Westing-house, shut out of international wireless telegraphy but **Westinghouse** holding the superheterodyne patent, among others, de- **Initiative** cided to compete with RCA in the field of domestic broadcasting. In Pittsburgh, Westinghouse engineer Robert Conrad began transmitting primitive programs. Amateur operators, of whom there were more than 6,000 nationally by 1920, were delighted to pick up vocal and musical broadcasts instead of just Morse code and encouraged his efforts. By May 1920, Pittsburgh newspapers were reporting on his regular Saturday evening concerts; in September a local department store began advertising $10.00 receivers capable of picking up Conrad's concerts; and at 8 P.M. on November 2, 1920, Westinghouse station KDKA, which had just obtained the first U.S. government license to operate a general broadcasting service, began regular transmissions from the roof of the company's factory.

KDKA's first broadcast, which went on until after midnight, reported the results of that day's presidential election won by Republicans Warren Harding and Calvin Coolidge over Democrats James Cox and Franklin Roosevelt. The broadcast was heard by people throughout the Pittsburgh area, many of them Westinghouse employees who had been given receivers for the occasion. Broadcasts continued, at first for an hour each evening but soon for longer periods, and Westinghouse quickly established stations at its properties in Newark, New Jersey, East Springfield, Massachusetts, and Chicago, Illinois. The company's plan was simple: use broadcasts to create demand for radio equipment, then profit through the sale of sets.

The Westinghouse effort prompted a quick reaction from RCA. Seeking to retain control of the domestic radio market, RCA offered Westinghouse a million shares of its stock and a 40 percent share of the radio equipment market (the rest would belong to General Electric) in return for Westinghouse's radio patents and operations. Westinghouse accepted in March 1921, and RCA gained a dominant position in the newborn industry.

Home and Car Radios When commercial broadcasting began in 1920, most radio receivers were simple, homemade crystal sets that could be put together for about $2 and used with a $4 set of earphones. By 1922, however, RCA began to manufacture the Radiola, a device with six vacuum tubes, amplifiers, and a superheterodyne tuner that had a superior sound, required no external antenna, and was very simple to operate. As loudspeakers were improved and especially before 1928—when plug-in electric circuitry began to replace batteries interchangeable with automobile batteries and recharged by switching back and forth—radios were fitted into bulky, often ornate wooden cabinets and sold as living room furniture. Console sets big enough to hold a large battery and often also a phonograph dominated the market until the 1930s when economic conditions created a demand for cheap table models and portable sets.

In 1928, William Lear designed the first car radio. Within a year, the Motorola Corporation was in business producing it. Early car radios were bulky, however, and their reception was poor. Not until after World War II would the technology improve sufficiently to make car radios widely popular.

With the advent of broadcasting, radio quickly went from being a specialized and limited technology for private com- **A New** munications of interest to a small civilian and military profes- **Craze** sional community and a handful of amateur enthusiasts to a new craze in which a great mass of Americans could participate. Eight months after KDKA's reports on Harding's election, another broadcast event was much more widely heard and had an even greater effect in stimulating further interest in radio. Sarnoff decided that RCA should promote the market for its receivers by broadcasting a major sporting event, a heavyweight boxing championship match between American Jack Dempsey and Frenchman Georges Carpentier to be held in Jersey City, New Jersey. Already heavily publicized by the leading sports promoter of the era, "Tex" Rickard, who anticipated selling 90,000 tickets, the fight was attracting nationwide interest. RCA established a transmitting station, installed receivers and loudspeakers in a hundred theaters and social clubs from Maine to Florida, and arranged for the proceeds from ticket sales at these locations to be donated to charity. The live broadcast of the fight on July 2, 1921, was heard by an estimated 300,000 listeners, including a crowd of 100,000 gathered around loudspeakers in New York's Times Square.

The Dempsey-Carpentier fight boosted the already substantial interest in radio. Luckily for RCA, Dempsey knocked out Carpentier in the fourth round moments before its overheated transmitter blew up. Three months later a successful broadcast of the World Series between the New York Giants and the New York Yankees created even more enthusiasm for radio.

By the end of 1921, ten stations, including the four Westinghouse stations, four others in the New York and Pittsburgh areas, and single stations in Dallas and Los Angeles, were licensed for general broadcasting. In the first six months of 1922, nearly ninety more stations went on the air, and by the end of the year, almost 350 had been established. Sales of radio sets and parts likewise skyrocketed, totaling $60 million in 1922. The figure doubled the following year, and by 1924 it reached $358 million.

WHAT LISTENERS HEARD

Americans quickly seized the opportunity provided by radio to participate in public events and enjoy entertainments without having to leave their own homes. Elections, heavyweight fights, and World Series did not occur frequently enough, however, to begin to occupy the hours available for radio broadcasting. The question of what to put on the air confronted the new radio industry from the start. Regular news coverage, as opposed to reports on a few special events, was beyond the capacity of early radio and would remain so until the 1930s. Music, live performances as well as phonograph recordings, quickly became the most popular way of filling the airwaves. Children's bedtime stories, educational programs, and weather reports also became standard fare.

Broadcasters   With all the uncertainties involved in early programming, a need arose for radio announcers with good voices and a gift of gab who could describe sporting events, introduce studio acts, and, perhaps most important, fill airtime with a continuous stream of interesting patter when something went wrong. One member of this new craft, desperate for something to say when three performers in a row failed to appear at the studio, thrust his microphone out a window and declared, "Ladies and gentlemen, I give you the sounds of New York!"[1]

A few radio announcers found themselves pressed into service to cover the sporting events that drew large audiences from the outset. KDKA broadcast a University of Pittsburgh–West Virginia University football game even before the Dempsey-Carpentier fight took place. Before long football and baseball games, boxing matches, and horse races were all being covered, greatly expanding the audience and creating new enthusiasm for competitive sports. Announcers, many of them without much athletic background, needed to develop techniques and language to describe the action vividly, enthusiastically, and accurately. An even greater challenge was to fill the airspace when nothing much was happening. Quickly, the still-familiar practice evolved of having two announcers team up to report on games. One would describe the play-by-play action on the field, the other would provide analysis, background information on players, and "color." Football also required a "spotter" to identify the large and constantly shifting cast of players involved in the action. For all their challenges, sports broadcasts drew huge audiences as Graham NcNamee discovered when he received over 50,000 fan letters after he covered the 1925 World Series.

Music,
Music,
Music   From the outset, music filled much of radio's available broadcast time. Live performances of the parlor piano and vocal music of recent decades were most common at first, but classical music, especially opera and orchestral performances, enjoyed frequent broadcast. While many Americans had joined in or at least heard the former sort of music at home, in saloons and vaudeville theaters, or elsewhere, few had attended an opera or symphony concert. The audience that heard classical music with the low sound quality of early radio was soon eager for live performance. Between 1928 and 1939 the number of major professional symphony orchestras increased from

ten to seventeen; the total number of orchestras, including part-time less professional ones in smaller cities, grew from sixty to two hundred and eighty-six. Perhaps more significant, whereas musical instruction in public schools was almost unheard of in 1920, two decades later it was widespread. Thirty thousand school orchestras and twenty thousand bands had sprung up.

Radio was much more effective than the earlier technological innovation, the phonograph, in building an audience for classical music. Until the long-playing record was developed in 1948, phonograph records could only hold about five minutes of music per side, creating difficulties in the presentation of all but the shortest classical works. Furthermore, by 1924, superheterodyne radios were producing better quality sound than phonographs. Radio therefore took the lead in presenting classical music. The phonograph industry went into a radio-induced slump that lasted through the 1930s.

Radio also promoted the popularity of other forms of music. Both jazz and country music reached beyond the audiences they had known and evolved significantly as a result. Music that could be and often had been performed at home in the parlor included sentimental songs, ballads, vaudeville and musical comedy tunes, and less-challenging operatic pieces. Such parlor music was familiar, traditional, and remained widely enjoyed by early radio audiences. The limitations of radio, however, reshaped this sort of music. Intense voices, especially high sopranos, had a tendency to blow out the tubes on radio transmitters. As a result, a number of singers developed a new, soft, gentle style that came across well and soon became known as "crooning." Female singers such as Vaughn De Leath and Kate Smith as well as males such as Rudy Vallee and Bing Crosby built large and loyal audiences as they perfected the "crooning" style.

Radio did not at first embrace jazz, a musical genre ripening rapidly in the 1920s. Jazz had its origins in dixieland, ragtime, **Jazz** blues, and other musical forms that had evolved in the pre–World War I urban south, particularly in the African American community of New Orleans. Jazz migrated along with its practitioners to Chicago and elsewhere during the war and enjoyed growing popularity throughout the urban north in the 1920s. Since jazz was not considered altogether respectable, whether because of its African American roots, its spontaneous, improvisational nature, its pulsating and often passionate style, or its frequent association with prohibition era speakeasies, most radio stations were at first reluctant to broadcast it.

Band leader Paul Whiteman did a lot to change attitudes toward jazz, less because he was a classically trained musician and actually wrote down parts for his musicians than because he favored a soft, sweet, and smooth style of jazz. When he commissioned composer George Gershwin to write a jazz composition for piano and orchestra and first presented "Rhapsody in Blue" in February 1924, jazz acquired instant respectability. Whiteman's orchestra and his style of jazz became a regular feature of radio music for the next quarter century. Other bands led by Guy Lombardo, Ozzie Nelson, Rudy Vallee, Duke Ellington, Glenn Miller, and Tommy and Jimmy Dorsey followed in Whiteman's path, helping to make jazz an important part of radio broadcasting, especially in the 1930s and 1940s.

Country Music   Radio helped foster the evolution of another musical form in the 1920s: country music. While not encountering the initial resistance that faced jazz, country music at the time consisted of a range of nonprofessional, traditional folk music often referred to as "hillbilly." Early southern radio stations experimented successfully with fiddle tunes, gospel songs, and other localized forms of folk music. In April 1924, the Sears, Roebuck station in Chicago, named WLS for World's Largest Store, began a fiddle and square dance music program called *The National Barn Dance.* It was an instant hit. Nineteen months later, station WSM in Nashville, Tennessee, followed with a variety show named *The Grand Ole Opry.* Before long, the "Opry" had proved so popular that it was being broadcast four hours a night every Friday and Saturday. These programs, which could be heard throughout the South and Midwest, and a number of imitators called attention to country music and made celebrities out of its best performers. Innovations in style, such as the combining of fiddle, guitar, mandolin, and banjo to make "bluegrass music," soon followed. Radio lifted country music from its highly localized roots and encouraged its evolution as widely popular and distinctive American music.

Religious Broadcasts   Religious services became another early staple of radio broadcasting. Sacred music represented only part of the appeal. Radio preachers reported receiving a flood of letters of gratitude from farmers, the elderly, invalids, and others unable to attend church services. While most radio preachers reached only a local audience, by the late 1920s and 1930s a few gained a national following. Evangelist Aimee Semple McPherson in Los Angeles and Father Charles Coughlin in Royal Oak, Michigan, were the first to emerge and quickly became the best known. Whether religious observance became more common and less communal and intense because of radio broadcasts remained ambiguous, however.

Political Broadcasts   Radio's impact on American politics, likewise, proved an uncertain blessing from the outset. Broadcasts of the 1924 Republican National Convention in Cleveland and the Democratic National Convention from Madison Square Garden in New York gave radio listeners a sense of national party politics unlike anything available before. The Republican convention was broadcast first, but with the nomination of the incumbent, President Calvin Coolidge, a foregone conclusion and little thought given to the radio audience, it was a tedious affair. Unfortunately for the Democrats, the broadcast of their convention two weeks later called attention to deep party divisions between urban and rural, northern and southern, and progressive and conservative factions. The convention dragged on for an unprecedented fourteen days and 103 ballots before a presidential nominee was selected. While their radio performance was not the only cause of the Democrats' subsequent election loss to their Republican rivals (who had their own problems with recent Harding administration corruption scandals), it did initiate a new era in which radio brought national politics more vividly into the lives of ordinary Americans.

As the radio boom accelerated, more broadcasting stations as well as more powerful ones whose signals traveled further went on the air. At first, every station was supposed to broadcast on the same federally assigned frequency (as a result of the 1912 Federal Radio Act which envisioned military and government radio communication but not commercial broadcasting). In late 1922, a second frequency was allocated. This change was hardly enough to keep stations from interfering with each other. While nearby stations worked out agreements to alternate periods that they would be on the air, this compromise did not solve the problem. Some stations simply altered their frequency on their own. When warned against doing this, Aimee Semple McPherson sent Commerce Secretary Herbert Hoover a telegram saying, "PLEASE ORDER YOUR MINIONS OF SATAN TO LEAVE MY STATION ALONE STOP YOU CANNOT EXPECT THE ALMIGHTY TO ABIDE BY YOUR WAVE LENGTH NONSENSE STOP WHEN I OFFER MY PRAYERS TO HIM I MUST FIT INTO HIS WAVE RECEPTION." Unrestricted high-power stations, broadcasting at 100,000 watts or more, could literally blow their lower-power competitors off the air.

Government Regulation

Since only the number of radio frequencies was limited, broadcasters soon called for federal regulation. Reluctant to restrict private business, Hoover's Commerce Department at first tried to get broadcasters to reach agreements among themselves. Problems continued, however, and with the number of stations increasing to nearly 700, Congress finally adopted the Radio Act of 1927, declaring that the airwaves belonged to the people and the government must accept responsibility for managing them in the common interest. The new Federal Radio Commission (replaced in the mid-1930s by an expanded Federal Communications Commission) defined a radio broadcast band at 500 to 1,500 kilocycles, licensed stations to operate at specified frequencies and transmission power up to 50,000 watts, and set standards of good practice for license holders.

Larger commercial broadcasters welcomed government rationalization and regulation of the radio business. Meanwhile, the many small non-profit stations operated by educational institutions complained about being assigned poor frequencies and restricted to daytime operation. Four out of five of the educational stations licensed in the 1920s went off the air by the following decade, leaving only about forty across the nation to pursue programs of academic lectures, agricultural reports, and domestic advice. The effect of the Radio Act of 1927 was, therefore, to enhance the commercial potential of radio while undermining its educational possibilities.

THE RISE OF NETWORKS

Although government intervention made possible a multitude of radio stations and, therefore, the possibility of a great variety of choices for listeners, other developments—networking and advertising—before long came to standardize what most people heard. Experiments with linking stations by telephone lines so that they could simultaneously broadcast the same program began with the 1922 World Series, carried by a New York City and a Schenectady station. By the following summer, a similar arrangement made it possible for a St. Louis speech by President Harding to be heard in New York. An enthusiastic newspaper reporter predicted that "it might not be too long before farmers at the four corners of the Union may sit in their own houses and hear the President of the United States."[2] At the same time, experiments with short-wave transmission of programs that would then be rebroadcast by local stations came to offer an alternative mode of creating radio networks.

NBC   Negotiations between RCA and AT&T, two pioneers in the creation of networks, led in 1926 to the establishment of the National Broadcasting Company (NBC) which went on the air in November 1926. Because of its origins as a merger, NBC actually operated two networks, the Red and the Blue, until the latter was sold and became the American Broadcasting Company (ABC) in 1943. The first four-hour NBC broadcast involved a New York orchestra, a Chicago soprano, and the comedian Will Rogers from Kansas City; more significant, the audience was estimated at twelve million.

The next year, the NBC network was able to link fifty stations in twenty-four states for the largest broadcast ever: all-day coverage of a Washington, D.C., celebration honoring Charles Lindbergh with a parade, a presidential medal, and other festivities for his recent trans-Atlantic flight. Enthusiasm for "Lucky Lindy," already immense, grew even greater as excited announcers extolled his virtues to an estimated nationwide audience of thirty million. Americans had known national figures before, political leaders, military heroes, even athletes; but with

Lindbergh, national radio networks began to demonstrate their ability to turn a person of accomplishment into a celebrity by transmitting the sound of his or her voice as well as information about him or her. Hundreds of thousands of people who would never come close to Lindbergh could feel that they knew him as well as they knew a neighbor. Lindbergh, not the first pilot to fly the Atlantic, though the first to do so alone, achieved what would become lifelong public prominence, not merely for his aerial feat, but for his good fortune (or ill fortune, depending on one's viewpoint) in being the first national radio celebrity.

The potential of radio networks led quickly to the creation of a second. The Columbia Broadcasting System (CBS) lacked the fi- **CBS** nancing of NBC, but aggressive development (including the 1929 acquisition of a West Coast network) and imaginative programming forged it into a substantial nationwide rival to NBC before the end of the decade. From 1927 onward, therefore, radio listeners who had heretofore commonly experienced only local broadcasts gained access to and choice in national radio network programs. Another network, the Mutual Broadcasting System, appeared in 1934. With radio networks, Americans, wherever they lived, became able to hear simultaneously the same information, entertainment, and commercial messages. No doubt as a result, radio sales accelerated further after 1927, reaching $650 million in 1928 and $842 million in 1929, more than double the total five years earlier.

Both CBS and NBC responded to growing interest in classical music. CBS began regular broadcasts of the Chicago **Classical** Civic Opera in 1927 and established its own orchestra the **Music** same year. The NBC Symphony Orchestra, founded in 1936, was led by the renowned conductor Arturo Toscanini; it broadcast weekly from its own specially built studio, the most acoustically advanced of its day. Broadcasts of New York's Metropolitan Opera began in 1932, underwritten by Texaco Oil Company, and continue to this day under the same sponsorship. The early efforts of radio networks furthered a lasting nationwide interest in classical music outside a tiny, urban, wealthy elite, but before long broadcasters' attention turned from the introduction of generally unfamiliar music to the presentation of popular forms assured of creating an audience for advertising messages.

ADVERTISING ON THE AIRWAVES

In 1922, WBAY in New York (it soon changed its call letters to WEAF) announced that it would be a "toll broadcasting station," selling time to anyone wanting to speak or perform over the airwaves. At first the charge would be $50 for fifteen minutes in the evening, $40 for the same time in the afternoon. Amazingly, a month went by before time was purchased for an August 28 program that promoted a Queens apartment development during breaks in a thirty-minute talk about novelist Nathaniel Hawthorne. By the end of the year, the number of toll broadcasts was increasing but not enough to support the station.

Financing Broadcasts
Advertising did not represent the only means of financing radio broadcasting. Annual license fees on radio receivers as a means of funding state-run systems became common in Europe. In the United States, there was talk of municipal governments paying for radio or endowment of stations by wealthy philanthropists. Resolution of the question of how to pay for radio broadcasting would, of course, influence its content, as is now evident in the contrast between public radio and television and commercial broadcasting. Promotion of radio equipment sales and the self-financed efforts of early amateurs could not carry broadcasting very far. Since at the time, widespread resistance existed to any expansion of government activity, not long into the 1920s commercial advertising became a principal and profitable means of financing radio and a shaping influence on content.

Sponsored Programs
Radio advertising at first consisted primarily of sponsoring programs. Advertisers counted on the goodwill generated by having their brand name associated with a popular program to boost sales. Broadcasters and advertisers alike were reluctant at first to intrude upon an audience by describing a specific product, much less proclaiming its virtues or indicating its price. Such "direct advertising" might be appropriate in a newspaper or magazine but was thought to infringe too much on the radio audience. Debate even went on as to whether such a personal and private product as toothpaste should be advertised in a medium that could easily impose on an unsuspecting audience.

Marketing Power
The potential power of radio as a marketing instrument gradually overcame such early hesitation. Before long, advertisements were encouraging listeners to consider new products and reconsider ones already on the market. Perhaps the most striking example of the impact of radio advertising was the Lucky Strike cigarette campaign. Before the mid-1920s smoking was a predominately male activity. Few American women smoked and even fewer dared to do so in public. Alert to the potential for doubling its market, Lucky Strike began broadcasting endorsements by foreign opera stars. The ads conveyed glamour, sophistication, not to mention the safety of cigarettes for valuable voices. Before long, the notion that cigarettes could help women keep slim and attractive began to be implied. Propelled by huge advertising budgets, the message got through to millions of women.

The sale of advertising became a driving force stimulating and shaping network broadcasting. Advertisers were attracted by the larger audiences and better programs that networks offered, while the networks in turn saw the potential for profit. Decisions on what to send out over the air came to be made on the basis of what would draw the largest or most desirable audience for the advertiser. Furthermore, the desire not to offend any part of the audience that might be listening led broadcasters to avoid controversial material. Music, sports, comedy, and drama were much better suited to this objective, in the eyes of most advertisers and broadcasters, than educational programs or discussions of public affairs and politics. An early experiment with having H. V. Kaltenborn, an editorial writer for the *Brooklyn Eagle,* deliver on-the-air current affairs commentary was soon abandoned when his strong opinions seemed as likely to offend as to attract listeners. The first consideration in determining broadcast content and schedule remained that of attracting the largest possible audience.

Initially radio broadcasts were limited to the evening hours, but as their popularity (and profitability) increased, **Broadcast** programs of diverse character occupied more and more **Hours** hours of the day. Stations started going on the air for a couple **Expand** of hours at midday with some music, weather information directed at farmers, and some sort of program designed for housewives; they might return in the late afternoon with programs targeted at early elementary school children and women before aiming at a more general audience from 6 to 11 P.M. The earliest morning "wake-up" programs concentrated on calisthenics. *New York Daily Graphic* publisher Bernarr Macfadden, a physical fitness enthusiast, began, in 1925, to buy time on WOR from 6:45 to 8 A.M. every morning so that he could personally conduct an exercise program. By the 1930s, weather reports, recorded music, and talk had become the standard morning fare. A few stations tried late-night programs featuring mellow music and announcers with particularly soothing "bedtime" voices. Since relatively few stations remained on the air and signals traveled further late at night, some of these stations gained unusually far-flung audiences.

SERIALS, SOAPS, AND *AMOS 'N ANDY*

The last hours to be filled with radio programming were the hours of the usual workday. By the late 1920s, **Serial Dramas** however, these periods came to be recognized as times **and Comedies** when housewives might listen and could be targets of specialized advertising. Cooking, child care, gardening, and other advice programs thought by male advertisers to be of particular interest to women were first to be broadcast; romantic dramas soon followed. By the early 1930s serial dramas such as *Ma Perkins* and *The Romance of Helen Trent,* designed to attract regular listeners with their continuing stories, began to appear. These were often sponsored by domestic product manufacturers such as Proctor and Gamble, and hence scornfully labeled "soap operas."

Although it was a new and untried form in radio programming, the regular dramatic or comedy program with a constant setting and ongoing cast of characters emerged remarkably quickly in the late 1920s. Serial dramas and situation comedies attracted enormous and faithful audiences and thus became popular with advertisers. They would retain their popularity, both with listeners and those trying to get their attention, until the advent of television (which borrowed the format) after World War II. Regularly scheduled, ongoing programs, situation comedies in particular, became the backbone of network radio.

No radio program of the era achieved greater popularity than *Amos 'n Andy*, which evolved as a local Chicago program over several years and began its national broadcast on the NBC Blue Network in August 1929. At its peak in the early 1930s, an estimated 40 million people, almost one third of the nation's population, listened to *Amos 'n Andy* between 7 and 7:15 P.M. every weeknight. The characters of Amos and Andy were two African American men who had migrated from Atlanta to the south side of Chicago and were perpetually confused by city life. Simple and trusting Amos, domineering Andy, and their good friend, a rascal who went by the nickname "the Kingfish," as well as many other characters were all played by the show's two white creators, Freeman Gosden and Charles Correll. While much of the show's humor centered on the characters' distortions of language ("What a sitchiation," "Ain't dat sumpin," "I'se regusted," and the Kingfish's favorite phrase, "Holy Mackerel!"), Amos and Andy were portrayed as decent and likable fellows dealing with universally perplexing situations. Many black listeners seemed to enjoy the show as much as whites, though some resented its characterizations. In Pittsburgh, Robert Vann's newspaper aimed at African Americans, the *Courier*, circulated petitions to have the show banished from the air. Vann obtained 740,000 signatures and stirred thought among white liberals, though the petition did not achieve its goal. When Britain's George Bernard Shaw was asked what he found most memorable about the United States after a visit in the early 1930s, he replied without hesitation, "the Rocky Mountains, Niagara Falls, and 'Amos 'n Andy'. "

Amos and Andy entertained their listeners with their efforts to explain situations they confronted, such as the onset of the Great Depression.

Andy: Well, Lightin', 'course I would like to give you a job but de bizness repression is on right now.

Lightin': What is dat you say, Mr. Andy?

Andy: Is you been keepin' yo' eye on de stock market?

Lightin': Nosah, I ain't never seed it.

Andy: Well, de stock market crashed.

Lightin': Anybody git hurt?

Andy: Well, 'course Lightin', when de stock market crashes, it hurts us bizness men. Dat's what put de repression on things.[3]

Amos 'n Andy spawned a number of imitators in the 1930s. Some of these programs followed the formula of rooting their humor in a minority group's perplexities with mainstream America. *The Goldbergs*, a show about Jewish immigrants in New York, was one of the more popular. Others, such as *Fibber McGee and Molly*, concentrated on addressing the ordinary problems of daily life to which a broad audience could relate.

RADIO AND THE REAL WORLD

While political leaders starting with Warren Harding and Calvin Coolidge spoke on radio, none appreciated its potential for establishing a sense of personal, informal contact with **"Fireside Chats"** the vast number of Americans until Franklin D. Roosevelt became president in 1933. FDR began a series of what came to be called "fireside chats" in which he explained the nature of depression conditions and his administration's response to them. With four of every five American newspapers editorially hostile to FDR, radio became Roosevelt's best means of explaining his positions to the public. Huge audiences listened; and his resounding reelections in 1936, 1940, and 1944 were, in one respect, a measure of the impact on most Americans of what they heard on the radio. Even Roosevelt's most notable and effective political opponents achieved their position largely through radio. Charles Coughlin, a Roman Catholic priest with a weekly broadcast from "The Shrine of the Little Flower" in Royal Oak, Michigan, and Louisiana Senator Huey Long built national followings for their critiques of the New Deal on the basis of their compelling radio presentations.

Not until the mid-1930s did radio networks begin to broadcast regular and substantial news programs. Earlier, newspapers, **Radio News** fearing competition, refused access to their news wire services. Radio lacked the incentive and resources to gather news on its own until the CBS and NBC networks decided to do so. News programs quickly became popular with the listening audience. Rising international tensions caused by the Spanish Civil War, the Japanese invasions of Manchuria and China, and Germany's invasions of numerous European

Scott's Run, West Virginia, couple listening to the radio, 1938. Photo courtesy of the Library of Congress.

countries under the leadership of Adolph Hitler gave news reports and analysis a growing presence and importance.

"War of the Worlds" At first the audience for radio news was rather trusting of what it heard, a fact that became evident on Halloween eve 1938 when CBS broadcast Orson Welles' vivid dramatization of "War of the Worlds." Presenting H. G. Wells' tale of alien invasion as a series of eyewitness news reports interrupting a dance band performance, the program's effectively contrived realism panicked a large and far-flung audience that either missed or ignored an introduction identifying it as fiction. The nationwide uproar over "the night the Martians landed" demonstrated the significant role that radio had come to play in shaping Americans' sense of what was going on beyond their immediate view.

Radio seldom fused the entire American population into a single audience, however. Even when a FDR fireside chat, an **Ending** *Amos 'n Andy* program, a Joe Louis championship fight, or the **Isolation** World Series was being broadcast, people could and did choose to listen to other programs. Not everyone heard "War of the Worlds," though its fame became such that few might later admit that they were not tuned in to its first broadcast. While *Fortune* magazine surveys in 1937 and 1938 found radio to be the nation's most popular pastime, edging out movie going and far surpassing reading, individual listening habits varied widely.

In any case, whether the listener was a Chicago worker or a Great Plains farm wife, radio reduced his or her sense of personal isolation. The worker might tune in to the Chicago Federation of Labor station WCFL or an ethnic station offering traditional music from the homeland. The farm woman meanwhile might listen to stations offering household hints, commodity price quotations, and weather reports along with soap operas and music. In either case, radio brought a variety of information and entertainment into the home, allowing people an escape from their daily routine and a chance to feel that they were connected to others in a vast unseen audience.

NOTES

1. Nathan Brokenshire quoted in George H. Douglas, *The Early Days of Radio Broadcasting* (Jefferson, N.C.: McFarland, 1987), 63.

2. Quoted in Douglas, *Early Days of Radio*, 130.

3. Ibid., 203.

5

Cinema and the Extension of Experience

Another important means of communication, unlike radio broadcasting, was not altogether new in the 1920s. Motion pictures did, however, change fundamentally during the decade. The addition of sound to on-screen images transformed the moviegoing experience. With 95 million movie tickets being sold each week by the end of the decade and movie attendence remaining very popular during the depression years that followed, cinema, like radio, had an enormous impact on American daily life. The combination of visual and aural images provided vivid multi-dimensional experiences that could be shared by a scattered mass audience. Movies, as much or more than radio, served to break down provincialism, increase awareness of the unfamiliar, and create a national community with a specific set of shared experiences.

THE RISE OF MOTION PICTURES

American enthusiasm for motion pictures began to take shape in the 1890s with the introduction of single-viewer Kinetoscopes and, in 1896, large-screen projection. Within **Nickelodeons** a few years, middle-sized and large cities all had "nickelodeons," a made-up word combining the price of admission with the Greek term for theater, offering fifteen- to twenty-minute programs composed of a potpourri of unconnected black-and-white scenes. Brief presentations of dancing, travel scenes, speeding locomotives, historical recreations such as the beheading of Mary, Queen of Scots, or the raising of an American flag during the 1898 war in Cuba, and, increasingly, films with sexual themes filled nickelodeon screens. Vaudeville theaters, competitors in the business of inexpensive mass entertainment, began showing motion pictures interspersed with their live acts. Nickelodeons were slower to be established outside of urban centers. However, companies such as the Cook and Harris High Class Moving Pictures Company of Cooperstown, New York, used portable projection equipment to bring two-hour shows, at least occasionally, to hundreds of small towns in the northeastern and midwestern United States until nickelodeons began to appear in towns throughout those regions with as few as 1,000 residents. By the end of the first decade of the twentieth century, the motion picture business was well established

Early Films

In 1903, an eleven-minute film helped inaugurate a more complex style of filmmaking. *The Great Train Robbery* told a dramatic story using a dozen locations, twenty different camera placements, and new techniques such as a striking close-up of a bandit firing a gun directly at the camera. Soon all manner of exciting fights and high speed pursuits became commonplace cinema fare. By 1915, the narrative film attained its full development with the three-hour *The Birth of a Nation*, a drama that switched rapidly from one element to another of an elaborate story portraying the Ku Klux Klan as a restorer of peace and order to the South following the Civil War.

Early films relied on the pure visual excitement of moving images to entertain an audience. Chases, fights, and rescues were easy to photograph and, furthermore, did not require their audience to speak English or even to know how to read. Along with physical comedy that required no explanation, such scenes became the backbone of a motion picture industry that in its early years aimed at and became most popular among the urban working class.

Not until the introduction of more complex films such as *The Birth of a Nation* with frequent captions and musical accompaniment along with a thrilling climactic gun battle and rescue did large numbers of middle- and upper-class Americans begin to join the moviegoing audience. By the 1920s, surveys reported that high school and college graduates, although they together composed only one-fourth of the nation's population, had become the largest component of the audience. The majority of filmgoers were under thirty-five, and people with higher incomes were attending more often than workers and farmers. While men and women went to the movies with equal frequency, it was females who were buying and reading the growing flood of movie fan magazines.

MOVIE THEATERS AND PICTURE PALACES

By the early 1920s, feature-length as well as shorter silent films, often accompanied by live vaudeville acts, **Popular Cheap** had become a popular form of cheap entertainment in **Entertainment** large- and medium-sized cities. In January 1923, the United States had 15,000 silent movie theaters with an average capacity of 507 and a weekly attendance of 50 million, leading one historian to conclude that going to the movies had developed into a normal feature of life for every segment of society. One region represented a clear exception to this generalization: the South. The highly conservative, mostly rural, and deeply impoverished region had few theaters outside of its larger towns and cities. As late as 1930, for instance, Georgia had only one-third as many movie theater seats per thousand population as any state outside the region. Rural southerners with little cash as well as few automobiles to get to a theater in town were, whether black or white, for the most part left out of the growing national film audience until after World War II. Racial segregation further inhibited African Americans from going to the movies, except in cities (northern as well as southern) large enough to support theaters catering particularly to them; in those circumstances movies became highly popular among African Americans as the least oppressive white-dominated form of entertainment. Because only a relatively few "race movies" reflected their own culture, African Americans, as well as Hispanics and Asians in the Far West, saw mainly mainstream American films if they saw anything at all.

Approximately 1,000 American theaters were "picture palaces," large, elegantly decorated, air-conditioned auditoriums located in urban centers. Picture palaces generally seated 1,500 or more, and appealed to a middle-class audience willing to pay 30 cents or more to see a movie and, usually, live vaudeville acts—singers, dancers, comedians, acrobats, jugglers, or magicians—in extraordinary surroundings. Many came equipped with a "mighty Wurlitzer" organ to accompany the motion picture as well as provide independent entertainment. Even grander picture palaces termed "atmospherics" were built later in the decade, with expansive lobbies; thick carpeting; statuary and paintings; exotic Spanish, Moroccan, or Byzantine styling; and ceilings that seemed to resemble open skies with moving clouds or twinkling stars. Smaller, less elaborate versions of picture palaces in smaller cities likewise sought to make the experience of going to the movies a departure from ordinary life, yet the motion picture itself accomplished this feat even in the plainest theaters which were the norm in urban neighborhoods and small towns.

**Audiences
Grow**

Movie audience continued to grow. Muncie, Indiana's, nine movie theaters sold 31,000 tickets each week in 1924, while church attendance averaged 20,600, helping to explain religious hostility to motion pictures already seen as frequently immoral and decadent. Sunday, in fact, was the biggest day of the week for Muncie's theaters. By 1928, 65 million tickets were being sold nationally each week to a population slightly less than twice that number. With many theaters changing their presentation two or more times a week and urban areas having many theaters, some people were buying tickets more often than once a week. Other people seldom if ever went to the movies during the 1920s or afterwards, but moviegoing was becoming very much a commonplace aspect of American life.

**Minority
Theaters**

Wherever there was a significant minority population, either African American or Hispanic, theaters generally segregated the seats. Minority patrons were required to sit in a separate area, usually a balcony. In some cases, minorities were simply excluded. No wonder that separate theaters catering exclusively to minority audiences, offering opportunities to go to the movies without discomfort, cropped up in places with sizable African American or Hispanic populations. The Asian population was too small to sustain much of a movie culture of its own, although a few Japanese theaters, importing films from Japan and employing *bench* (film explainers who performed beside the screen), struggled along in southern California.

WHAT AUDIENCES SAW

**Material
Opulence**

By the early 1920s, the vast majority of silent films had settled into a few subject categories: the crime story, the Western, the historical costume drama, the contemporary domestic melodrama, or romance. As the audience shifted from nearly all working class to increasingly middle and upper class, so too did the settings of the stories. Increasingly, films pictured a society where, in the words of cinema historian Robert Sklar, "nearly everyone (who was not a cowboy or a cross-eyed comedian) dressed in evening clothes, lived in an elegant home, and passed the time in cabarets."[1] Films of this sort encouraged audiences to think of material opulence as widespread. This ideal of consumption was reinforced by the increasingly popular movie magazines. Fan magazines called attention to the extravagant homes and life styles of the Hollywood community as well as to the biographies of movie stars who had risen from modest circumstances to achieve positions that, the implication was clear, were to be envied.

The portrayal of women in 1920s films reflected what movie makers thought audiences would find acceptable in the years immediately following the adoption of woman suffrage. **Women's Roles** Films with contemporary urban settings were especially likely to feature restless young women, single or married, eager to escape the home and obtain a status equal with men. Positions of superiority over men were shown as a waste of women's true talents. At the same time women should not be *Manhandled* (the title of a 1922 film) and lose their virtue, vital to a successful marriage. Even a free-spirited and apparently sexually liberated female such as Clara Bow in *The Plastic Age* (1925) or *It* (1927) must demonstrate chaste goodness underneath her naughty behavior in order to win her man. The triumph of conventional virtue, often after some audience-attracting misconduct, proved to be a constant theme.

Many of the most popular and memorable silent films of the early 1920s did have strong sexual themes. Between 1921 when he appeared in *The Sheik* and 1926 when he died suddenly at **Sexual Themes** age thirty-one, Rudolph Valentino was the most popular screen actor, playing role after role in which his character's aggressive sexuality was explained by his Latin or Arab or European background. Swedish-born Greta Garbo became the silent screen's female equivalent of Valentino in films such as *The Temptress* (1926) and *Flesh and the Devil* (1927). The films of Garbo, Valentino, and others conveyed to the large audience eager to watch them that non-Americans were more free and open in their sexual behavior. Even the hugely popular silent film comedians of the early 1920s, Charlie Chaplin, Buster Keaton, and Harold Lloyd, earned many of their laughs through inept and ludicrous efforts at courtship. Yet at the same time, a couple of sex scandals within the California film community caused a nervous industry to start a program of self-censorship that sharply curtailed the sexual content of most films and inaugurated a forty-year period in which most sexual messages were subtle, indirect, and modest.

Still, in the 1920s a growing national audience received a great deal of information about sexual matters through film, information not previously available. For a pioneering study of the influence of movies, young people testified over and over that they learned a great deal about how to act from what they saw on the screen. One young women reported that she imitated movie actresses who closed their eyes while kissing. A young man reported, "It was directly through the movies that I learned to kiss a girl on her ears, neck, and cheeks, as well as on the mouth." And the rapid pace of silent movie romances convinced other young people that romance occurred quickly; they reported that kissing and necking were happening earlier than before in their relationship. "I know love pictures have made me more receptive to love-making," said one sixteen-year-old high school sophomore; "I always thought it rather silly until these pictures, where there is always so much love and everything turns out all right in the end, and I kiss and pet much more than I would otherwise."[2]

Not all films offered uncomplicated endorsements of romance between attractive males and compliant females. In the ambiguously titled 1920 silent film *Why Change Your Wife?* director Cecil B. DeMille presented the beautiful Gloria Swanson as a frumpy housewife who was losing her husband to a glamorous, well-made-up and well-dressed interloper. The wife responds by acquiring a wardrobe of sexy, sleeveless, backless dresses of gold lamé and feathers, and, of course, wins back her husband. On one level the film conveyed the message that married as well as single women needed to pay attention to their appearance. At the same time, viewers were at least as likely to carry away Swanson's memorable observation, "The more I see of men, the better I like dogs."

Prohibition Flouted
Another theme in 1920s films helped shape perceptions as to how people beyond the audience's personal experience were dealing with national prohibition. Although few films in the early 1920s depicted drinking or bootlegging, by mid-decade a wave of films about contemporary urban jazz-age "flapper" society did so. "No such picture would be considered properly finished," observed one New York film reviewer, "without a number of scenes depicting the shaking up and drinking down of cocktails and their resulting effect on those who partake of them." In a representative sample of 115 films from 1930, liquor was referred to in 78 percent and drinking depicted in 66 percent. Further analysis of forty of those films reveals that while only 13 percent of male villains and 8 percent of female villains could be seen consuming alcohol, no less than 43 percent of heroes and 23 percent of heroines were shown doing so. Moviegoers could hardly avoid the impression that drinking was widespread and that prohibition violation was socially respectable.[3]

THE ADVENT OF TALKIES

Attending a movie seldom involved sitting in complete silence, in part because most theaters presented silent pictures accompanied by a piano player, an organist, or even an orchestra. Shortly after mid-decade, however, thanks in part to the technological advances made with radio, films with their own synchronized sound accompaniment began to appear. In 1926, Warner Bros. premiered its Vitaphone sound system in short, predominantly musical films. In October 1927, they brought out the first feature length "talking picture," *The Jazz Singer*, starring vaudeville performer Al Jolson in a story, appropriately enough, about a young man caught in a cultural conflict between his traditionalist family and his own modern tastes and opportunities. An immediate sensation, *The Jazz Singer* drew audiences as fast as movie theaters could be equipped to show it.

With the instant popularity of talking pictures, most theaters found they could drop the practice of interspersing **Vaudeville** vaudeville acts and live music with silent motion pictures. **Era Ends** The grand picture palace, which had the upper hand as long as theaters presented a combination of film and live entertainment, lost its economic advantage as full programs of sound motion pictures became available. A few vaudeville troupes, such as the Three Stooges and the Marx Brothers, were able to transfer their style of entertainment to film, but for the most part vaudeville faded. Warner Bros. and other studios (e.g., Fox, Metro-Goldwyn-Mayer, and Paramount), quick to seize the opportunity to make "talkies," soon gained dominance in a movie industry transformed during the late 1920s. These studios profited spectacularly as well as gained control over much of what the millions of moviegoers throughout the country would thereafter be able to see.

The rapid switch from silent to sound motion pictures altered the behavior of moviegoers, historian Robert Sklar **No Talking** points out. It was considered quite acceptable for silent movie audiences to react out loud to what they saw on the screen. An ongoing series of comments could create a bond among members of an audience sitting in the dark, furthering a sense of community among those in a neighborhood or small town theater or even creating one temporarily in an urban picture palace. Talking by viewers made silent movie going a shared experience and rendered each screening a unique and personal event. With talking pictures, however, audience conversation served to distract from the film dialogue, and audience members who spoke aloud were promptly hushed by ushers or fellow patrons. As Sklar observed, "The talking audience for silent pictures became a silent audience for talking pictures."[4] As a result, moviegoing soon became a much more private and passive experience even in a crowded theater.

The addition of sound offered filmmakers new ways to attract and excite audiences. The very fact that films could **New Movies** make their points with sound as well as visual messages allowed them to become much more fast paced and complex, thus inherently more compelling. By 1930, the year the Census Bureau counted 123 million Americans, the weekly sale of movie tickets, stimulated by the popularity of talkies, reached three-fourths that number. Despite the severe economic problems of the 1930s, movie attendance, while slipping somewhat, remained strong throughout the decade.

Shooting and Screams The sounds of shooting and screams as well as the noise of galloping horses, creaking doors, and thunderous explosions seemed guaranteed to generate thrills and sell tickets. Stories set in wartime became far more popular than they had been in the silent era, especially after a film set in World War I became the biggest hit of 1930. Ironically, *All Quiet on the Western Front* was based on a German novel stressing the universal destruction and tragedy of war. Horror films, such as *Dracula, Frankenstein,* and *King Kong,* likewise attracted crowds. *King Kong* proved particularly popular. The story revolved around a clash between modern science and a powerful force of primitive nature. The filmmakers shrewdly kept the contest even until the last scene when warplanes finally destroyed the giant ape as he climbed to the top of New York's newest and tallest skyscraper, the Empire State Building. The sounds of shooting and pounding horses' hooves helped Westerns, which had been slipping in popularity but which were relatively inexpensive to produce, regain an important position in Hollywood's output.

Crime Dramas Contemporary crime dramas offered other opportunities to exploit sound using gunfire, breaking glass, squealing tires, and wailing sirens. While crime stories had long been a staple of motion pictures, the films of the silent era tended to focus on solitary murders. At the outset of the sound era, gangster movies took over. Fables of big city bootlegging, films such as *Little Caesar, The Public Enemy,* and *Scarface,* offered more opportunity for violence—and noise. These films tended to present gang leaders as principled, even noble characters, ambitious young men striving to succeed in a chaotic and violent social environment. The motion picture industry's self-imposed morality, reinforced after 1934 by the Roman Catholic Church's firm insistence that Hollywood measure up to its standards or face a ban on its worshippers' attendance, required that wrongdoing be punished in the end. Nevertheless, gangster films often left audiences with the impression that prohibition laws, not the bootleggers themselves, were ultimately at fault.

Suggestive Dialogue Sound also made possible films that depended on shocking or clever, fast-paced dialogue, often with subtle sexual double meanings that could titillate audiences but escape censorship. The comedies of the Marx Brothers and Mae West in the early 1930s first exploited the humorous possibilities of sound. Increasingly as the decade wore on and as the industry put in effect a 1934 self-censorship production code, filmmakers turned away from overt sexuality and toward much more subtle, so-called "screwball" comedies. Films such as *It Happened One Night, My Man Godfrey,* and *His Girl Friday* combined wacky situations, witty talk, and romance.

Films that featured singing and dancing offered additional opportunities to exploit sound. Some of the most popular **Song and** films of the decade, from *Gold Diggers of 1933* to *The Wizard* **Dance** *of Oz* in 1939, involved song and dance. Even gangster movies often took the opportunity to show a nightclub chorus line, although they were not just intending to provide musical entertainment as cameras lingered leeringly over long-legged, scantily clad female dancers.

THE DEPRESSION AT THE MOVIES

The Great Depression and the public's perceived attitude about it shaped 1930s films a great deal. In the early **Morality and** 1930s, films tended to portray contemporary societies **Optimism** thrown into chaos, whether because of the emergence of gangsters, the presence of zany figures such as Groucho Marx, or the arrival in New York of King Kong. As the political and economic situation appeared to improve after Franklin Roosevelt's election as president, films began to take on a more optimistic tone. A large number of historically or literary-based films from *David Copperfield* in 1935 to *Gone with the Wind* in 1939 offered images of people coping successfully with other and even worse circumstances. Screwball comedies always concluded happily in marriage. Even Frank Capra's popular political melodramas such as *Mr. Deeds Goes to Town* (1936) and *Mr. Smith Goes to Washington* (1939) ended with the triumph of traditional morality. A new form of film, the animated cartoon pioneered by Walt Disney, offered perhaps the most resolutely optimistic storylines of all. The triumph of the most industrious of the *Three Little Pigs* conveyed this confident message in a short 1933 film whose theme song, "Who's Afraid of the Big Bad Wolf?" became an early New Deal anthem. In 1937, Disney offered essentially the same message, though this time using human outcasts living in a forest rather than barnyard animals, in the hugely popular first feature-length animated film, *Snow White and the Seven Dwarfs*.

Escape from the reality outside the theater became another commonplace in 1930s movies. Many films portrayed con- **Escapism** temporary drama or romance that could easily have been played out against any background. Significantly, they were most often set in upper-class environments with glamorous women in evening gowns, relaxed and confident men in tuxedos, expensive automobiles, and even more luxurious homes. Whether this was done to cheer up audiences, inspire consumption, or simply reflect the Hollywood lifestyle remains unclear.

Other forms of cinematic escapism were likewise popular. Busby Berkeley produced a series of elaborately choreographed and imagina-

tively photographed musicals that also involved upper-class lifestyles but achieved their effect as much from their dancers' complete departure from the conventions of real life. Meanwhile, child actress Shirley Temple starred in a series of films that showed her singing, dancing, and cheerfully triumphing over adversity, often in exotic settings and usually assisted only by some elderly male companion. The plump preteen-age girl with curly hair, deep dimples, and an ever-present sunny smile became so popular that mothers all over the country rushed to dress their daughters in Shirley Temple outfits and give them Shirley Temple hairdos.

Perhaps the most escapist film of the decade was the 1939 hit *The Wizard of Oz*, which transported a young girl from depressed black-and-white Kansas to the vivid color (new to film) of Oz, a land populated by talking scarecrows, lions, tin men, wicked witches, and other fantastic creatures. The film contained the populist message of L. Frank Baum's novel on which it was based that simple human virtues of honesty, courage, sensible thought, mutual support, and affection were more to be relied on in times of difficulty than hocus-pocus in the capital city. Most audiences, however, no doubt left the theater more caught up in the dazzling color, music, and fantasy than the subtle political message.

Gone with the Wind, another huge 1939 hit, also provided an escape from reality, particularly for Southerners still mired in the worst poverty in the nation, a condition that could be traced back to the outcome of the Civil War. *Gone with the Wind*, based on an immensely popular 1937 novel by Margaret Mitchell of Atlanta, was a timeless story of fickle romance. Set in Georgia, the story portrayed an antebellum South that never was, a gracious society of considerate masters and happy loyal slaves. In the film's reconstruction of the past, the Civil War destroyed property and lives but not the Southern spirit. Fantasy it was, especially in its positive treatment of race relations and opportunities for strong independent women in Southern society, but far less inflammatory than the previous Civil War epic, *Birth of a Nation*, with its myth of a heroic Ku Klux Klan. In part because of the reputations of its stars, Clark Gable and Vivien Leigh, and in part because it was among the first all-color feature films, *Gone with the Wind* became an enormous success.

Not only did the economic depression affect what was on the screen, it influenced what went on in the theater. **Ticket Sales** Ticket sales fell 25 percent between 1930 and 1933, and **Struggle** though they began to recover the following year, all of the industry's ingenuity was required to avoid economic disaster. The silent-era practice returned of showing serials—short, intensely thrilling films that invariably left Flash Gordon or another central character suspended in a perilous situation until the next episode a week later would produce an escape followed by entrapment in yet another predicament. Bank

The Lyric Theater, Shenandoah, Pennsylvania, 1938. Photo courtesy of the Library of Congress.

nights, which involved the drawing of lucky ticket stubs for cash prizes, became similarly popular, as did giveaways of cheap glassware and china, one piece a week so that only regular customers could build a set.

Theater operators struggling to hold onto their audiences not only continued the practice of changing what they were showing one, two, or more times a week, but they also began offering double features—two full-length films for the price of one. Producers and distributors disliked this latter practice but were powerless to stop it. By the mid-1930s half the theaters in the United States were showing double features. Also, theaters that once disdained selling popcorn and candy because it seemed cheap and undignified now discovered that candy returned a 45 percent profit and popcorn three or four times its cost. In many theaters the sale of food and drink represented the difference between profit and loss, and snacking while watching a movie became commonplace.

The Drive-in   Another innovation was the drive-in movie theater, which made its first appearance in New Jersey in 1933. Intended to take advantage of the American enthusiasm for automobiles, drive-ins allowed customers to park on a carefully designed incline and watch a movie without ever getting out of their cars. Providing sound in sizable, open-air theaters was a problem (and a nuisance to those nearby but not in the drive-in) until the development of the individual car speaker in 1941. Nevertheless, many large urban areas had at least one drive-in movie by the end of the 1930s, though the brief boom time for such theaters would not occur until the 1950s.

Going to the movies, despite a small decline due to the economic hard times, remained the most widespread form of commercial entertainment during the 1930s. Along with listening to the radio, watching movies became a routine way of learning about the world beyond one's own immediate view. **Mass Cultural Appeal** The image of life beyond the neighborhood, small town, or farm might not be accurate, but it was far more vivid and detailed than any earlier available impression. Thus film, together with radio, had a profound influence in connecting people's daily lives to a larger national culture.

The end of the 1930s brought color films and FM radio broadcasting. At the 1939 New York World's Fair, RCA engineers unveiled their new technology of television, although they would not be able to make it commercially viable until after World War II. Thus, important technological improvements were occurring that would soon have consequences for mass communication of sight and sound. However, the fundamental shift in the daily lives of ordinary people from a relatively isolated existence to easy participation in a centrally defined mass culture had already taken place. Information about appropriate behavior, taste, fashion, and, above all, what was going on in the world beyond one's immediate experience was available as never before.

NOTES

1. Robert Sklar, *Movie-Made America*, rev. ed. (New York: Vintage, 1994), 138.
2. Ibid.
3. David E. Kyvig, *Repealing National Prohibition*, 2nd ed. (Kent, Ohio: Kent State University Press, 2000), 28.
4. Sklar, *Movie-Made America*, 153.

6

Carrying on Day by Day: Life's Basics

Routine aspects of life appear at first glance to change very little from day to day or even year to year. People seem to eat, dress, and take care of themselves in much the same way from one generation to the next. Fashions in food and apparel appear to change only superficially and practices of keeping clean even less. Usually only after the passage of considerable time does it become possible to look back and recognize that significant changes have taken place in these routine features of daily life. But while small and slow alterations in mundane matters of life are not as apparent, not to mention as exciting as earth-shaking events or technological revolutions, they are just as much a part of historical transformation. The details of how life's ordinary practices are conducted help distinguish one historical era from another. In this respect, the 1920s and 1930s are as distinctive as any other time.

CHANGING DAILY LIFE

Sometimes gradually and at other times with surprisingly rapidity, Americans in the 1920s transformed some of the ways in which they carried out their daily lives. Urban growth and technological innovations stirred by the automobile, radio, and cinema brought about many of these changes. Those living in an expanding urban America encountered and embraced change more rapidly than did those in more rural areas. Rural dwellers were not so isolated, however, that they were unaware of developments elsewhere. Indeed awareness of growing differences helped persuade some small town and rural dwellers to move to the city and others to oppose an urban society they regarded as increasingly unsatisfactory. During the next decade, both rural and urban Americans would find themselves making further adjustments in day-to-day life in response to the economic conditions imposed by the Great Depression. In both decades, however, innovations assumed at first to be unimportant if not merely temporary would leave lasting marks on the manner in which Americans lived their daily lives.

THE AMERICAN DIET

During and after World War I, Americans experienced what historian Harvey Levenstein has properly called a "revolution at the table," the peak stages of a dietary transformation that had been slowly accelerating for several decades. From the colonial era until past the middle of the nineteenth century, Americans had eaten a heavy British-style diet based primarily on roasted or fried meat, boiled potatoes and cabbage, grain-flour breads and baked goods, and sugar, foods easy to acquire, preserve, and prepare as well as capable of addressing the energy needs of strenuous agricultural labor. Americans consumed a great deal of meat, starches, fat, and sugar but few fruits and vegetables. Cooks used salt liberally but employed few other seasonings and hardly any spices. Until the 1830s, fermented cider and beer and distilled grain spirits were more common beverages than comparatively expensive coffee and tea. Thereafter, as its price fell, coffee in particular gained in popularity, especially with urban workers. Milk, considered unsafe in the days before pasteurization, was used primarily by infants and small children. Altogether, American food was heavy, bland, monotonous, and, especially for poorer people with the most restricted range of choices, nutritionally inadequate. The American diet produced a variety of dietary deficiency diseases and made constipation the most common, although not so deadly national affliction.

Urban Diet In the later decades of the nineteenth century, the eating patterns of urban dwellers began to change. Well-to-do Americans made French cuisine fashionable. With its elaborate entrées and sauces, soups, salads, and desserts, French food required servants for the preparation and service of meals. Thus, to choose a French diet served to proclaim one's economic success. The American middle class, seeking to copy society's elite with less domestic help, found it possible to do so by simplifying the menu and making use of a rapidly developing variety of commercially processed foods. Meat packers developed disassembly lines to turn livestock into table-ready cuts of meat. Professional bakers, breakfast cereal manufacturers, and brewers converted grain into edible forms. Other food processors refined

A steelworker's family at dinner in Aliquippa, Pennsylvania. Photo courtesy of the Library of Congress.

sugar, created condensed soups, and canned or pickled fruits and vegetables. As railroads conveyed fresh as well as processed foods quickly and cheaply to distant markets, urban diets became more varied as well as more nutritious.

Rural Diet The rural diet lagged far behind because of economics and isolation. In the South, the most economically disadvantaged area, a black or white tenant farmer's normal diet consisted of little more than ground corn meal made into mush or bread, fried salted pork, molasses, and, in season, some local greens. Pellagra, a serious disease resulting from a vitamin B deficiency in niacin and protein, was widespread. In the more prosperous Midwest, most farmers ate a considerably better diet. Even there, however, farmers depended largely on what they could raise themselves and what was in season. Only the "summer diet" included much in the way of fruits and vegetables. These foods were consumed while they were fresh rather than preserved. The "winter diet," as a result, centered around pork and grains (mainly wheat or corn), supplemented by some potatoes, beans, and a little dried fruit. On the farm and elsewhere, getting enough to eat was far more of a concern than what was eaten.

New ideas about proper diet began emerging in the decades
Changing   on either side of 1900. Detection of the presence of bacteria,
Ideas   discovery of pasteurization, and formulation of a germ theory of disease occurred during the latter decades of the nineteenth century. Only in the 1910s and 1920s, however, did dietary
problems resulting from the absence of vitamins and minerals come into
view and become a concern. At the end of the nineteenth century, the
first generation of scientific nutritionists began to perceive a need for
better dietary balance, but not until World War I created a food shortage
did the idea spread that Americans could afford to eat less as long as
they ate wisely.

Prior to World War I, eating a lot was thought to be sensible and being plump was regarded as a sign of good health as well as prosperity.
Early nutritionists suggested that an adult male ought to consume 3,000
to 3,500 calories each day. Faced with an army and allies to feed as well
as a reduced agricultural labor force, the U.S. government in 1917 began
telling people they could remain healthy if they ate less as long as they
consumed the proper proteins, carbohydrates, minerals, and vitamins.
Claims that fewer calories sufficed for working adults were reinforced
by rationing programs and campaigns for voluntary "wheatless" and
"meatless" meals each day and entire days each week. During and after
U.S. participation in the European war, a fundamental shift began taking place in American eating habits, especially among the middle and
upper classes. Southern and immigrant soldiers who had been exposed
to much more varied meals while in the military contributed to the
change as well. By the end of the 1920s Americans were better fed, yet
consumed 5 percent fewer calories per capita than they had on the eve
of the war, a very significant overall drop during a period of general
prosperity.

Commercial food processing companies consolidated, ex-
Food   panded capital investment and operations, and persuaded
Industry   consumers to try new products to such an extent that by the
end of the 1920s, the food industry was the largest sector of
American manufacturing. Large-scale dairies and bakeries rapidly
emerged to drive out of business or at least place at a severe competitive
disadvantage many smaller milk and baked goods producers. Improved
production methods helped to increase sharply the sales of canned fruits
and vegetables, not to mention condensed soups, beans with pork, sugar,
and tomato sauce, and spaghetti in tomato sauce. The C.W. Post cereal
company acquired over a dozen other companies, including the Jello
Company, and used management and advertising skills to enlarge the
market for the products of its new conglomerate, General Foods. Another
expanding food processor, this one started by Minneapolis flour millers,

called itself General Mills. It became very successful in encouraging the use of its products by creating a fictional housewife, Betty Crocker, who offered recipe recommendations in magazine and radio advertisements. Agricultural producers formed trade associations, some of them pooling and marketing their produce under common labels such as Sunkist oranges and Sun-Maid raisins. In these and countless other cases, the intent was to get the public to eat unfamiliar foods.

In 1925, Clarence Birdseye discovered how to quick-freeze fresh foods in cellophane packages (itself a new product developed by the DuPont chemical company). Birdseye was not the first to freeze food, of course, but he developed the means of doing it rapidly on a large scale. Quick freezing avoided bursting cells and causing the food to turn to mush when thawed as had been the case with earlier, slower methods. Within three years, restaurants and the few Americans with home freezers were starting to purchase frozen foods in significant quantities. By 1934, they were buying 39 million pounds a year. It was not until after World War II, however, with the spread of electric home refrigerators and the sudden success of frozen concentrated orange juice that the frozen food industry would become a major aspect of commercial food processing.

A great variety of foods were promoted in the 1920s on the basis of health claims, some valid and others of questionable **Health** legitimacy. Breakfast cereal makers, who had in the previous **Claims** half century weaned the country away from heavy breakfasts of meat, potatoes, eggs, and bread with effective advertising about their products' superior convenience, cleanliness, and nutrition, now exploited the new interest in vitamins and minerals. "It is possible to give children all the food they can possibly eat—and still their little bodies can be under-nourished," proclaimed General Foods. Fortunately, Post's Grape-Nuts contained "iron, calcium, phosphorus, and other mineral elements that are taken right up as vital food by the millions of cells in the body." Fleischman's Yeast, facing a decline in home baking, advocated eating two or three yeast cakes each day. Morton's Salt became "health salt," while virtually all-sugar Welch's Grape Juice extolled its "health values" as well as its "laxative properties you cannot do without." Even chocolate bar manufacturers acclaimed their candy as vitamin-packed.

Both the consolidation of food processing and an increase in health assertions were evident and effective in the dairy **Dairy** industry. Giant holding companies, most notably Sealtest and **Industry** Borden, gained a dominant position in the industry, especially in urban markets. Efforts to assure product purity together with advertising claims that milk was not merely for infants and small children, but was a vitamin- and mineral-rich essential health drink and recipe additive for everyone, helped reverse the prewar pattern of limited and declining dairy product consumption. In 1925, Americans consumed a record 800 pounds of milk and milk products per capita.

Bakery Goods Bread, meat, and sugar remained staples of the American diet. Bread was more of a mainstay for the working class than for higher income groups. Working-class families had been the first to turn from homemade to store-bought bread, and they preferred the white breads that they associated with upper-class tastes. Soft white breads made from highly refined, and thus less nutritious flour soon constituted 70 percent of bakery production. The small bakery turning out at most a few hundred loaves a day, long a fixture of urban neighborhoods, was by the 1920s losing ground to large, high-volume commercial bakeries. Bakery goods, once thought inferior and only for the working class, were widely embraced by the middle class in the same way as other commercially canned, processed, and prepared foods.

Commercial Foods The virtual disappearance of servants after World War I contributed to the trend toward the middle class's greater reliance on convenient, commercially obtained foods and simpler meals. Elaborate French cuisine, also burdened by its reliance on now-illegal alcohol, faded from the scene. Most food continued to be prepared and eaten in the home. "Mealtime" was usually a time when families gathered together though even that ritual was threatened as school and factory cafeterias, men's and women's luncheon clubs, not to mention after-school and community activities, the movie theater, and, above all, the automobile drew family members away from the table. "Eat and run" was becoming acceptable behavior to the point that one Muncie, Indiana, father complained, "It's getting so that a fellow has to make a date with his family to see them."[1]

While food preparation was generally considered one of a married woman's chief responsibilities, less time and effort were being spent on cooking. Home baking of bread, a time-consuming routine for most women a half century earlier, was routinely being done by fewer than one-in-four housewives by the 1920s. Likewise, the use of electric kitchen appliances as well as commercially processed food reduced the effort spent on home food preparation.

Simple meals became the general standard in the 1920s. Breakfasts were commonly built around citrus fruit, dried cereal, or eggs and toast. Students and workers carried light lunches to school or workplace while the more affluent bought hot lunches at restaurants or lunch counters when they were away from home. The main meal of the day was usually eaten late in the day or early in the evening except on farms and in small towns where dinner at noon remained the custom. Dinners tended to center on roast or broiled meat or poultry, potatoes, a vegetable, and a simple dessert.

Before World War I old-stock Americans, those who pre- **One-Dish**
ceded the post-1870s wave of immigration, often thought it **Dinners**
unappealing, indigestible, and perhaps even likely to stir immoral passions to use spices and seasonings other than salt
or to mix various foods together in the same dish of stew, casserole,
goulash, borscht, minestrone, or pasta the way new immigrants routinely
did. In the 1920s, most Americans continued to avoid much seasoning
of food. However, the "one-dish dinner" including some combination of
meat, potatoes, pasta, beans, rice, and vegetables, often held together and
flavored with condensed tomato soup, processed "American" cheese, or
other milk products, gained acceptance as nutritionally sound and easy
to prepare. Salads of various sorts became popular as main courses as
well as side dishes, many of them adorned with canned fruit or vegetables, Jello, and/or bottled mayonnaise. Sweet desserts, cakes, pies,
cookies, and puddings remained standard dinner items.

As food processors seeking to encourage the use of their
products published more and more recipes in the growing **A National**
number of women's magazines, not only did the trend to- **Diet**
ward easy-to-prepare meals increase, so did the trend toward a standardized national diet. New immigrant and regional food
specialties did not disappear, but they became more common as special
occasion meals, Sunday and holiday dinners, or community events. "I
have eaten in Florence, Alabama, in Logan, Utah, in Mansfield, Ohio,
and Penobscot, Maine," wrote a reporter for a 1928 restaurant trade journal. "Is there any difference in the meals served in one locality from
another? No." Kansas newspaper editor William Allen White agreed,
observing of the nation's most popular meal, "A good beefsteak is the
same on every American table."[2]

Americans eating away from home immediately felt
the effects of national alcohol prohibition on what was **Lunchrooms and**
available to them. First, the liquor ban devastated **Italian**
upper-echelon restaurants with their emphasis on **Restaurants**
French cuisine. It was not only the difficulty of cooking without wine, but also the problem of turning a profit without alcoholic beverage sales that rapidly put most French-oriented restaurants
out of business. At the same time, prohibition largely eliminated the
inexpensive (though not quite "free lunch") food services of male-
oriented urban saloons. Simultaneously, however, an expanding urban
workforce, including a growing percentage of females for whom the saloon had not been an appealing option, created a demand for restaurants
providing moderately priced meals and rapid service.

Overall, the number of restaurants tripled during the 1920s and of the
new ones that opened, 48 percent were lunchrooms, 26 percent were
coffee and sandwich shops, 8 percent were cafeterias, and only 11 per-

Angelo's Lunch, Columbus, Ohio, 1938. Photo courtesy of the Library of Congress.

cent were full-service restaurants. Cafeterias, diners, and lunch counters emerged as the fast-food restaurants of the era. Along with more conventional restaurants, they provided a menu of traditional American items. By the 1930s, eastern urban areas were beginning to sprout chains of franchised restaurants (Howard Johnson's New England seafood restaurants, the Wichita-based White Castle chain, Toddle Houses, and the more working class oriented, Detroit-based White Tower five-cent-hamburger stands being the most widespread). Also growing in popularity were Italian restaurants with names such as "Italian Village" or "Roman Gardens," decorated with red-and-white checkered tablecloths and displaying pictures on the walls of Venetian gondolas or the Leaning Tower of Pisa. Unfortunately, they served little besides standard American fare and, perhaps, spaghetti with bland tomato sauce. Most Americans were more interested in mildly exotic restaurant decor than in eating unfamiliar food.

Baby Foods   The special issue of what to feed infants was ages old, at least among those who could afford an alternative to mothers' breast milk. The use of wet nurses by the upper class had been in decline for several decades as servant girls became harder to find. Since the nineteenth century, middle-class women experimented with cow's or goat's milk or the new, processed sugar-fortified condensed milk, but sanitation problems hampered this practice. Working-class and especially immigrant women were most likely to continue to rely on breast feeding, for both economic and cultural reasons.

In the 1910s, new methods for large-scale pasteurization of milk were rapidly adopted by commercial dairies serving large cities. Start-up costs were high but since large dairies could quickly sell pasteurized milk at competitive prices, smaller dairies with a less hygienic product were soon driven from the market. A significant decline in infant mortality followed, leading most pediatricians by 1921 to recommend that babies be fed pasteurized cow's milk diluted with water and supplemented with sugar. Physicians also advised a small amount of orange juice to provide vitamins. By the end of the decade, children of six months and older also were being fed commercially prepared as well as home pre-pared mashed and pureed fruits, vegetables, cereals, and even meats. Except among impoverished families, infant diets had been transformed in a lasting fashion.

As notions of nutrition and health changed, the concept that a slim body was more attractive than a plump one caused some **Dieting** people at the upper end of the economic scale to adopt an entirely new approach to food consumption: dieting. While early advice books offered roughly equal amounts of guidance on gaining and losing weight, in the early 1920s weight loss became their overwhelming focus. Especially among middle-class women, concern over excess weight be-came commonplace. Popular novels for young middle-class females rou-tinely had a fat comic character as a contrast to the popular, smart, and always slim heroine. Seeking to remain or become slender became a fre-quent preoccupation. Systematic efforts to lower one's weight through exercise and especially diet became widespread.

Gimmick diets proliferated in which every meal consisted of no more than half a grapefruit, melba toast, and coffee; a baked potato and but-termilk; or raw tomatoes and a hard-boiled egg. Advertisements for var-ious foods, among them United Fruit Company bananas, Wonder Bread, and Welch's grape juice, assured readers that the products provided "quick energy" but were "never fattening." In this diet-conscious era tobacco companies successfully promoted their cigarettes as a means to avoid weight gain as well as improve digestion and escape "jangled nerves." Cigarette sales, especially among women, soared.

Ultimately, changes in the American diet could be mea-sured in the size as well as the shape of American bodies. **Slimmer and** College women in 1930 were slimmer than their mothers, **Taller** yet averaged more than an inch taller. Upper-middle-class Boston schoolboys in 1926 stood no less than three inches taller on av-erage than their predecessors a half century earlier. Likewise, men from a wider range of backgrounds entering the armed forces in World War II would turn out to be significantly taller than their World War I counterparts. These measurable physiological changes certainly confirmed the notion that "you are what you eat" and underscored the significance of the alteration of the American diet.

BUYING FOOD

Local Food Stores
Until the 1920s, most food stores were small. Even the pioneering A&P Tea Company chain carried a limited range of goods. People expected to go to several different stores to acquire their food. Not only bakeries, but also butcher shops, greengrocers, confectioneries, delicatessens, and grocery stores were separate, small operations. Store clerks would take a customer's order, assemble the various requested items from the store's bins, cabinets, cold-storage lockers, and tall shelves, and deliver it to the customer's home. Normally food stores provided credit to their regular customers as well.

Urban Retail Markets
While most residents of towns and cities patronized nearby food stores, major urban areas also had large central retail food markets with a variety of stalls and vendors and a high sales volume. Faneuil Hall Market in Boston, the Reading Terminal Market in Philadelphia, and the Pike Place Market in Seattle were among the 174 markets that the Bureau of the Census found in cities with a population over 30,000 in 1918. The biggest yet of the central markets, the 68,000-square-foot Crystal Palace Market in San Francisco, opened in 1922 at a location served by 80 percent of the city's street car lines. It drew 150,000 people a week to its 110 departments.

Self-Service Supermarkets
In 1916 in Memphis, Tennessee, Clarence Saunders opened a "self-service grocery store." In reality, Saunders' new-style store provided few traditional food store services, but it did reduce prices and offer a greater variety of goods. It accepted a smaller profit margin on its products and sought to prosper on the basis of high volume sales. Customers in this new-style store would walk along aisles with a basket and choose items without assistance. A checker at the exit would add up the purchases, put them in bags, and collect the customer's money. Saunders quickly built his new design into a chain of owned and leased stores. Called Piggly Wiggly Stores, the chain included 400 stores by 1920. By 1928, just before it was sold to Safeway and Kroger, the Piggly Wiggly chain had grown to 2,700 stores.

Self-service grocery stores quickly became the new standard. In May 1918, self-service came to Akron, Ohio, where customers had long been used to white-shirted, white-aproned Acme Grocery Company clerks

Clerk stocking grocery store shelves, San Angelo, Texas, 1939. Photo courtesy of the Library of Congress.

gathering the items that they requested from tall shelves along narrow aisles and delivering their orders to their homes. In Los Angeles, Ralph's Grocery Company, which had operated since 1872, switched from clerk- to self-service in 1926. Before the end of the decade it had opened sixteen large stores, calling them "supermarkets." Ralph's provided automobile parking lots rather than delivery service. In Houston, Texas, Henk & Pilot was another grocery store that expanded in the 1920s and added large parking lots.

Even less expensive supermarkets sprang up, especially in the East, in the early 1930s. By offering "loss-leaders" to attract shoppers into the store, settling for a lower overall profit, and seeking to move a high volume of goods, they sharply undercut smaller food stores regardless of whether they were independents or chain stores. The A&P Company operated a chain of 15,150 small stores in 1929 that averaged only $1,317 in weekly sales. A&P began opening supermarkets in 1935 and by 1940 operated 1,400 such stores; only 4,100 of its smaller, older stores re- mained.

The accessibility and declining cost of an ever-wider variety of food throughout the 1920s and 1930s meant that   **Eating Less**
the diet of most Americans improved significantly during   **but Better**
this era. By 1930, average Americans not only consumed 5
percent fewer calories than before World War I, they ate much more
fruit, particularly citrus, many more vegetables, especially green ones,
significantly more milk and cheese, less flour and corn meal, fewer potatoes, and less red meat. Beef consumption went down from 72.4
pounds per capita in 1899 to 55.3 pounds in 1930.

Positive dietary developments continued into the 1930s, despite the
depression. A 1935 study reported that, compared to those in 1918,
American meals were now more varied and nutritious. Consumption of
milk was up 25 percent, commercially baked goods had increased 40
percent, canned fruits and vegetables had risen nearly 400 percent, and
oranges had soared 1,000 percent. Ironically, the very idea that eating
less could mean eating better, especially if vitamin-rich foods were included in the diet, served middle-class Americans well in adjusting to
an economic depression.

Not every American ate well in the 1920s, much less
during the 1930s. While food was generally cheap and   **Not Everybody**
available even during the depression, throughout these   **Ate Well**
two decades an estimated 40 percent of the population,
especially those at the lower income levels, remained underfed. While
the rural poor people in Appalachia and the South consistently suffered
the most severely from inadequate diets, urban workers also often struggled, especially when confronted with unemployment, as was routinely
the case for at least a few weeks a year, even in the prosperous 1920s.
A typical laid-off Muncie worker in 1923 sought to feed a family of four on
$5 a week, $2 of which was spent on the cheapest cuts of meat and the
rest of which went for bread, potatoes, and beans. Fruits and vegetables
were simply out of reach, as was milk for the two children and anything
else. As the number of unemployed grew in the 1930s, the same grim realities would confront greater numbers of people. Nevertheless, higher
dietary expectations, even when not always met, had become common
during the 1920s and 1930s, distinguishing that period from earlier times.

MAKING AN APPEARANCE

As the notion of what was an attractive human figure
Dressing for   changed, so too did ideas about dress. The time was
Status and Style   long past when Americans thought of clothing simply
in terms of warmth and protection from the elements.
Since clothing reflected economic status and cultural values, it served as
a barometer for change in such matters. As always, most Americans re-

mained far behind the cutting edge of fashion, but even if they were unaware of or indifferent to the latest developments in the fashion center of New York, their wardrobes before long came to show the influence of changing styles. Clothing displayed on movie screens or in magazines and mail-order catalogues made possible the transformation of fashion more rapidly and universally than in earlier decades.

Machine-made, mass-produced clothing had started to become common in the late nineteenth century, but was at first largely confined to exterior garments for adult males. Much women's and children's clothing con- **Ready-to-Wear Clothing** tinued to be made at home. Making their own and their children's apparel had long been considered one of women's major responsibilities, absorbing several hours of their time each week and creating a mass market for sewing machines after they appeared in the 1850s; but this practice declined rapidly in the 1920s, especially among middle-class women previously most reluctant to adopt manufactured, "ready-to-wear" clothes. In fact, the growing resort to mass-produced clothing in the latest styles led one Muncie businessman to observe that he was losing his ability to judge the background of job applicants by the way they dressed. Standardized fashion sold in ready-to-wear clothing stores helped create at least the appearance of a society of equals.[3]

The last type of clothing to make the transition from predominantly homemade to manufactured proved to be underwear. For undergarments, both men and women began with winter flannel and summer cotton "union suits," with knee-length or longer underdrawers (sometimes lace trimmed for women) and shirts (long-sleeved for winter, sleeveless for summer). By the early twentieth century, the fashion for girls and women was starting to shift away from the stiff corsets of fabric, bone, and steel designed to severely pinch the mid-section and heighten the impression of ample hips and chest. The corset was at least loosened if not replaced by a less-restrictive one-piece fabric waist or camisole still intended to accentuate a small waist and larger bust. A new-style undergarment, given the French name *brassiere*, came into use shortly before World War I. The first bras also sought to flatten the chest for the chemise or flapper dress just beginning to be popular, especially among women who wished to deemphasize their reproductive function and assert their independence. Gradually, as fashion evolved and designs again emphasized motherhood, bras to shape and emphasize the roundness of the breasts were developed, and in the 1930s bra cups in standard A, B, C, and D sizes appeared.

World War I dietary changes inaugurated nothing short of a revolution in standards of attractiveness and attempts to achieve them. In the late nineteenth century when getting **Changing Standards** enough to eat on a regular basis was often still a challenge and understanding of nutrition was limited, being stout was regarded as a sign of health, success, and beauty. Actress Lillian Russell, widely regarded as the Great American Beauty of the 1880s, tipped the scales at 200 pounds, while U.S. presidents, presumably widely respected for their judgment as well as their achievements, tended to be stocky men. Even health conscious (and husky) Theodore Roosevelt had no qualms about supporting as his successor the heaviest man ever to occupy the White House, 325-pound William Howard Taft.

Late-nineteenth-century clothing had tended to emphasize or even help create a plump figure. Both men's and women's clothing had featured layers of heavy fabrics, padded shoulders, and a loose fit. Women's dresses, normally with flared and pleated ankle-length skirts made fuller by being worn over petticoats, used yards of cloth. As more young women began working outside the home in the cities of the 1890s, simpler styles of tailored suits or long, dark skirts (without petticoats) and white blouses or "shirtwaists" became common. Just prior to World War I, fitness rather than girth started to become the standard for male attractiveness. The somewhat more slender (though still robust) silhouette of the Gibson Girl, named for the popular magazine drawings of Charles Dana Gibson, took hold as the female counterpart. The war, however, prompted tremendous change in thought and fashion.

Wartime shortages of both food and fabric stirred government conservation efforts. The Wilson administration sought to educate people on the advantages of eating less and, consequently, weighing and wearing less. Good nutrition was reflected in erect posture, healthy looking skin, and shiny hair. These characteristics rather than plumpness became signs of beauty, not to mention patriotism. Likewise, simpler clothing with fewer layers, single- instead of double-breasted suits, and shorter skirts saved fabric and aided the war effort. After the war ended, the slender image of the "flapper" girl and the soldier "doughboy" continued to be idealized as the epitome of attractiveness.

Flapper Styles   Women's clothing styles in the postwar era, at least those favored by younger women, were the most notable symbol of the new fashion. Flapper-style dresses used light fabrics that hung straight from the shoulders and gathered low on the hips rather than at the waist. This style sought to deemphasize both the bust and the hips in order to create a slim profile. Corsets disappeared almost altogether, and multilayered petticoats gave way to single-layer slips, or just "knickers," under skirts. Hemlines, which had only during the war risen from ankle to mid-calf, rose to the knee and beyond as the 1920s proceeded. Exposed lower legs acquired further emphasis from sheer silk stockings.

Cosmetics   Wearing cosmetics in moderate amounts to enhance one's appearance became an acceptable fashion for the first time in the 1920s. Women, especially younger ones, abandoned long-standing views that those who wore cosmetics were "painted la-dies" of loose morals who were probably trying to cover up signs of sexually transmitted diseases. Face powder to conceal uneven skin, cover a shiny nose, and give the face a smooth, pale appearance became in-dispensable among middle-class women. In turn, rouge for color in the cheeks, lipstick, eyebrow pencil, and finally eyelash curlers also became popular. A variety of "skin lighteners" appeared as many African Amer-icans sought to achieve the "white is right" complexion that was an outgrowth of racism. By the middle of the decade the cosmetics industry was booming. Sales soared for "compacts," small hand-held cases with powder and a mirror to allow frequent scrutiny and touch-up of facial makeup.

The explosion of cosmetics to enhance beauty stemmed in part from an effort to conceal facial acne and its scars. Concern with skin blemishes also stimulated the marketing of additional remedies: soaps, lotions, yeast cakes, and even unfiltered X-ray treatments. This last practice, med-ically dubious but unregulated, later would be identified as causing can-cer. The equally unsupervised cosmetics industry put some products on the market that were also dangerously unsafe. Burning and scarring, even several fatalities due to cosmetic poisoning, would be reported be-fore the federal government moved to regulate the industry in the 1938 Food, Drug, and Cosmetic Act.

The fashion of "bobbed" hair became another central ele-ment of the flapper style. Not only did extremely short **New** cropped hair emphasize the slender look, it served as a sym- **Hairstyles** bol of a break with tradition. During the nineteenth century, long hair was a standard of beauty, not to mention a sign of propriety. Hair was regarded as a woman's crowning glory, and so the more she had the better. Only young girls were permitted to wear their long hair loose; after puberty hair was carefully and elaborately arranged. For a mature woman to "let her hair down" was considered an invitation to intimacy and appropriate only when she was alone with her mate. Even as the Gibson Girl set new standards of dress, she retained abundant hair, pinned and piled on top of her head. To cut one's hair very short, as an increasing number of women did in the 1920s, was to defy these traditional standards.

Women with bobbed hair set themselves visibly apart. College women defended the new style as less inhibiting and less troublesome to care for than long hair and thus a parallel to their newly acquired gender equality with men at the ballot box. Even though it required attention to set and maintain the waves and curls thought attractive, bobbed hair was indeed liberating when compared to carefully tied or pinned hair-styles that restricted vigorous activity if a proper appearance was to be preserved.

Men also tended to wear their hair shorter than they had before World

MODERN FROCKS IN THE NEW SILHOUETTE—

AS NEW YORK WEARS THEM

EXTRA FINE QUALITY

Ⓐ
RAYON AND COTTON FLAT CREPE
$5.98
POSTPAID

Ⓑ
ENSEMBLE OF RAYON AND COTTON FLAT CREPE
$6.98
POSTPAID

EXTRA FINE QUALITY

Ⓒ
ALL SILK FLAT CREPE
$8.98
POSTPAID

Ⓓ
"GEM-O-SHEER" RAYON CHIFFON
$8.98
POSTPAID

SEE OPPOSITE PAGE FOR DESCRIPTIONS OF THESE STYLES

WE PAY THE POSTAGE

Ⓔ
ALL SILK FLAT CREPE
$9.98
POSTPAID

Ⓕ
"TWIN PRINT" ENSEMBLE
$7.98
POSTPAID

Ⓖ
PRINTED ALL SILK FLAT CREPE
$9.98
POSTPAID

8 P156 B-C-K-MN
A-M-D-S-LA POSTAGE PAID BY SEARS, ROEBUCK and CO. THE WORLD'S LARGEST STORE

"Modern Frocks in the New Silhouette" from the Sears, Roebuck and Co. Spring 1930 catalogue. Reprinted by arrangement with Sears, Roebuck and Co. and protected under copyright. No duplication is permitted.

"Fashion Tailored Suits" from the Sears, Roebuck and Co. Spring 1930 catalogue. Reprinted by arrangement with Sears, Roebuck and Co. and protected under copyright. No duplication is permitted.

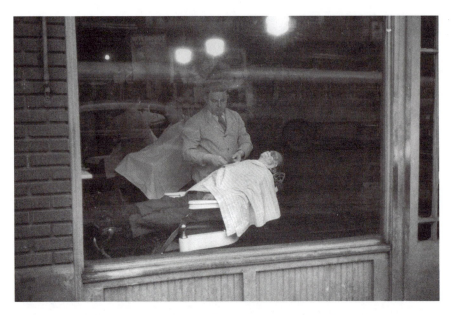

Man being shaved in an Aliquippa, Pennsylvania, barber shop. Photo courtesy of the Library of Congress.

War I. Hair slicked down with water, oil, or gel in imitation of movie stars such as Rudolph Valentino became the favored fashion. Full beards had largely disappeared. Sideburns and mustaches seemed to be following. The clean-shaven look was both fashionable and practical. Fewer and fewer faces bore smallpox scars that required concealment and the availability of inexpensive mass-produced safety razors made possible a daily shave at home.

Appeal to Youth   For the most part, young adults were ahead of their elders in adopting new fashions. Students lagged not far, if at all, behind. By the time they reached high school, students demanded store-bought clothes in the current fashion and insisted that they could no longer wear the same clothes two days in a row. Silk dresses and stockings, along with sweaters, were the ideal for middle-class girls who now complained about gingham dresses and cotton stockings. The male equivalents of acceptability were slacks and sweaters. Silk party dresses, often with bared shoulders and backs, and suits were also regarded as middle-class high school or college wardrobe essentials.

Clothing Hides Hard Times   The economic downturn of the 1930s had a limited effect on dress. People feeling the economic pinch made clothing last longer. Hard times brought plumpness back into fashion as a sign of success, but not nearly to

Women shopping for hats in Harmony, Georgia. Photo courtesy of the National Archives.

the extent as before the turn of the century. Designs for women once again called attention to hips and busts in contrast to the pencil-thin styles of 1920s. Hemlines fell to the ankle and fitted waistlines returned. Men's suits once again acquired padded shoulders. Fuller cuts reemerged as the standard for men as well as women. But the trend toward mass-produced clothing continued and with it the ability to disguise, at least to some extent, one's individual economic situation by conforming to standard patterns of dress.

KEEPING CLEAN

In order to resemble the examples of beauty and fashion presented in poster art, movies, newspapers, **Personal Hygiene** and magazines, Americans who could afford to do so quickly embraced the new standards of diet and dress. In particular, one historian observed, film and fashion encouraged the "unveiling of the female body, baring arms and legs and putting the body on display as never before."[4] Altered expectations of appearance in turn encouraged new approaches to personal hygiene in the 1920s, particularly among the middle class.

Ever since the Civil War, a belief in the importance of keeping clean had been spreading in the United States as a result of new theories that diseases were carried by dirt, decayed food, and sewage. The increasing availability of piped water and indoor plumbing made frequent washing more convenient and common. Setting aside an entire room in the house for a separate toilet and bathroom, a practice that began appearing in middle-class home design in the early twentieth century, provided one important measure of a growing commitment to cleanliness.

World War I stirred further concerns about personal hygiene. The shocking rejection as physically unfit of nearly one-third of all World War I draftees drew attention to deficiencies in American hygiene. Further anxiety was aroused by the influenza epidemic of 1918–1919. This worldwide scourge cost perhaps 500,000 American lives, most of them in urban areas. An alarmed society began devoting more attention to matters of health and hygiene.

Schools Promote Cleanliness Public schools began instructing all children to bathe regularly, wash their hands before meals, and brush their teeth twice a day. Immigrants thought to present problems to themselves and dangers to others because of a lack of cleanliness became particular targets. Adult education programs for immigrants focused on English, civics, and hygiene. Elementary school texts dealing with hygiene and biology shifted from devoting 65 percent of their content to anatomy and physiology and 4 percent to sanitation in the 1890s to 5 percent on anatomy and physiology and 40 percent on sanitation by 1925. In New York City, public high school physical education classes with a component of personal hygienic instruction did not exist before 1922 but enrolled over 50 percent of all students by 1934.

Body Odor and Bad Breath Commercial advertising gave new prominence to cleanliness and introduced the new social diseases of "body odor" and "bad breath." Lifebuoy soap ads featured a man with "b.o." who luckily discovered "what they're saying behind my back!" before losing friends and a job promotion. The ads also showed a young woman with underarm odor whom men avoided until she was rescued by the proper (you guessed it! Lifebuoy) soap. Toothpaste was also heavily promoted. Colgate was the early leader, but Pepsodent sales skyrocketed when it began sponsoring the *Amos 'n Andy* radio show. Expectations of a fragrant aroma as a measure of personal cleanliness quickly took hold.

Fighting Filth The war against filth was also fought on the urban battlefield with the new weapons of electric vacuum cleaners and washing machines. In cities and electrified towns, standards of household and apparel cleanliness reached new heights in the 1920s. In rural America such change came more slowly. With dirt roads, coal and wood stoves, and farm animals, rural houses were hard to keep clean. The lack of electric appliances made the situation more difficult. Laundry was the farm woman's most time-consuming and backbreaking chore. The lack of running water and the sheer bulk of farm dirt in clothing rendered the task of cleaning clothes, bedding, other fabrics, and kitchen equipment daunting, if not impossible. The distinction between urban and rural America in this respect was, quite literally, a clean break.

Changes in diet, dress, and social attitudes regarding cleanliness converged in the post–World War I period in one particular case: feminine hygiene. Historian Joan Brumberg has observed that understanding their bodies and sexuality was **Feminine Hygiene** quite limited but increasing rapidly for early-twentieth-century boys and girls. Inferior nutrition and health standards caused nineteenth-century adolescents to mature later, with a middle-class girl of the 1890s likely to reach menarche (age of first menstruation) at fifteen or sixteen and a working-class girl even later. As menarche declined and menstruation became less erratic and more frequent as a result of improved diet and health, parents and physicians struggled to understand what was happening as well as to how to deal with their daughters' and patients' onset of reproductive capacity. Girls normally received little or no sex education because adults thought it best to protect them from sexuality as long as possible and, frankly, because their own knowledge was limited. Other than as a signal of fertility, menstruation was not well understood before the 1920s when hormonal stimulation of the menstrual cycle was discovered, incidentally eroding the Victorian notion that a woman's life was defined by her ovaries—not her brain.

Dealing with menstruation as a practical matter changed according to individual circumstance. Traditionally, menstruating females used and reused washable rags to capture the blood flow. By the 1890s, upper-middle-class women, stirred by new ideas about germs and the spread of disease, began purchasing gauze and cheesecloth to make their own sanitary napkins or bought the first mass-produced napkins from the Sears & Roebuck catalogue. By World War I, disposing of, rather than reusing, napkins had become the standard middle-class routine; this practice soon came to be thought of as a measure of refinement and success, often one out of the economic reach of working-class and especially immigrant girls. In the 1920s, when the Kimberly-Clark Company began advertising a mass-produced disposable sanitary napkin it called "Kotex" in *Ladies Home Journal* and *Good Housekeeping*, it started taking over what was often an uncomfortable discussion for mothers with their daughters. Like earlier, not so widely circulated advice pamphlets, ads stressing the need to avoid fatigue, strenuous exercise, and exposure to disease during "that special time of the month" carried a subtle message of female disability and weakness.

The "feminine hygiene" products industry grew rapidly in the 1920s and 1930s. In 1936, the first commercial internal tampons were marketed under the brand name "Tampax." Because of early perceptions that they might be either dangerous or immoral, tampons were slower than sanitary napkins to win acceptance, especially among not-yet-married women. Only after World War II transformed women's social and economic circumstances would the use of mass-produced feminine hygiene products of one sort or another become nearly universal.

Pattern of Change

Like other aspects of routine day-to-day life such as food, dress, and standards of cleanliness, female hygiene long received little attention from historians. All of these matters, however, represent significant if perhaps not terribly exciting aspects of ordinary living. Important alterations in these aspects of everyday life occurred in the era of the 1920s and 1930s and reflected shifts in thought, manufacturing, consumption, and social customs. By the end of the 1930s, evolution in every one of these areas added up to a pattern of existence for most Americans that differed from their experience only twenty years earlier.

NOTES

1. Robert S. Lynd and Helen Merrill Lynd, *Middletown: A Study in Modern American Culture* (New York: Harcourt, Brace and World, 1929), 154.

2. Quoted in Harvey Levenstein, *Revolution at the Table: The Transformation of the American Diet* (New York: Oxford University Press, 1988), 170–72.

3. Lynd and Lynd, *Middletown*, 161.

4. Joan Jacobs Brumberg, *The Body Project: An Intimate History of American Girls* (New York: Random House, 1997), 98.

7

Carrying on Year to Year: Making a Life

Not only everyday routines but also activities that people enter into rarely or only once go into making a life. Courtship, family formation, childbearing, and dealing with illness, aging, and death head the list of such infrequent but fundamental activities. Acquiring an education, raising children, and dealing with family relationships are ongoing processes rather than singular events but are likewise a series of discoveries rather than repetitions of familiar acts. Whether such activities happen only once or evolve over time, they remain central elements of people's lives that change from one era to another.

Midway between the everyday and the rare or unique activities of life are those matters that for most people are common but occasional concerns. Dealing with issues of health, or more likely its absence, is one. Addressing spiritual interests, usually through some form of organized religion, is another. Seeking a temporary escape from normal routines through a wide range of activities labeled most simply the pursuit of leisure is yet another. These matters, too, are essential components of daily life that in the details of their practice distinguish one era from another.

The new technologies of the automobile, electricity, and mass communication affected these aspects of life during the 1920s and 1930s. So, too, did the widespread economic prosperity of the first decade and distress of the second. Not all shifts were simply due to external influences. Modifications also took place within the culture of personal relationships, education, health care, religion, and leisure. Whatever the motivation, however, these aspects of daily life were clearly, if subtly, continuing to evolve.

CYCLES OF FAMILY LIFE

American family life underwent fundamental alterations in the early twentieth century. Shifts occurred at an earlier time and faster pace in urban areas but gradually spread throughout the nation. Courtship, the process of identifying and engaging a life partner, changed most dramatically, but other aspects of family life, ranging from childbearing to marital expectations and responses when they were not fulfilled, evolved as well.

Courtship and Dating   As recently as the first decade of the century, much courtship had taken place in the home according to well-defined customs. A young man would be encouraged to "call" on a young woman. In doing so, he would meet her parents, talk to her in the family parlor, perhaps be offered refreshments, possibly be entertained by her piano playing or singing, and ultimately be encouraged to call again or discouraged from doing so. This social ritual, originating with the upper class, common within the middle class, and copied insofar as possible by families of more modest means, gave eligible women and watchful parents some power over the courtship process. Men could, of course, decline to call, but if they did proceed, they ventured into the woman's environment. If the courtship progressed, the couple might move from the parlor to the still highly visible front porch or attend a public function together, but only well along in the process could a young lady properly consent to the privacy involved in going for a buggy ride alone with her suitor.

"Dating" began to replace calling early in the twentieth century. Homes in the urban environment, in which more and more people found themselves, provided, especially for those of lower income, less space for receiving and entertaining guests. At the same time, cities offered greater possibilities outside the home. Gradually, courting couples began going on dates, prearranged excursions to soda and coffee shops, movie theaters, restaurants, and other places where, even in the midst of a crowd, they experienced less supervision and greater privacy than in the parlor. The automobile further extended the range of possibilities for dating couples, not only as transportation to entertainment but as a place for private intimacy. As the possibilities of a nonmoving automobile began to be appreciated, the term "lover's lane" entered the vocabulary.

Since dates cost money and males were far more likely to be able to earn cash for such purposes, dating tended to give men greater control over courtship. Since they were now the hosts, men gained control over their choice of partner and the entire process; indeed it was considered improper for a women to propose a date, though she might hint that she would welcome a man's invitation. As costs mounted, so too did the female sense of obligation and the male expectation of appreciation.

In the 1920s, dating became common practice among the nation's youth. It prevailed not only in the cities where it started but in suburbs and smaller communities as well. Young urban men and women who had left school but had not married or acquired a steady companion, found that they could meet at dance halls, speakeasies and bars, skating rinks, and other public places. Only in rural areas and especially in the South where there was little surplus income, access to automobiles, or commercial entertainment did dating fail to develop and older social patterns persist.

Dating soon ceased to be just a search for a mate. It became a primary means for casual social entertainment for adolescents and postadolescents. Robert and Helen Lynd observed that in Middletown, frequent dates using the family automobile had become one of the most common sources of tension between teenagers and their parents. At colleges, and also at high schools as the practice spread, dating came to be regarded as a means of demonstrating popularity. The more numerous and varied the dates and the higher the standing of the persons dated, the higher one's status. Thus, continual and diverse dating became an ideal, and often a practice. For many young people, dating served as general recreation and social self-affirmation, not necessarily courtship of a potential life companion.

The shift from calling to dating encouraged greater sexual exploration and intimacy. Long before the rise of the dating system, young people regularly experimented with kissing games. Engaged couples often enjoyed **Greater Sexual Freedom** what was coming to be called "heavy petting," and enough people engaged in premarital intercourse that nearly one-in-ten late-nineteenth-century brides went to the altar pregnant. Dating, however, brought with it freer attitudes about sexuality and more freedom to explore them. Movies provided "how to do it" guides for the inexperienced, and the culture of high schools and colleges, which more were attending, encouraged young people to try things for themselves. Prolonged kissing and embraces became accepted aspects of romantic relationships. Necking and petting (the distinction depended on whether the contact was above or below the shoulders) were customary if not universal practices; evidence compiled later pointed to a sharp rise in premarital sexual intercourse after World War I with over four-fifths of males and nearly half of females acknowledging participation. These gender differences reflected the persistence of the "double standard," the widespread attitude that sexually active mles were just "sowing wild oats" and couldn't be expected to be faithful to a single mate, while women who behaved in the same fashion abandoned their virtue. Although gender distinctions and sexual attitudes in general were beginning to change, most of the sexual activity that did take place was only with a single partner whom the individual expected to marry.

Love and Marriage As courtship practices evolved and dating exposed many young people to a greater variety of potential partners, the decision to marry was cast in a new light. Marriage had traditionally been regarded as a partnership for economic, educational, and welfare purposes as much as a social relationship. The most common justification offered in court for the few divorces of the 1880s was that "he wasn't an adequate (or reliable) provider" or "she didn't carry out her duties at home." By the 1920s, however, fewer persons participated in family economies such as farming, other institutions were taking over educational and welfare responsibilities, and more people were involved in work settings where cash wages allowed individuals to purchase daily necessities. The mutual dependency in dealing with various basic life functions that had hitherto held couples together began to diminish. A mate's lack of attention, consideration, or romantic appeal came to be mentioned far more often in divorce petitions as a reason for marital dissatisfaction.

A new notion emerged, popularized by psychologists, social service professionals, and educators, that a successful marriage was based primarily on affection and companionship. Denver judge Ben Lindsay, in a 1925 book, wrote that "companionate marriage" succeeded because of mutual devotion, sexual attraction, and respect for spousal equality. Pressure from society, church, or state to stay together could not produce a happy marriage in the absence of personal emotional fulfillment, he continued, and in fact could be prove harmful to a couple and any children they might have. Marriage could not be expected to be tension or conflict free, but husbands and wives who were loving companions could communicate and resolve difficulties. Couples unable or unwilling to do so, Lindsay concluded, were better off separating.

Divorce Some but not all states eased divorce requirements, their legislators saying that marital happiness was more important for couples (and their children) than family economic security (and the risk of adults and children having to be supported by the state). Divorce skyrocketed, increasing from one per eighteen marriages in the 1880s to one per six in the 1920s, but remarriage likewise became common. In 1930, census takers found only slightly more than one percent of adults listing their current status as divorced, far fewer than at one time had been divorced. The figures had grown fractionally since 1920 and would rise minimally further by 1940, but overall the percentage of the population that divorced and did not remarry remained quite low. People were not turning against marriage, as some concerned observers grimly suggested. Instead they had come to desire a happy and fulfilling family life and, if disappointed in an attempt to achieve it, proved increasingly willing and able to start over rather than accept less. Simply put, emotional and sexual satisfaction was replacing economic security as the standard of marital choice and contentment.

A few states, most notably New York, maintained highly restrictive divorce laws, while South Carolina refused to allow divorce at all. In many locales the Roman Catholic Church and other influential conservative voices opposed easier divorce as a threat to family stability. Residents of such places did not forego divorce but often had to resort to exaggerated claims of spousal misconduct to satisfy legal requirements. Others traveled out of state to dissolve their marriages.

Nevada, which permitted anyone who had resided in the state for six months to divorce easily even a spouse who had never set foot in the state, became the most popular destination for migratory divorce. Realizing that divorce seekers were spending millions of dollars in the state's hotels, restaurants, and gambling parlors and that other poor rural states, Arkansas, Idaho, Oklahoma, and the Dakotas in particular, were competing for this business, Nevada reduced its residence requirement to three months in 1927 and then slashed it further to six weeks in 1931. By far the least populous state with only 77,000 residents in 1920 and 110,000 in 1940, Nevada granted 1,000 divorces in 1926, five times that many in 1931, and continued to have the highest divorce rate of any state. Even with relaxed rules, however, a migratory divorce remained inconvenient and expensive, and only a small fraction of divorce seekers, mainly the wealthy, pursued this route.

Marriage remained the norm for most American adults throughout the 1920s and 1930s. According to the U.S. **Marriage Age** Census Bureau, more than three of every five people age fifteen or older were married, and when widowed and divorced individuals were added in, the ratio reached nearly seven in ten. Such figures include a large number of persons who were below the median age for first marriage, which in 1920 was 24.6 for males and 21.2 for females. During the 1920s, the median for males slipped slightly and remained almost steady for females. In the following decade, the median age for males remained at 24.3, while for females it rose further to 21.5. Economic hard times forced many couples during the 1930s to delay setting up the separate household that was the standard expectation for married couples. Some postponed marriage, while others shared living quarters with parents or siblings.

While marriage rates remained fairly steady, childbearing continued its longtime decline. During the nineteenth cen- **Declining** tury the average number of children born to American white **Birthrate** women had fallen by half, from 7 to 3.5. Between 1900 and 1929, the birthrate dropped by another third. The birthrate decline was greater among middle-class than working-class families, white than nonwhite families, and native-born than immigrant women. The drop reflected decisions to limit family size and practice birth control to do so. The Lynds discovered that in Middletown almost every upper-class couple used some means of contraception, male condoms primarily, though increasingly, female diaphragms. Far fewer working-class couples understood or practiced birth control. One significant result of these deliberate actions was that growing numbers of women completed their childbearing by their early 30s and spent more of their lives in other pursuits.

The typical family, especially of the middle or upper class, had already grown smaller before the depression. Economic hard times caused a further sharp drop to the lowest birthrate of any decade between the founding of the United States and the end of the twentieth century. As many potential parents determined that they could not afford more or any children and others decided that the economic risks were too great, the generation born in the 1930s turned out to be the smallest in American history, much smaller than either the preceding generation of the 1920s or the subsequent generation of the 1940s.

Leniency toward Children
Relationships between parents and their children struck observers such as the Lynds as different from those prior to World War I. Change occurred, most notably, though not exclusively, in middle-class families. The shift stemmed from the growth in the 1920s of a school-centered and automobile-liberated youth culture and the decline during the following decade in parental authority linked to the ability to provide economic security. In general strict discipline and harsh punishment became less evident, two-way communication more so. Younger children came to be treated with more open affection, while adolescents were given greater freedom than in earlier decades. As in other eras laden with change and instability, young people often dealt more easily than their parents with new circumstances, and thereby older children in particular gained greater influence within the family.

Life Expectancy Increases
The American population continued to increase despite the falling birthrates because people were living longer. Over the course of two decades average male life expectancy increased by a notable 6.5 years from 56.3 in 1920 to 62.8 in 1940. Female life expectancy rose by an even more remarkable 8.8 years from 58.5 to 67.3. A nearly 50 percent decline in the infant mortality rate from 86 per 1,000 births in 1920 to 65 per 1,000 by 1930 and 47 per 1,000 by 1940 helps account for this change, but mere escape from infant or childhood death does not account for the entire change. Among those who survived to age twenty, males could expect to live,

on average, 2.2 years longer (to 67.8 years of age) in 1940 than in 1920. In the same span of years, female life expectancy grew by 4.9 years (to 71.4 years of age). Taking race into account and with it the differences in economic circumstances between the average white and nonwhite sheds further light on life expectancy. Whereas in 1920 the average for all white females was 55.6 years and white males was 54.4, for nonwhite males it was 45.5 and nonwhite females 45.2. The increase by 1940 was universal but uneven; white females had risen to 66.6 years and white males to 62.1, while nonwhite males rose only to 51.5 and nonwhite females registered the greatest proportional increase to 54.9, still far behind their white counterparts.

Longer life had many implications, particularly for those with limited resources, in an age when many employers preferred young, quick workers. When older workers lost their jobs, few had disability benefits, pensions, or adequate savings. With women tending to live longer, widowhood bereft of resources became a particularly widespread problem. In 1920, over 5.5 million people, 6.1 percent of all adult males and 14.6 percent of females, had suffered the death of their spouse; by 1940 the number grew to 7.8 million though the percentages slipped to 4.8 and 12.9, respectively. Reliance on one's children was common but often humbling; not being able to turn to children or relatives made the situation even more difficult for the aged or infirm. Poverty among the elderly, especially women, was a problem that grew more serious as lives lengthened. Not until the Social Security system was adopted in 1935 and fully implemented in 1942 did the situation begin to improve.

The end of life had to be dealt with sooner or later by every family. While the nature of grief might vary with the individual death, certain common patterns had developed in funeral **Funeral Practices** practices. Mourning and burial had come to be guided by professional funeral directors, of whom there were 24,000 by 1920 and 40,000 twenty years later. In the South the old practice of wrapping and rapidly burying the corpse remained the standard. Outside the South, however, it had become commonplace to embalm the body and display it in a open casket at home or, increasingly, at a "funeral home." Everywhere, burial of the remains in a cemetery was usual and cremation rare. Funeral services allowed family and friends to express sorrow and honor the departed, but prolonged periods of formal mourning thereafter, with widows wearing all black for a year or more, had become less customary

HEALTH CARE

Staying healthy was an ongoing challenge and a daily uncertainty that most Americans addressed with limited knowledge and resources. During the previous half century, scientific discoveries of bacterial transmission of diseases had produced great advances in the treatment of cholera, smallpox, typhoid fever, tuberculosis, and syphilis. Between 1900 and 1930, the first three almost disappeared, tuberculosis fell from second to tenth as a cause of death, and syphilis was brought under control. The limits of this advance in the understanding of contagious diseases became evident, however, as the influenza epidemic of 1918 claimed a death toll that in the United States alone may have exceeded 500,000 (record keeping was far from perfect), primarily in urban areas.

Germn Free In the aftermath of the flu epidemic, consciousness spread and concern deepened about the need to ward off germs.

Cleanliness took higher priority in many Americans' daily lives than ever before. Concern with sanitation, especially in urban areas, led municipalities to initiate or expand regular street cleaning and garbage pickup. Similar concerns became evident within the home. As indoor toilets and consolidated bathrooms became common, especially in middle-class homes, disinfectant cleaning solutions such as Lysol were heavily promoted and widely used. In 1921 the Johnson & Johnson Company developed a sterile bandage held in place by adhesive tape. Marketed for use over small cuts and sores, it was promoted as the "Band Aid."

Eating Healthy Marketers of new products, and even older ones, took advantage of health concerns to promote sales. Pre–World War I discoveries of their nutritional importance led to the promotion of foods and dietary supplements rich in vitamins and minerals. Milk consumption in particular soared; two national dairy holding companies, Borden and Sealtest, emerged to buy up, modernize and standardize many local dairies, and encourage adults and especially growing children to drink "a quart a day." Sales of citrus fruit soared as California growers extolled the healthful qualities of their Sunkist brand. Equivalent success was achieved in a similar manner by California Sun-Maid raisin producers, while the asparagus section of the Canners League of California was able to introduce a previously unknown vegetable into the American diet. Health claims did not have to be unimpeachable to be effective, as the Morton Company proved when it promoted its product as "health salt."

Medical Care Overall improvements in their diets, mentioned earlier, contributed a great deal to healthier and longer lives for most Americans. More serious health problems could not be solved so easily. Modern hospital-centered medical care provided by physicians with specialized training was limited, expensive, and generally used only by the wealthy. People who consulted doctors tended to prefer general practitioners who dispensed a wide range of diagnostic and treatment services from their offices or on home visits, usually at modest cost. Between 1920 and 1940, the number of physicians grew

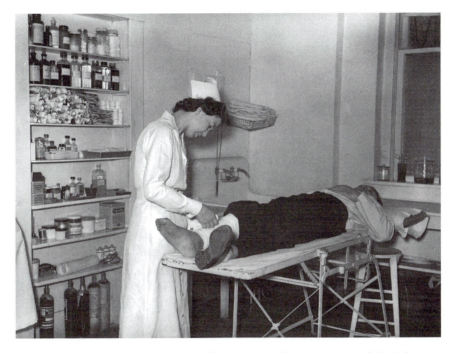

Hospital emergency room, Herrin, Illinois, 1939. Photo courtesy of the Library of Congress.

about 7 percent, but slipped from 137 to 133 per 100,000 people in a population that was growing three times as fast. It was easier to gain access to a doctor in urban areas. By 1930, 27 percent of the population lived in cities of 100,000 or more, but 44 percent of all doctors practiced there. The concentration of health care facilities and medical expertise in urban centers already well underway would continue.

The most universal circumstance putting health at risk was childbirth. Until 1938, a majority of births took place at **Childbirth** home with the mother typically attended by female relatives, friends, neighbors, or a midwife, and, increasingly, a physician. Husbands generally were excluded. By the 1920s, however, urban women, particularly those of middle-class status, turned more often to hospitals to give birth attended by physicians and nurses specializing in obstetrics. Before World War I, hospitals had been widely viewed as unhealthy places, and in fact as recently as 1912, the death rate among children delivered in hospitals was three times that of those born outside of them. Improvements in hospital sanitation and care rapidly altered those conditions and made hospitals the preferred location for childbirth.

Faith in doctors and hospitals rather than traditional practices at the most risk-filled moment for both women and their children reflected a general growth of confidence in medical science. "Slowly but surely," declared *Good Housekeeping* magazine, "childbirth is being lifted out of the realm of darkness into the spotlight of new science." Male physicians encouraged this shift, regarding birth as a dangerous, pathological process best handled in a hospital where forceps, episiotomy, and anesthesia could ease the process. Most expectant mothers, their natural apprehensions reinforced by their doctors, were happy for the drug-reduced awareness of the delivery followed by the rest and service of a hospital stay. They cheerfully surrendered authority over the birthing experience to male strangers and impersonal hospital routines. Only in later decades would women realize that with safety and comfort came loss of control over an important experience in their lives. Most rural women far from hospitals and poor women unable to afford them continued to give birth at home. The change in middle-class childbirth practices, however, played a great role in the dramatic drop in infant mortality from 86 per 1,000 births in 1920 to 65 per 1,000 by 1930 and 47 per 1,000 by 1940.

Doctors Oppose Medical Insurance   If illness or injury struck, the majority of Americans with modest incomes or less during the 1920s and 1930s most often turned to home remedies and accepted considerable suffering. Medical and hospitalization insurance was practically nonexistent. In 1940, the federal census found only 91,000 people out of 132 million with hospitalization coverage and did not even ask about broader medical coverage. The medical profession resisted any suggestion that might impose external supervision or controls. It resisted the Sheppard-Towner Maternity- and Infancy-Protection Act of 1921. When the possibility of national health insurance as a part of the New Deal social welfare program was broached, the American Medical Association convened a special meeting of its house of delegates to denounce the idea. Consequently, medical care and especially a catastrophic emergency remained a possibility that every family or unattached individual had to confront by themselves. Professional care was either an unpredictable burden or completely out of reach.

EDUCATION

Educating the younger generation was a task that parents and other elders confronted in every era. Once viewed as a family responsibility, by the start of the twentieth century education had come increasingly to be seen as a matter in which the whole society had a stake to insure that young people became capable workers and good citizens. Mandatory school attendance laws intended to insure at least a minimum of literacy among a state's citizens appeared as early as the 1840s in New England.

By 1900 compulsory attendance at public or private school was almost universal outside the states of the old Confederacy but nonexistent there—in large part because of white opposition to spending on black schools. Only in the era of World War I did states such as South Carolina, Georgia, and Mississippi adopt even weak school attendance requirements. By 1920, 85.7 percent of five to seventeen year olds were in public or private schools, a proportion that would rise steadily over the next two decades to 95.5 percent by 1940. Nonpublic, mainly parochial schools accounted for 10 percent of total enrollment by 1940.

Although most young people during the 1920s and 1930s had at least some experience with school, the nature of that experience depended on who they were and where they lived. About 10 percent more nonwhite than white children **School Attendance** did not attend school at all, due mainly to the woeful state of schools for African Americans in the segregated South. With schools funded predominantly from local resources, the length of the school year varied widely. In the poorest rural districts, the school year was as short as three months. At the same time the national average school year lengthened from thirty-two to thirty-five weeks, and student average attendance went from twenty-five to thirty weeks per year.

Segregation of schools was not unique to the South. Residential segregation together with the custom of neighborhood-based schools and carefully drawn school district lines meant that most children only saw other students of their own race. And while African Americans were graduating from teacher-training colleges, the racism of parents and school officials meant that white schools would not accept African American teachers. Therefore only African American students had the experience of teacher role models and authority figures who were African American.

Desire or need to enter the world of work as well as a sense of having gained what one could from school led many students to make what from a later perspective seems like an early departure from school. Males left school a year earlier than females on average, and nonwhites left three years earlier than whites. As of 1920, only 17 percent of the population was graduated from high school, though that was nearly three times the percentage that was graduated at the start of the century.

World War I sent shock waves through the United States regarding the inadequacy of its schools. In the **Improvement Needed** midst of a severe manpower shortage, the country discovered that many young men were unfit for military duty because of inadequate education. Two-of-five recruits tested were below average on the Yerkes Alpha Test designed to identify potential officers and weed out those unsuited for service. Often referred to as an

A one-room schoolhouse in Grundy County, Iowa, 1939. The teacher is at the blackboard with the only second grade student in the class. Photo courtesy of the Library of Congress.

intelligence test and used to argue that immigrants, blacks, and lower economic class people in general were incapable of higher reasoning and unworthy to participate in a democracy, the test was in fact a measure of the individual's education, particularly his schooling in English and mathematical reasoning. The need to improve American education became evident.

Nearly one-in-four students in 1920 attended a school in which there was only one teacher. Two hundred thousand such schools were spread across rural America, most notably in the South where racial segregation further reduced the number of students gathered in any one school. Students often had to walk a mile or more to reach these schools. When they arrived, they were greeted by a teacher who had to provide instruction in all subjects at all grade levels. Many of these rural teachers had only a high school education, or less, themselves. The stock of schoolbooks and equipment was equally meager.

The School Bus   The 1920s saw a great movement toward school consolidation. The advent of the school bus made it possible to bring together in a central location students from a wide area. A consolidated school allowed teachers to concentrate on particular subjects or age groups. Busing permitted students to attend classes with others of the same age and ability. With enough students in one place to justify it, high schools in particular could offer a wider range of courses. The school bus became a symbol of significant educational improvement. By the end of the 1920s the number of one-teacher schools had fallen by a quarter and within another decade by almost half. Only Southern schools for African Americans, stifled by segregation and neglect, failed to share in the progress.

Consolidation raised expectations and rewards for teachers as their numbers grew from 700,000 to 912,000. **Teachers** At least a two-year course at a state teachers' college or **Become** normal school became standard and, especially at the **Professionals** high school level, a four-year college degree became commonplace. Teachers began thinking of themselves as professionals. At the end of World War I only one-in-seventy teachers belonged to the National Education Association; on the eve of World War II nearly one in four did so. Salaries, never high in the predominately female profession, did nevertheless improve considerably from an average of $871 in 1920 to $1,441 by 1940.

For students, the typical school day included a combination of study periods for reading textbooks, writing, and **Instruction** solving math problems and recitation periods. During rec- **and** itation sessions students told their teacher what the book **Curriculum** had said or how the problem should be worked out. Some progressive school systems were beginning to shift from a common, lockstep curriculum for every student to more individual instruction. Projects, in which a range of subjects such as mathematics, vocabulary, science, geography, and history might all be taught in combination as a part of a special inquiry into some topic such as ships, frogs, or Italy, began replacing recitation, especially at the elementary level. Most schools, however, either did not change their basic approach or went no further than the intermediate step of dividing students into slow, average, and rapid learner sections. Parochial schools changed more slowly than public ones. Textbooks became more colorful and attractive, more up-to-date, and more often supplemented by flash cards, workbooks, and filmstrips in schools that could afford them. However, all schools, as they grew in size, acquired administrative bureaucracies, adopted common practices, and became increasingly impersonal.

Larger urban or consolidated rural schools gave their expanding population of students with differing abilities and goals a more diverse range of courses from which to chose. English, history, math, and science remained at the core of the curriculum. The most notable expansion occurred in the area of vocational education. Agriculture, typing, home economics, and mechanical arts, such as wood- and metalworking, received particular attention. Physical education, art, and music also increased.

Foreign language instruction, on the other hand, decreased, hard hit by the World War I concern that English become the universal American language. As late as the early 1920s, more than a quarter of all students learned Latin, 15 percent took French, and 11 percent studied Spanish, but those figures fell sharply over the next dozen years, and no other languages received much attention. With the foreign-born population decreasing as well, the United States had turned a corner on the path to becoming a society that overwhelmingly comprehended only English.

Extracurricular Activities

As important in the daily life of students as changes in the school curriculum was the rise of an extra- or co-curriculum. Adult-supervised organizations in which adolescents could learn skills and values became an important part of the schools of the 1920s. Some of these organizations, such as the Boy Scouts, Girl Scouts, and Young Men's or Women's Christian (YMCA, YWCA) or Hebrew (YMHA, YWHA) Associations, had started a decade or more earlier to keep maturing males and females away from each other, occupy them in outdoor activities and crafts for hours each week, and give them moral instruction. Athletic teams, drama societies, and other interest groups using school facilities and extending the school day for students became a noteworthy part of the educational system. For instance, by 1929, there were 750,000 young people in 4-H clubs, which taught moral values and social skills as well as encouraged members to participate in county and state fair livestock- or plant-raising competitions. Schools also sponsored and chaperoned social activities for their students such as dances and proms. Together with an increase in an informal after-school social life with their peers and away from their families, extracurricular activities kept young people engaged in the culture of school more than ever before. By 1940, half of all eighteen year olds were staying in school long enough to obtain a high school diploma, triple the percentage who had done so merely twenty years earlier.

Colleges and Universities

The increase in high school graduates together with the growing demand for better-educated teachers helped stimulate a significant rise in college attendance during the 1920s and 1930s. As the percentage of eighteen to twenty-one year olds attending college doubled from 8 to almost 16 percent, the overall enrollment in American colleges and universities grew from 600,000 to 1.5 million. Most of the enrollment growth involved middle-class students attending nonelite public universities in the Midwest and elsewhere. During these decades, two-out-of-three students attended schools that were coeducational and catered to full-time residents. The private universities and colleges more prominent in eastern states, generally smaller to begin with and often restricted to a single sex, grew more slowly. These elite schools regularly excluded or severely limited admission of immigrants, Jews, and African Americans; all but the latter found public institutions, especially urban schools such as the City College of New York, the University of California Los Angeles, and the University of Cincinnati, more hospitable. Also slow growing were the more socially conservative small colleges operated by many religious denominations and the handful of colleges for African Americans.

Like secondary schools, colleges and universities under-went curricular reform and expansion in the years between the world wars. As the number of faculty tripled, the variety of courses increased proportionally. Courses and programs **A Variety of Courses** in business, engineering, fine arts, and education and new approaches to the study of human society such as anthropology, political science, and sociology were added to the traditional arts and sciences, medicine, law, and theology. Courses designed to prepare students for the ordinary routines of everyday life, gradually becoming as straightforward and frank as the popular Indiana University course on marriage begun by Professor Alfred Kinsey in 1938, also entered the catalogue.

Paralleling that in secondary schools, collegiate social life flourished in the 1920s. As growing numbers of young adults enrolled in colleges and universities to spend a few hours each week in the presence of learned professors, they **College Social Life** were left with substantial amounts of time to spend with each other free from the company of their elders. Such social opportunities no doubt attracted some to enroll in the first place and shaped the collegiate ex-perience of even those who were more serious about their studies. Young people clustered together on campuses, possessing plenty of free time, and, generally supplied by their middle-class parents with at least some disposable income, devoted themselves to their own entertainment. At-tendance at school athletic events became popular; going to movies and dances became even more so. Disdain for "old-fashioned ways" and the thrill of doing something that their parents and other elders might dis-approve of led many to patronize speakeasies and bootleggers. Dating and sexual exploration remained at the top of most students' list of fa-vored diversions. Altogether, student social life set the collegiate culture apart, drew attention to innovations in fashion and conduct, and pro-vided a model for the behavior of young people already at work or still in high school.

College life took on a more serious note in the 1930s. More, though hardly all, students became involved in po-litical discussions and some were drawn by their professors **Enrollment Increases** or their own analysis to advocate reformist or even radical solutions for the nation's economic difficulties. Many families and stu-dents had less money to spend on frivolity. More students had to find part-time jobs on or off campus to make ends meet. Campus social life continued but with greater attention to its less expensive aspects. Still, despite the depression, students in ever increasing numbers continued to enroll in institutions of higher education. Four hundred thousand more students were in colleges and universities at the end of the depression decade than at its outset, continuing the surge in education so evident in the 1920s.

RELIGION

Religion played a role in most American lives in the 1920s and 1930s, but, for the most part, a limited one. In Middletown, as throughout the country, most people belonged to a church, almost always a Christian church and usually a Protestant one. The Lynds observed, however, that membership vastly exceeded the number of individuals who attended services on a weekly basis or provided financial support. In turn, churches contributed little to community charities, far less than they spent on foreign missionary work. Questioning of dominant Christian beliefs was rare, but at the same time there was much, in the Lynds' words, "outwardly conforming indifference."[1]

Variety of Denominations While church membership was taken for granted, choice of creed varied. Christian denominations prevailed overwhelmingly, with Jews the only statistically significant exception. The Roman Catholic Church, drawing primarily on the large nineteenth-century Irish immigrant population as well as more recent arrivals from southern and Eastern Europe and Hispanics in the Southwest, was the largest Christian denomination. A sizable Orthodox community existed as well among recent Eastern European immigrants. Two-thirds of Christians, however, affiliated with one or another Protestant sect. Baptists were especially prominent in the South, Lutherans in the upper Midwest and Northwest, and Mormons in the intermountain West. The largest denominations, the Methodists, Congregationalists, Episcopalians, and Presbyterians, could be found almost everywhere, though often not as the largest group in one location. The Protestant community was further fragmented by north-south divisions within the Baptists and Methodists and by the existence of numerous smaller churches that had declared independence because of some theological or other dispute. By the 1920s, Middletown, a typical example, had forty-two churches catering to twenty-eight different Christian denominations (and one Jewish congregation) for a city with less than 40,000 residents. People tended to stay with the church into which they were born and almost never switched to a different faith.

Despite doctrinal differences, religious practice shared many common features. Homes, more often than not, contained religious decorations,

A Sunday service at the Irwin, Iowa, Lutheran church. Photo courtesy of the National Archives.

pictures, or artifacts such as crosses, crucifixes, or menorahs. Most families routinely paused before meals for a brief prayer asking that they and their food be blessed. Otherwise, religious matters were normally centered in the church. Clergymen reported that they visited homes at times of bereavement, when called upon to provide counsel, and often simply to stay in social contact with their members. Conducting prayer services in the home, however, was increasingly a thing of the past.

Sunday was the day most given over to religious activities. Religious education programs had developed over the previous half century: graded curriculums were patterned after secular education but centered on Bible study and conducted **Religious Education** by church volunteers. "Sunday schools" had shifted the focus of religious training from the home to the church. By the 1920s parents more often sent their children to Sunday school than attended services themselves, and male involvement on Sunday morning, while not uncommon, was proportionally least frequent of all. Two-thirds of the adults in Middletown's churches on a normal Sunday, the Lynds noted, were female.

Christian churches held services on Sunday mornings and, with declining frequency, on Sunday and Wednesday evenings as well. The extent of formal ritual varied, but congregational singing as a part of the service was nearly universal. Especially in Protestant churches, the minister's sermon was the centerpiece of the service. Ministers acknowledged that they devoted a great deal of their time to preparing their sermons, which for the most part dealt with the need for faith and conduct according to principles linked to the Bible. They tended to avoid comments on current affairs with which their congregation might disagree.

Religious Division   Controversy within a congregation might be unusual, but differences among denominations and even within them were more common. The issue of alcohol divided Baptists, Methodists, and other firm prohibitionists from most Catholics, some Lutherans, and others who, largely because of ethnic background, were not opposed to drinking. Liquor, religion, and politics intertwined in 1928. Southern Methodists and Baptists became unusually outspoken in their hostility to Democratic presidential candidate Alfred E. Smith, a Catholic governor of New York, son of immigrants, and open opponent of national prohibition; these normally Democratic Southerners threw their support to Smith's presidential rival, the prohibition-supporting Quaker Republican, Herbert Hoover. Northern urban Catholic voters responded by rallying around Smith. Religious tension and mutual distrust became a central factor in the contest that Hoover eventually won by a comfortable margin.

Race created other religious divisions throughout the period. Largely white Protestant denominations, principally the Methodists and Baptists, could count a half million African American members by 1940. However, 99 percent of them worshipped only with other African Americans in segregated congregations. Most African Americans, 15 times as many in fact, belonged to their own entirely separate churches. Most of these were small churches in the rural South, but the largest Protestant congregation in the nation was Harlem's 14,000 member Abyssinian Baptist Church. Harlem was also home to the flamboyant mystic George Baker, who called himself Father Divine. He preached a strict code of conduct and attracted a large following among poor blacks (and some whites) who considered him God in the flesh.

Evangelists   Father Divine was not the only charismatic religious figure of the time. Evangelists who preached with extraordinary emotional fervor were popular, especially at the revival meetings that some churches held annually. Most evangelists were best known within their own denomination, but a few developed national followings with the help of radio and large urban revival meetings. Ex-Chicago White Stockings outfielder Billy Sunday, perhaps the most famous, held revivals in, among other places, New York City's Madison Square Garden. Aimee Semple McPherson created her own Church of the Four Square Gospel in Los Angeles. In the 1930s, Detroit's Catholic Father Charles Coughlin gained a radio audience in the millions for broadcasts highly critical of the New Deal from his "Shrine of the Little Flower."

Among more conventional churches, the most no-
ticeable distinction was whether they embraced a view **Fundamentalism**
of society conditioned by modern science or clung to
older traditions of belief. The latter stance was coming by the 1920s to be called fundamentalism after a 1910 religious tract, "The Fundamentals." This widely distributed pamphlet advocated a literal interpretation of the Bible, including the creation story, the virgin birth and resurrection of Jesus, and the Second Coming. Fundamentalism was embraced by various theological seminaries as well as by a number of highly successful evangelists, including Billy Sunday and former presidential candidate William Jennings Bryan. It gained a large following particularly, but not exclusively, in the South and Midwest and other more rural and conservative parts of the country.

The most spectacular head-on clash of fundamentalism and modernism took place in Dayton, Tennessee, in 1925, after the Tennessee legislature, sympathetic to the fundamentalist viewpoint, adopted a law banning the teaching of Charles Darwin's scientific theory of evolution in public schools. A challenge to the law by the American Civil Liberties Union through Dayton teacher John Thomas Scopes led to a courtroom battle in which civil libertarian Clarence Darrow defended Scopes and the unrestrained teaching of science. William Jennings Bryan, defending the antievolution law and the fundamentalist views on which it was based, found himself called to testify as an expert on the Bible. Darrow got Bryan to express some uncertainty about the literal truth of biblical stories such as the creation of the universe in six earth days and the swallowing of Jonah by a whale. As a result, fundamentalism came in for much ridicule in more modern circles. Scopes, however, was convicted, the Tennessee law remained in place, and fundamentalist views held firm in more conservative areas of the country. The highly publicized *Tennessee v. Scopes* trial deepened the rift between modernists and fundamentalists, leaving each side thinking the other not merely thoroughly mistaken but actively hostile to the truth.

For most Americans, however, religion did not involve
such intense disputes over theology and civil liberty. In- **Americanized**
stead, it consisted of a general approval of things as they **Christianity**
were, with success explained as a reward for virtue and
difficulty as a test of character. The contented pro-business views of dominant Protestantism were reflected in Bruce Barton's 1925 book, *The Man Nobody Knows*, which quickly became one of the decade's best-sellers. Barton depicted Jesus as a dynamic leader "who picked up twelve

men from the bottom ranks of business and forged them into an organization that conquered the world," a swell guy anyone would enjoy
knowing and following.[2]

Dominant American Christianity involved learning Bible stories and
memorizing verses of Scripture as a child, holding some general but not
deeply examined religious beliefs, and participating in church rituals of
baptism, marriage, and death. Not only were Sunday schools and "vacation Bible schools" common, but public schools routinely conducted
brief prayers and hosted activities by the YMCA and other religious
groups. No wonder that when the Lynds surveyed high school juniors
and seniors in Middletown they found that 83 percent of boys and 92
percent of girls agreed that Christianity was the one true religion; of the
balance as many expressed uncertainty as rejected this view. Perhaps a
better measure of the depth of these beliefs was that 58 percent of males
and 68 percent of females agreed that the Bible was a sufficient guide to
all the problems of modern life, while only 26 percent of boys and 20
percent of girls disagreed; the balance of respondents were uncertain.

LEISURE

American churches found themselves facing growing competition for
the attention of the public during the 1920s and 1930s. Sunday was the
one day when work was generally set aside. In recent decades, the middle class and some workers had shifted to a half day of labor on Saturday, but not until the passage of the Fair Labor Standards Act in 1938
would the two-day weekend become standard and Sunday lose its
unique status as a full day of leisure.

Sunday a Day for Recreation
In early America, Sunday was a day for putting aside
secular activity and concentrating on worship and
prayer. Gradually, however, more and more Americans'
devotion was shifting to secular pursuits and recreation.
By the 1920s golf courses were reporting more players on the links Sunday morning than at any other time of the week. Sunday also had become the most popular day of the week for moviegoing, though one
survey showed that a third of the working class and one-sixth of the
business class still thought it was wrong. Amateur baseball and gun
shooting were other popular, if somewhat disputed, Sunday pursuits.
Professional baseball teams had steadily chipped away at "blue laws"
banning Sunday games for which admission was charged. Midwestern
cities led the way before the turn of the century but were not joined by
New York and Washington until World War I. Boston held out against
professional Sunday baseball until 1929, while Philadelphia and Pittsburgh remained steadfast until 1934. The single most common Sunday
activity appeared to be taking a drive in the family automobile, for the

Family picnic in Grant's Pass, Oregon, 1939. Photo courtesy of the Library of Congress.

purpose of visiting friends or family, sightseeing, or travel to a picnic site, a museum or park, or some place of entertainment. Stores remained closed, but otherwise Sunday was becoming a day for leisure rather than piety.

Many churches sought to hold the attention of their members and attract others by offering a range of Sunday activities that included recreation and social life as well as traditional religion. The effort soon spread to weekdays as well. Weeknight church suppers became common. Clubs for men, women, and adolescents that combined a large measure of sociability and entertainment with a small dose of religious education and worship went by different names but arose in most denominations. Young Men's or Women's Christian or Hebrew Associations carried the initiative further, especially with athletic activities. But churches struggled to hold the attention of people increasingly inclined to think of Sunday as a day for enjoyment. In the 1930s, a Middletown radio station reported an upsurge of listeners when it switched from religious to popular music on Sunday afternoon.

Social Organizations   The use of leisure time became an unprecedented issue for families and individuals as shorter work weeks and automobiles permitted enjoyment of diversions outside the home. Radio and motion pictures together absorbed a great deal of attention. Voluntary organizations and clubs, both church sponsored and secular, allowed men, women, and teenagers in communities of practically every size to explore shared interests, concerns, and backgrounds. Men had business clubs such as Rotary and Kiwanis as well as fraternal associations such as the Knights of Columbus, Masons, Moose, Lions, and Elks. Women belonged to various clubs and informal social, educational, and charitable groups, while the Boy Scouts and Girl Scouts headed the list of membership organizations for younger people. For the middle class especially, voluntary organizations became so numerous and their activities so frequent that some complained of being "clubbed to death."

Leisure Activities Increase in Variety   The use of leisure time varied by place, season, and class. Conversation, reading, listening to the radio, and attending movies were by far the most common recreations in Middletown, the Lynds observed, and that was no doubt true elsewhere as well. Drinking, which never died out entirely during prohibition, became more affordable and thus commonplace, after repeal in 1933. The working class patronized taverns, while the middle class increasingly drank at home. Otherwise, dancing was perhaps the most widely shared pleasure, though in some conservative Protestant communities it was frowned upon. Urban street festivals and picnics in the countryside were common warm-weather pastimes. Until the depression put many of them out of business, amusement parks, from New York's Coney Island and Ohio's Cedar Point to small ones at the end of the local trolley line, drew crowds to their mechanized thrill rides, games of chance, and dance pavilions. Traveling carnivals and circuses also thrived. Bowling, billiards and pool, and small stakes gambling were all popular, especially among the urban working class. Prohibition repeal expanded access to saloon-based pool tables, not to mention nickel slot machines. Penny-a-card bingo also gained favor in the 1930s. While card playing was very common, the games varied from urban working-class poker and blackjack and middle-class bridge to small-town cribbage. A board game originally developed to demonstrate how capitalism worked and played in college economics classes was modified in the 1930s by the Parker Brothers Company and renamed Monopoly. The opportunity provided to players to amass a fantasy fortune helped account for the game's great popularity.

Men playing pool in the Irwin, Iowa, pool hall. Photo courtesy of the National Archives.

Sporting contests had long been occasions for social-izing, wagering, and admiring the performance of race **Sporting Events** horses, hunting dogs, and skilled athletes. World War I military experience had exposed many men to baseball, boxing, and track and field. American Legion programs kept many veterans engaged in these sports, both as players and coaches of younger participants. Middle-class involvement in hunting and fishing increased. Vastly more expensive elite sports such as golf and tennis gained popularity as well. However, the most notable growth in sports during the 1920s was in the size of the audience. Not only the number of spectators at sporting events but the radio audience for them propelled sports forward as leisure ac-tivity.

Baseball drew the largest audience. The "Big Leagues" of professional baseball were confined to the northeast quarter **Baseball** of the country where the proximity of urban centers and the convenience of rail transportation made two eight-team leagues possible. The American League had been around since the turn of the century, the National League considerably longer, and their only direct competition with each other, the World Series, since 1903. Professional baseball was damaged by the scandal that swirled around the 1919 Chicago White Sox, eight of whose players were convicted of taking bribes from gamblers to lose the World Series to the Cincinnati Reds. Establishment of a baseball commissioner to police owners and players restored faith that the games were fair contests. A tighter, harder, "lively" ball was introduced along with new rules to assure frequent replacement of the ball so that it could not be softened up. These changes aided hitters, increased the possibility of home runs, and attracted more fans than ever before. Larger crowds, not to mention stadiums built in the 1920s to hold them, marked the growing popularity of what fans already called "the national pastime."

Radio and newspapers carried accounts of big league baseball far beyond the ten cities where it was played (New York had three teams, Boston, Chicago, Philadelphia, and St. Louis two each, and Cincinnati, Cleveland, Detroit, Pittsburgh, and Washington the others). Minor league professional teams existed in smaller cities and towns of the South, Midwest, and Pacific coast. Additional legions of semiprofessional and amateur baseball teams made it difficult for Americans to remain entirely unfamiliar with the game. Star players became celebrities whose exploits were widely known and admired. The most famous of all, home run slugger Babe Ruth of the New York Yankees, answered criticism that his 1930 salary was higher than President Herbert Hoover's by saying, "I had a better year." Most agreed.

Football   Football had, since the 1890s, become extremely popular at high schools and colleges with the playing fields and resources to support it. As enrollments grew and physical education became part of curricular and extracurricular activity, football increased its following. While standard teams put eleven players on the field, low enrollment schools often adapted the rules to permit games with five or six on a side. Not only did students and alumni flock to games but so too did people whose only connection to a school was an enthusiasm for its teams. Recognizing a potential publicity and financial bonanza, universities built stadiums seating several times their enrolled student body and began hiring talented players with "athletic scholarships." Excellent teams and outstanding players or even the opportunity to have a good time watching a losing effort drew huge crowds, unprecedented throngs of 60 to 80 thousand and even more, to college campuses on fall Saturday afternoons. By the end of the 1920s, college football brought in an estimated $21.5 million, $4.5 million more than professional baseball during the same year. Professional football, employing ex-college stars, began attracting large crowds in the same cities that supported major league baseball but generally remained a sidelight to the enormously popular college game.

During the winter months between fall football and spring and summer baseball, school and college gymnasiums **Basketball** housed a sport only invented in the 1890s. Basketball had almost instantly become popular with both males and females through-out the country. Rules differed for five-member men's teams and six-member women's teams; and, except in a few midwestern states, women's basketball did not become the spectator sport that the men's game did. Men's basketball drew fans to high school and college games and even to industrial leagues. Businesses hoping to advertise them-selves and build employee morale would recruit and reward workers who were talented ballplayers. For basketball players and fans alike, this was the extent of professionalism in the 1920s and 1930s.

Except for boxing, baseball, horse racing, and football— professionalized sports that attracted crowds of spectators **Other Sports** and quickly gained radio audiences as well—most sports **Activity for** remained predominantly kids' games. Large numbers of **the Young** children and younger adults played baseball, bicycled, swam, ran, and, in northern regions, ice skated and skied. But these sorts of leisure-time activities tapered off rapidly after high school, the Lynds noted in Middletown, a victim, they surmised, of the popularity of the automobile.

One notable exception to the general pattern of reduced adult sports activity was the rise in the popularity of golf in the 1920s. **Golf** The game was restricted to the wealthy because of equipment costs, the time required to play a round, and the expense of maintaining a large and carefully groomed grass course. Media reports of the tri-umphs of Atlanta attorney Bobby Jones, an amateur who regularly de-feated professional competitors, together with the opening of more private and even public courses boosted interest in golf. By the end of the decade, an estimated three million players could be found on some four thousand courses nationwide.

The depression caused enthusiasm for golf to sag but gave rise to an alternative, miniature golf. It required much less exertion, skill, and time to play, was far less expensive, and thus was accessible to more people as a leisure-time activity. A wide public took up miniature golf, a game not invented until the late 1920s. So popular did it quickly become that by 1930 there were an estimated 30,000 courses in operation across the United States. Among other things, miniature golf's popularity suggests that many people looked more for relaxation and amusement in their daily lives than for strenuous exercise.

By the 1920s, middle-class Americans were also beginning to enjoy annual vacations, long a pleasure of only the **Vacations** wealthy. Salaried workers increasingly benefited from a two-week annual paid release from their duties. Rarely did hourly wage earners enjoy such a respite, though some employers would allow workers to take an unpaid leave of a week or two without losing their jobs. Vacations for farmers were even rarer as livestock feeding and other chores had to be done every day.

For those fortunate enough to be able to take vacations, automobile trips to visit distant family or sites were popular. Natural attractions from Cape Cod, Niagara Falls, and the wooded lakes of Michigan and Wisconsin to national parks such as Yellowstone, Yosemite, and the Grand Canyon became favored destinations. The primitive quality of roads, directional signs, and accommodations in many areas made automobile travel a challenge. Out of necessity, vacationers often took along camping equipment or pulled a small camping trailer behind their car. Others patronized the clusters of tiny cabins cropping up along main traveled roads that were at first called motor hotels and, starting in the mid-1920s, motels.

Holidays

For many Americans, holidays represented the high points of their leisure time. Christmas was the most important holiday for the nine out of ten who were Christian. Protestants had traditionally devoted more attention to Easter; but within the previous century, American Christmas celebrations had come to combine Catholic and Orthodox religious festivities, Anglican feasting, the German and Scandinavian tradition of decorated Christmas trees, domestically evolved traditions of greeting cards and the "jolly old elf" Santa Claus, and, at the center of the celebration, extensive gift giving. New Year's Day, Easter, Memorial Day, Fourth of July, and Thanksgiving were other generally important holidays, while children enjoyed Halloween, and ethnic groups celebrated their own special occasions from St. Patrick's Day to Yom Kippur.

Leisure practices evolved for most persons from year to year as their individual state of affairs and economic situation changed. The normal progression of family life together with alterations in health and educational circumstances likewise played a role in how people carried on their lives. For most Americans most of the time life was filled with the routine and conventional. Only rarely would some occurrence so consequential and disruptive that it might later be called "historic" intrude on the day-by-day and year-to-year rhythms of existence.

NOTES

1. For a detailed discussion of religious practices in Muncie, see Robert S. Lynd and Helen Merrill Lynd, *Middletown: A Study in Modern American Culture* (New York: Harcourt, Brace and World, 1929), 315–409.

2. Bruce Barton, *The Man Nobody Knows* (Indianapolis: Bobbs-Merrill, c. 1925), x.

8

Conflict, Crime, and Catastrophe: The Disruptions of Daily Life

While for most people most of the time, each day was generally similar to the day before and the one to follow, exceptions did occur. The placid continuities of daily life could be thrown into turmoil. Personal disputes erupted into emotional confrontations and sometimes violence. So too did social, racial, ethnic, economic, or political conflicts, often on a much larger scale. In these cases, life's ordinary routines could be upset in distressing and sometimes terribly threatening ways, not merely for a few individuals but for a vast number of people as well. Criminal activity not only affected the victim and perpetrator but also challenged the defined standards of socially acceptable behavior and thereby the sense of security that came with being able to assume the safety of one's person and property. Meanwhile, law enforcement efforts affected a much wider range of the population, not only those involved in crimes but many entirely innocent. Large-scale catastrophes, perhaps, most thoroughly unsettled a community or region's daily life. Such occurrences were, after all, not the product of flaws in human behavior but rather the result of utterly unpredictable and overwhelming forces of nature. Furthermore, they indiscriminately impacted everyone in their path.

Episodes of conflict and crime, not to mention natural catastrophes, provide distinctive punctuation to the normal routines of every age. However out of the ordinary they may be, they become the aspects of a period most widely remembered and deemed historic. Although they may be uncommon rather than typical experiences, they do possess great significance. They not only indicate the stresses and fears faced by the people of the time, but also the manner in which the society dealt with life's disruptions. In these respects, the conflicts, crimes, and catastrophes of the 1920s and 1930s stamped their mark upon the era.

CONFLICT

Underlying Tensions
Several decades of rapid industrialization and urbanization, heavy immigration, and contentious efforts at political and social reform had preceded the 1920s. The accumulated strains of these developments had crested in the tumult of the Great War of 1914–1918. Tension between those encouraged and those alarmed by change, heightened by the United States' entry into the European war in 1917, did not altogether dissipate with the November 1918 armistice. The November 1917 Bolshevik Revolution in Russia together with postwar domestic labor unrest, both greeted unsympathetically by American business and government, generated the Red Scare of 1919. The legacies of these recent experiences and the continuing bitterness they spawned subsequently manifested themselves in large-scale social conflicts during the following decades.

Differences in the circumstances and daily life experiences of various Americans underlay the conflicts of the 1920s and 1930s. Race continued its long history as a primary American social cleavage. The disparities of urban and rural life generated deep mutual suspicion between those who dwelt in the two dissimilar environments, especially when reinforced by economic, ethnic, religious, and racial differences. Hostility between Protestants and Roman Catholics, which often incorporated other clashes as well, attained high visibility in the 1920s. Suspicion and distrust between North and South, old-stock residents and recent arrivals, traditional enemies, and new rivals for jobs, housing, or other measures of social acceptance caused animosities to linger close to the surface and occasionally flare into ugly outbursts.

The "American Dream"
Cultural differences stirred more direct confrontations than did economic disparities, though the latter no doubt exacerbated the former. Demarcations clearly existed between the small minority who had achieved abundance and security, the much larger number who had gained only an insecure grip on financial comfort, and the largest segment of the population who at best enjoyed limited and irregular comfort and more often wrestled with poverty. Nevertheless the long-standing and ongoing notion that in America hard-working individuals could improve their lot and achieve economic success continued to obscure the reality that most did not. Yet the myth of the "American dream" helped account for the failure of most lower- and middle-income Americans to perceive themselves as permanent members of an economic underclass with distinctive

interests at odds with the well to do. Not until the 1930s would conflict erupt that was particularly economic in nature, and even then it was remarkably limited under the circumstances because of the persistence of the American dream and the tendency of people to think in terms of individualism rather than class solidarity.

The American political system provided a means of ex- **Party Politics** pression and an outlet for social and economic conflict to some extent. At the same time, the peculiarities of American politics that had evolved in the course of the previous century tended to obscure and diffuse rather than resolve such conflict. The country's two long-standing national parties each had come to include in their ranks a broad spectrum of groups and interests. Internal party divisions often prevented a clear-cut stand on a particular issue. Furthermore, the ever-present prospect of attracting the modest amount of additional support necessary to gain victory often led both Republicans and Democrats to avoid taking sides when they could afford to do so. Both parties remained conscious of the small electoral margin between them. Each could usually contemplate attracting the additional support that might provide the margin of victory. At the very least, they usually preferred to avoid alienating a constituency whose loss might insure defeat. Consequently, much fundamental conflict in American life remained ill-defined by partisan politics and found other means of expression.

In the early 1920s, no outgrowth of the tensions within American society gained more visibility than the widespread **The Ku** popularity of the Ku Klux Klan (KKK). With national mem- **Klux Klan** bership estimates ranging from three to six million or beyond and with sizable ranks in such places as New Jersey, Ohio, Indiana, Illinois, Colorado, California, and the Pacific Northwest, the Klan in the twenties was not the limited Southern phenomenon of Reconstruction or the post–World War II civil rights era. Nor was it simply a racist organization. The Klan reflected many of the fundamental tensions that divided Americans at the time.

Originally a creation of white Southerners seeking to resist post–Civil War federal policy by intimidating blacks and conciliatory whites while preserving their own anonymity, the robed and hooded Ku Klux Klan had faded as Reconstruction ended. An exaggerated image of the masked Klan's effectiveness in preserving white authority arose with the publication of Thomas Dixon, Jr.'s popular novels, *The Leopard's Spots* (1902) and *The Clansman* (1905). The Klan myth increased in 1915 when D. W. Griffith based the first feature-length motion picture, *The Birth of a Nation*, on *The Clansman*. William Simmons, an Atlanta-based salesman of fraternal organization memberships and a former circuit-riding Methodist preacher, seized the opportunity presented by the film's appearance to create a new Klan in which he could sell memberships, costumes, and life insurance. Simmons' Klan grew to several thousand members by mid-1920. It expanded rapidly once he enlisted a pair of effective recruiters, Edward Clarke and Elizabeth Tyler, by offering them $8 of the initial $10 dues paid by every initiate they brought in. Clarke and Tyler in turn used most of their recruitment fee to motivate and assist an aggressive commission-based sales force.

The marketing of Klan memberships became a hugely profitable commercial enterprise for Clarke and Tyler as they struck a sympathetic chord with millions of Americans. Simmons' initial appeal to fraternity, secrecy, and white supremacy was supplanted by a message that broadly identified the Klan with any "one-hundred-percent American" who was a morally and legally upright white Protestant patriot. To defend such qualities meant to oppose and suppress their alternatives, the Klan insisted. Therefore not only did the KKK remain anti-black, it became anti-Jewish, anti-Asian, and especially anti-Roman Catholic. It expressed hostility to any group or individual, recent immigrants in particular but old-stock as well, that did not embrace what the Klan regarded as dominant American traits and practices. Klansmen vocally disapproved of prohibition violation, labor union membership, inflated retail prices, Sabbath breaking, political graft, immodest dress, bobbed hair, and all forms of unconventional sexuality. With fiery crosses, tar and feathers, and other means, it warned individuals and groups not meeting its standards to conform or leave. Joining the Klan was a means of asserting personal opposition to various changes taking place in American society. Those who enrolled did not think of themselves as bigots but rather as defenders of traditional standards in a battle with proponents of change.

While the membership of a secretive organization is difficult to assess, enough Klan records have survived to make possible some conclusions. Klan members came from large and medium-sized cities as well as small towns and the countryside. They were, in the words of Leonard Moore, a careful investigator of the Indiana Klan, from the mainstream of white Protestant society. Not disproportionately rural, fundamentalist, or lower class as is the stereotype, the Hoosier Klan represented a broad spectrum of Indiana's native-born population. Its ranks included many solidly middle-class individuals, white-collar and skilled workers, and farmers. A female counterpart organization, Women of the Ku Klux Klan, enrolled over a million women nationally. The only conspicuous absentees were the business and social elite who were adjusting to and benefiting from changes in American commerce and culture.

The average citizens who enlisted in the Klan seemed to share a concern that their communities were threatened by forces that ignored their traditions and upset their customs. The Klan's picnics, occasional acts of charity, and involvement in local politics and school administration sought to maintain traditional community culture. Its public parades and

Ku Klux Klan parade, Washington, D.C., September 13, 1926. Photo courtesy of the Library of Congress.

rallies attempted to both celebrate that culture and intimidate those who might seek to alter it. Cross burnings at the home of a suspected prohibition violator, union organizer, banker or businessman charging more than a "fair" price, or a person of questionable sexual morals served as a Klan warning not to violate approved standards. If flaming crosses failed to achieve the desired effect, floggings and tar-and-featherings sometimes followed.

The KKK prospered until the mid-1920s. Its pronouncements attracted support, and its local political endorsements often proved effective, especially in the Midwest. The Klan staged mass rallies and parades in Washington, D.C., as well as elsewhere. Its frightening outbursts of nighttime vigilantism, however, began to alarm bystanders as well as targets. In 1924, the Democratic party's national convention divided evenly over whether or not to condemn the Klan by name. The northern urban wing of the party saw the KKK as threatening its large Catholic, Jewish, and immigrant following, but lost a censure motion by a single vote to the southern and western delegates who either embraced the Klan or at least did not wish to offend its members. Democrats did poorly in the 1924 national elections, but in some areas Klan-endorsed candidates won local political office.

Soon thereafter Klan support declined sharply. Some of its followers became discouraged over its ineffectiveness in blocking change, obtaining prohibition enforcement, or preventing the evolution of morality and behavior. Episodes of brutality alienated others. Inept or corrupt leadership, financial mismanagement, and exposure of political bribery were recurring problems. Most damaging of all was the revelation of a spectacular crime in which the Grand Dragon of the Indiana Klan, David C. Stephenson, sexually assaulted a secretary on a train ride to Chicago and then, after the disconsolate young woman attempted suicide, kept her from obtaining medical attention so that she died painfully a month later from the aftereffects of poison and infected wounds. This gruesome story, and Stephenson's subsequent attempt to use his political connections to avoid punishment, offended thousands who had joined the Klan thinking that they were taking a stand against such behavior. Before the decade's end, the Klan was a tiny remnant of what it was at its 1924 peak.

Lynch Mobs The Ku Klux Klan did not hold an exclusive franchise on racial hostility in the 1920s and 1930s. Southern white society felt free to do spontaneously whatever it chose to keep African Americans, and occasionally others, in what it thought was their proper place. Throughout the South (where 90 percent of the African American population resided prior to World War I), whites had resorted to lynching more than a hundred times a year between 1885 and 1900 and between fifty and seventy-five times a year from then until 1920. Lynching of whites, briefly more numerous in the mid-1880s, thereafter fell to a tiny fraction of what blacks experienced. Occasional lynchings outside the South followed a similar pattern. Local authorities usually did little to restrain white mobs from seizing African Americans accused of crimes, especially those against white women. Dissatisfied with the state's ability to deliver sufficient punishment, such mobs would torture and mutilate their African American prisoners, sometimes set them on fire, and almost always hang them from trees. Although large crowds attended many lynchings, took bits of the victim's clothing as souvenirs, and posed for photographs, almost no one was ever punished. Law enforcement officers stepped aside, and coroners' reports usually indicated that death was the responsibility of "persons unknown."

Lynchings represented more than just the denial of the right to a fair trial and civil punishment. Even as they declined in number during the

"We Cater to White Trade Only." The sign posted in a Lancaster, Ohio, shop window provides evidence of customary racial discrimination even in areas of the country where Jim Crow laws were not in force, August 1938. Photo courtesy of the Library of Congress.

1920s before rebounding in the early 1930s, lynchings sent a stark warning to the black community not to challenge white supremacy. The message was clear: crimes by blacks against whites, whether murder or rape or even trivial behavior deemed "uppity," would be punished swiftly and brutally. African Americans carried the knowledge that, despite their every effort to be law-abiding, cautious, and polite, they could be the target of a lynch mob incited by false charges. In the late 1930s, singer Billie Holiday started singing "Strange Fruit," a blues song that stunned audiences with the image of lynching, the grim reality with which African Americans lived. It began:

> Southern trees bear a strange fruit,
> Blood on the leaves and blood at the root,
> Black body swinging in the Southern breeze,
> Strange fruit hanging from the poplar trees.

The National Association for the Advancement of Colored People began campaigning during World War I for a federal law against lynching. Anti-lynching bills passed the House of Representatives in 1922 and 1938 but failed to overcome Senate filibusters by southern opponents who talked of the need to limit the excessive power of the federal government and preserve the sanctity of states' rights. The specter of lynching thus persisted throughout the 1920s and 1930s and for another three decades.

Race Riots   White antagonism toward African Americans took other forms as well. Vivid memories remained of the 1919 flurry of race riots that produced extensive property damage, serious injury, and over 100 deaths. Violence against African Americans in 1919 had been by far most destructive and murderous in Chicago, but thereafter its focus shifted to the South. On May 31, 1921, the *Tulsa* (Okla.) *Tribune* published an inflammatory report of a young white woman's unproven and improbable claim of a mid-afternoon sexual attack by a black man in a downtown elevator. A white lynch mob formed, blacks armed themselves to resist, and shots were exchanged. Whites then rampaged through the black neighborhood of segregated Tulsa, setting fire to the Greenwood Avenue business district and over 1,000 homes. By the time the mob's fury was spent, black Tulsa smoldered in ruins. At least seventy-five residents, perhaps as many as 250, lay dead. While the Tulsa riot was the last large-scale outburst of racial violence during the 1920s, its grim message of continuing racial tension lingered.

Justice Denied   Perhaps even more devastating to African Americans' sense of security than the brutality of lynching or mob violence was their realization that they could not count on the southern legal system for protection. One highly publicized case drove this point home with particular force. In March 1931 near Scottsboro, Alabama, police arrested nine black teenagers hitching a ride on a slow-moving freight train. The two white women accompanying them, both prostitutes, immediately claimed to be victims of rape. Quickly indicted, the boys were provided no real legal representation, convicted in a one-day trial, and sentenced to death. The Scottsboro case attracted national attention, largely because American communists made it a symbol of American racism. Convinced that the women were lying (one admitted so within a year), the original judge ordered a retrial that produced more convictions and death sentences. This verdict was overturned by the U.S. Supreme Court. In *Powell v. Alabama* (1932) the Court said, for the first time, that states must provide an attorney to indigent defendants in death penalty cases in order to assure them the due process of law guaranteed by the Fourteenth Amendment. However, a third all-white Alabama jury again convicted the Scottsboro boys and sentenced them to prison. Eventually these verdicts were also overturned. The defendants finally all went free, but not until after spending, collectively, over a hundred years in jail.

Ethnic Conflicts   Not all of the conflicts that pitted one group of Americans against another during the 1920s and 1930s involved racial antagonism or physical violence. Some of the hostilities between groups with different backgrounds or values played out in legislative actions or election campaigns. Courts dealt with other contests for power and authority. Many differences remained unresolved and became constant irritants or burdens to people in the course of their daily lives.

In 1920, Congress responded to the widespread resentment by old-stock Americans to the wave of recent immigrants by considering proposals to limit further entry into the United States. On average more than a million newcomers a year, most of them non-English-speaking Catholics or Jews from southern and Eastern Europe, entered the country during the decade before the outbreak of World War I. War had reduced the influx of immigrants but not apprehensions among longtime residents about the presence of strangers with unfamiliar languages and customs, allegedly radical ideas, and what were labeled "un-American" tendencies. With the war's end both immigration and fear again began rising.

Consequently, efforts to reduce the number of immigrants gained support. The 1921 National Origins Act limited immigration in any year to 3 percent of the number **Limiting Immigration** of foreign-born members of a nationality group listed in the 1910 federal census. Complaints that this arrangement still admitted too many Italians, Greeks, Slavs, Poles, and Jews led to passage of the Johnson-Reed Act of 1924, further reducing quotas to 2 percent of a nationality's 1890 census representation. These immigration restriction laws ended a 300-year pattern of virtually unrestrained entry into the United States from Europe and reflected the unfriendliness of old-stock Americans to their recently arrived countrymen in the early 1920s.

The nativist-newcomer conflict scarcely ended with the passage of immigrant restriction laws. In the large **Newcomers** cities where many new arrivals congregated, newcomers **Build Political** began a political counterattack against their tormentors. **Alliances** Not only did they complain vigorously about the 1921 and 1924 entry laws, but they also began to agitate against other enactments they perceived as directed against them. National prohibition was a particularly sore point to those for whom alcohol use was a traditional and welcome custom. Various nationality groups, at first slow to abandon rivalries brought from abroad or developed as they struggled to gain a foothold in the United States, gradually built political alliances in their shared opposition to prohibition.

Boston provided an example of the complex evolution of social conflict and political alliances. Prosperous and powerful descendants of the city's seventeenth-century English immigrant **Boston** founders, often referred to as Yankees, set the social standards for New England. Among other things, these Yankees had helped establish the

Republican Party. The large population of nineteenth-century Irish immigrants, at first a working and servant class for the Yankees, had embraced the available political alternative, the Democratic Party. Italians,
Portuguese, and other new immigrant groups who, upon arrival, found
themselves in competition with the Irish, initially turned to the Republican Party. By the early 1920s, however, the realization that Yankee Republicans supported immigration restrictions and prohibition as well as
other things contrary to new immigrant interests led to new political
alliances with the Irish in the Democratic Party. Irish political leaders
reached out to the immigrants on the basis of a common Catholic faith,
a shared culture, similar political and economic interests, and a common
opponent. By the mid-1920s, the new Democratic coalition was winning
the battle with the Yankees and coming to dominate Boston's politics.

        The mix of ethnic groups was different but the pattern of cul-
Chicago   tural conflict was similar in Chicago. An old-stock business
        class, represented by a flamboyant and patronage-profligate
Republican mayor, William "Big Bill" Thompson, dominated the Windy
City in the 1920s. The mayor's isolationism and indifference to prohibition won favor with many ethnic groups that he actually did little to
assist. During the one term between 1915 and 1931 when Thompson was
out of office, however, reform mayor William Dever, also a Republican,
sought to enforce prohibition. Gradually an ethnic coalition formed
within the most heavily Catholic of America's big cities around bitter
opposition to prohibition and a desire for political power. Anton Cermak, a leader in the Czech community, built ties to other nationality
groups and constructed an effective organization to turn out supporters
on election day. Eventually Cermak's political machine elected him Cook
County sheriff and then swept him into the mayor's office as Thompson's
successor. In gaining the upper hand in Chicago's ethnic and economic
local politics, Cermak took control of a county Democratic party that he
quickly made effective enough to dominate Chicago politics for the rest
of the century.

Outside of large cities such as Boston and Chicago, new American
immigrants did not often prevail in the cultural conflicts of the 1920s.
Even within the Democratic Party where new immigrants were more and
more often finding a political home, the even split over the Ku Klux Klan
at the 1924 national convention showed the upper limits of their power
at that time. Yet new immigrant influence continued to grow.

        Other conflicts overlapped the clash between old-stock
Anti-Catholicism   Americans and new immigrants, though did not pre-
        cisely conform to it. Protestant-Catholic hostility was
mutual and intense, although both could fairly be termed conservative
churches in terms of their theology. Anti-Catholicism emerged as a core
Ku Klux Klan principle, often manifesting itself in attacks on parochial

schools as inhibiting the Americanization of immigrant children and warnings that the pope was conspiring to take over the U.S. government. When Catholic organizations such as the Knights of Columbus protested Klan intolerance, they became targets of abuse themselves.

In the complex crosscurrents of the cultural conflicts of the 1920s, New York Governor Alfred E. Smith became the lead-   **Al Smith** ing political hero of the new immigrants and the figure most reviled by conservative old-stock voters. Himself a son of immigrants who grew up in the poor, crowded Lower East Side of New York City, Smith was a devout Catholic, an ardent opponent of prohibition, and a champion of progressive reforms beneficial to the urban masses but not threatening to modern business. Northern urban Democrats gave him strong support for the 1924 Democratic presidential nomination, but conservative southern and western Democrats mounted just as powerful an opposition. By 1928, however, he swept a Democratic nominating convention more responsive to northern urban voices. As a presidential candidate, Smith brought the clash of cultures during the 1920s into sharpest focus.

The hostility of old-stock, rural, and Protestant Americans toward Al Smith and all that he seemed to symbolize to them attained extraordinary levels in 1928. Smith's Catholicism and his opposition to prohibition came in for particular attack. One fundamentalist publication charged that he wanted to make America "100 percent Catholic, Drunk and Illiterate," while evangelist Billy Sunday labeled Smith's supporters "the damnable whiskey politicians, the bootleggers, crooks, pimps, and businessmen who deal with them." Such comments were mild compared to the declaration of an Oklahoma City Baptist minister that "if you vote for Al Smith, you're voting against Christ and you'll all be damned."[1] Meanwhile Bishop James Cannon of the Methodist Board of Temperance, Prohibition, and Public Morals and Dr. Arthur Barton of the Southern Baptist Convention created an effective alliance to campaign against Smith throughout the South. As radio brought Smith's voice within range of millions who were otherwise unable to hear him, even his New York City accent alarmed those who in no way shared his background.

Smith's candidacy energized the urban and immigrant population. New immigrant women, who, despite woman suffrage, had taken little part in politics, turned out in large numbers to register and add their Smith votes to those of male family members. Whereas Republican presidential candidates had carried the ten largest cities by a combined margin of 1.5 million votes in 1920 and 1.25 million in 1924, Smith was able to carry, if only by 38,000 votes, these centers of immigrant culture. Smith cemented a bond between the mass of urban new immigrants and the Democratic Party that would endure. At the same time, he lost badly outside of those big cities to his old-stock, Protestant, and prohibition-supporting Republican opponent, Herbert Hoover. Thus, the 1928 election demonstrated how deeply ethnic and religious conflict continued to divide America, affecting every individual's sense of personal social standing and acceptance as he or she went about the business of daily life.

CRIME

Becoming the victim of a criminal act was a possibility, though a slight one, in the generally law-abiding society of the early twentieth-century United States. Worry about crime, if not crime itself, became a more widespread aspect of daily life in the decades after World War I. In some respects, crime and the response to it simply reflected the social conflicts dividing the country. In others, it was yet another function of growing urbanization, changing technology, and increased awareness of what was happening outside the local community. But perhaps more than anything else, crime patterns measured changing standards of acceptable behavior.

Sacco and Vanzetti The 1920s were barely underway when one crime took place that would epitomize the social conflicts of the era. In South Braintree, Massachusetts, in April 1920, two men shot a guard and the paymaster of the Slater and Merrill Shoe Company, then fled in an automobile with the company payroll. Police soon arrested two pistol-carrying Italian immigrants and charged them with robbery and murder. Nicola Sacco and Bartolomeo Vanzetti were interrogated for two days, mainly about their political beliefs, without being told the charges against them or their legal rights. Witnesses to the crime were asked to identify them standing alone, rather than pick them out of a lineup. None of these police procedures, declared by the U.S. Supreme Court decades later to be violations of constitutional rights to a fair trial, were uncommon at the time. Eleven years later, a federal report on law enforcement practices described "the third degree," or "the inflicting of pain, physical or mental, to extract confessions or statements" as "extensively practiced" by police across the country.

At the trial, Sacco and Vanzetti's political beliefs and their ethnic background appeared to carry more weight with the judge and jury than the weak case presented against them or the defense witnesses who placed Sacco miles away at the time of the robbery. The presiding judge, Webster Thayer, was heard to refer to the defendants as "those anarchist bastards." Once Sacco and Vanzetti were found guilty and sentenced to death, their lawyers failed repeatedly in efforts to persuade the prosecutor or judge to reopen the case on the basis of compelling new evidence. Even a confession to the crime by another death-row inmate who bore a striking resemblance to Sacco failed to impress Judge Thayer.

The Sacco and Vanzetti case gained the attention of the immigrant community as well as many legal experts and intellectuals, both inside and outside the United States, who came to see it as a terrible example of ethnic prejudice and a blatant miscarriage of justice. Despite eight separate appeals, one to the U.S. Supreme Court, the convictions stood. Large crowds turned out to protest in Boston and New York City. Nevertheless, Massachusetts put Sacco and Vanzetti to death in the Charlestown Prison electric chair in August 1927. The case fostered a sense of a harsh and socially uneven justice system, and the furor over the fate of Sacco and Vanzetti continued for years.

Despite a popular image of the 1920s as a lawless era, bank robbery, murder, and other serious felonies were **Serious Crime** comparatively rare occurrences, perhaps one reason why **Decreases** the Sacco and Vanzetti case received so much attention. The United States was in the midst of what many scholars agree was a long-term decline in serious crime that would not end until the 1960s. While the total volume of illegal activity is by nature difficult to determine precisely, one measure of the crime rate, admittedly far from perfect, is the number of convicted criminals who were imprisoned. In 1926, the first year for which U.S. Census Bureau figures are available, 96,000 inmates resided in state and federal prisons. By comparison, at the end of the twentieth century, over one and a quarter million prisoners were incarcerated. In proportion to population, the number of criminals imprisoned was over five times what it had been in the 1920s.

The rate at which crimes were committed did rise sharply during the 1920s, but only because an activity that earlier **Prohibition** and later would be considered legal was for the moment **Violations** labeled criminal. Prohibition law violations accounted for 65 percent of all cases in federal district courts during the era when the total liquor ban was being enforced. In 1921, federal officials prosecuted 29,114 prohibition cases, while by 1932, despite much diminished enthusiasm for the law, there were 65,960 such prosecutions. In the early 1920s, only seven percent of commitments to federal prison were for liquor law violations, but by 1930, with stiffer penalties in place, 49 percent were so. State governments, which shared responsibility for prohibition enforcement but often displayed much less enthusiasm for doing so, also saw their case load increase, though only at about half the rate of the federal justice system.

With a significant portion of the American people regarding prohibition as a mistake and not legitimately binding upon them, it is difficult to say whether statistics so heavily dominated by liquor cases show a real increase in criminality. Further complicating the situation, small-scale prohibition violations, such as possession for personal use, were usually either not prosecuted or plea bargained down to a fine or suspended sentence. Prosecution focused, especially later in the period, on professional bootleggers and speakeasy operators. When even this tactic failed to stem the growing alcohol trade, it was clear that, particularly in urban America, drinking was not considered much more of a crime than jaywalking or illegal parking.

The image of a crime wave nevertheless existed. In large part this was due to the volume and the particularly high visibility of prohibition violation. Sellers of bootleg liquor and operators of speakeasies had to make their presence known if they were to attract customers. Together with the many movies that, without disapproval, depicted drinking and the activities of bootleggers, real life evidence of prohibition violation certainly sent a mixed moral message to onlookers. Whatever citizens concluded about the wisdom of the alcohol ban or the morality of ignoring it, they no doubt acquired an impression that many people were breaking the law.

The FBI The activities of the Federal Bureau of Investigation (FBI) furthered the public sense of a crime wave. Reconstituted in 1924 under aggressive young director J. Edgar Hoover, the FBI strove to overcome a previous image of lethargy and corruption. Hoover sought to portray the FBI as an effective professional national crime-fighting force confronting a serious increase in criminal threats to society. The FBI began compiling national crime statistics in 1930 from local police reports of dubious reliability, raising consciousness and apprehension of criminal activity. Also the bureau began a campaign to collect the fingerprints of all Americans as a scientific means of solving crimes and protecting society from a variety of dangers. Hoover steadfastly avoided having the FBI take any part in prohibition enforcement, which he recognized as potentially threatening to the bureau's public image. Instead, he called attention to a series of small-town bank robbers such as John Dillinger, Bonnie Parker, and Clyde Barrow with whom the bureau could deal effectively, and he created the "Ten Most Wanted" list of criminals that brought more attention to FBI-targeted criminal activity. Hoover also worked closely with Hollywood filmmakers on their ever-popular crime dramas so that government agents, "G-men," would be portrayed as well-educated and trained, always proper and efficient, and inevitably successful at stopping crime. The director's tactics helped raise the FBI from obscurity to a well-known and respected federal agency by the end of the 1930s, yet at the same time stirred public concern about the threat of crime.

Police Methods Change Law enforcement practices changed in the 1920s and 1930s. The scientific professionalism advocated by various crime commissions and demonstrated by the FBI began replacing the "third degree." Also the new technologies of the telephone and automobile started to alter basic police

A small-town Ohio policeman talking to a local resident. Photo courtesy of the Library of Congress.

practices. Foot patrols continued in most cities, but more and more police took to automobiles to extend their range and speed of response. Summoned by telephone and dispatched by radio, they became more detached from the community's residents. This "mobilization" of police broke the everyday connection between the cop walking a beat and the neighborhood he patrolled.

Efforts to deal with bootleggers who also equipped themselves with automobiles and telephones shaped law enforcement and affected public perceptions of it. Cars and trucks allowed bootleggers to move liquor quickly and evade detection by the police. At least this was the case until 1925 when the Supreme Court ruled in *Carroll v. U.S.* that police could not be expected to obtain a search warrant to examine a vehicle stopped on a Michigan highway, which they correctly suspected was transporting illegal alcohol. Drivers of all sorts were thereafter much more at the mercy of police who halted them on the road. Just as unsettling to the public, the Supreme Court ruled in 1927 that wiretapping of telephones was constitutionally permissible as long as it took place off the target's private property. According to *Olmstead v. U.S.*, evidence collected by listening in at phone company headquarters and then used to convict a Seattle bootlegger was akin to overhearing a conversation in a pubic place. Both the *Carroll* and *Olmstead* rulings, along with others allowing police in disguise to encourage and entrap people in prohibition viola-

tions, permitting both state and federal courts to punish the same of-
fense, and sanctioning plea bargains instead of jury trials, caused worries
that prohibition was undermining traditional justice standards. The liquor ban struck many as an infringement on their legitimate rights, allowing police to intrude too much into private life.

Support for Prohibition Repeal   The reaction against prohibition became most notable
among educated middle-class women. Such women had
formed the backbone of the temperance movement; but by
the end of the 1920s, even larger numbers of them took up
the crusade to repeal the Eighteenth Amendment. The
Women's Organization for National Prohibition Reform, which by 1933
grew to three times the membership of the older Women's Christian
Temperance Union, claimed that prohibition encouraged crime, undermined respect for the American system of law enforcement, and endan-
gered the moral education of American children. As support for
prohibition repeal became irresistible, it clearly was driven by an overwhelming desire throughout society to reduce crime and at the same
time limit the need for police power sufficient to enforce standards of
conduct in the daily lives of the American people.

Prohibition's Legacy   The end of national prohibition in 1933 left a mixed legacy. On the one hand, public confidence in the law and
the necessity of unquestioning observance of it had been
shaken. On the other hand, the dry crusade accustomed
Americans for the first time to the federal government's enforcement of
laws bearing on individual conduct using customs officials, Coast Guard
agents, postal inspectors, national park rangers, and a new federal police
force, the agents of the Bureau of Prohibition. In the aftermath of prohibition, as concern about narcotics increased, federal policing of drug
traffic was accepted as appropriate with little question. At the same time
and perhaps most important, judicial sensitivity to the treatment of individuals in the criminal justice system began to increase. The Supreme
Court was much more sympathetic to the Scottsboro boys than it had
been to Sacco and Vanzetti. By the end of the 1930s, the Court was starting to show the concern for fair and equal legal treatment that would
characterize its efforts in the decades that followed.

CATASTROPHE

Natural disasters struck various regions of the United States during
the 1920s and 1930s. Some were the storms, fires, earthquakes, and other
unfortunate phenomena that occur in every era. Others, however, were
distinctive and unusually formidable disasters or plagues of biblical proportion. Forcing permanent changes in the lives of large populations and
whole regions, they deserved to be labeled catastrophes.

The first of these catastrophes was the pestilence of the boll weevil that began appearing late in the first decade of the **The Boll** twentieth century. A small insect that bored into cotton plants, **Weevil** turned the cotton boll black, and destroyed its value, the weevil proved relentless and irresistible. By the early 1920s, it was devastating cotton fields wherever it struck across the South. The southern economy, already the weakest of any region in the United States and heavily dependent upon cotton, felt the weevil's bite. Total cotton production in 1921 plunged to scarcely more than half of 1920's output, and while the price per pound rose by a fourth, that did nothing to compensate those individual farms that were completely ravaged. In 1922 and 1923, output improved only marginally, and it was 1924 before overall cotton production again reached the level of 1920. By then, the plague had forced many small farmers—independent and tenant, black and white—to abandon the land. Some turned to southern factory labor while others started the long trek to northern cities; but, in either case, their daily lives were transformed by the boll weevil.

Unusually heavy and prolonged rains across the nation's midsection in the spring of 1927 filled to overflowing the Ohio **Floods** and Missouri Rivers, other tributaries, and the great Mississippi River itself. Early on, Pittsburgh had eight feet of water in its downtown streets and Cincinnati soon had a similar experience. Man-made levies served to protect St. Louis and Memphis and other points along the thousand mile course of the Mississippi south of its junction with the Ohio at Cairo, Illinois. The force of millions of gallons of water, however, caused levies to break at Mound Landing, Mississippi, and Pendleton, Arkansas. Rushing through the breeches, surging river water flooded 2.3 million acres in Mississippi and affected over 170,000 people. One witness described the flood's approach "in the form of a tan-colored wall seven feet high, and with a roar as of a mighty wind."[2] The devastation was worse across the river where not only the Mississippi but also the Arkansas River burst through levies, inundating over 5 million acres.

To spare New Orleans, levies on the opposite side of the river were dynamited. Over 6.2 million acres of rural southwestern Louisiana ended up under water, and more than a quarter million Louisiana residents felt the impact. Before the waters receded, the "Big Muddy" sprawled to 100 miles wide at some points, over 160,000 homes were flooded, and $100 million worth of crops were ruined. The Red Cross cared for over 600,000 displaced persons, and as many as 500 lives were lost. Only a massive federal government rescue and relief effort involving 31,000 volunteers and 1,400 paid workers coordinated by Secretary of Commerce Herbert Hoover kept the death toll from spiraling into the thousands. The Mississippi River had often left its banks before and it would do so again, but 1927 represented by far the greatest and most damaging flood in its recorded history.

Drought and Dust

The torrent of water that produced the Mississippi flood soon had a counterpoint. The flood's equal in devastation but opposite in character was the multiyear drought that in varying degrees of intensity gripped two-thirds of the United States throughout most of the 1930s. This prolonged period of unusually sparse rainfall centered on western Kansas, eastern Colorado, and the panhandles of Oklahoma and Texas. The severe drought in the southern plains, combined with the strong winds that characterized the region and farming that had loosened the topsoil, turned the area into what came to be called the Dust Bowl.

From 1932 onward, windstorms swept the powder-dry soil a thousand feet into the air and created huge "black blizzards" that blotted out the sun, terrified those in their path, and left a thick residue of dirt in their wake. One such storm left a woman thinking it seemed like "the end of the world," while another said, "The nightmare is becoming life." In May 1933 alone, dust storms removed an estimated 300 million tons of soil from the plains and deposited it across the eastern United States from the Great Lakes to Washington, D.C., and New York City. As historian R. Douglas Hurt noted, "For the first time, many easterners smelled, breathed, and tasted soil that came from the Great Plains. Few liked the experience."[3] A year later, a single storm produced a dust cloud that for a day and a half severely reduced visibility from the Rockies to the Great Lakes and from the Canadian border to Oklahoma.

In 1935, the worst dust storms hit the plains with several deaths by suffocation reported. After a typical storm, one survivor reported, "Our faces were as dirty as if we had rolled in the dirt; our hair was gray and stiff and we ground dirt between our teeth."[4] Respiratory problems became common and chronic throughout the region with physicians reporting epidemic levels of pneumonia and other breathing difficulties. On a more mundane level, keeping a house clean proved virtually impossible as dust seeped through every crack and quickly covered furniture, food, and everything else. Some residents gave up and fled, but most chose to stay and hope for improved conditions. The "dust blows" continued through 1936, 1937, and 1938 before increased rainfall began substantially reducing the Dust Bowl problem in 1939.

Natural disasters, whether brought by insects, water, or wind, disrupted the lives of countless Americans. These catastrophes had to be borne just as did the social conflicts and crimes that also punctuated daily life. The impersonal nature of natural forces, however, caused people to react to them in a somewhat different fashion than they did to difficulties generated by the actions of individuals or groups. Human-induced calamities impacted the thinking of participants in them as to

Approaching dust storm, Amarillo, Texas, 1936. Photo courtesy of the Library of Congress.

their position in the overall culture of the United States. For instance, the victims of a race riot and those who more or less voluntarily took part in it derived starkly contrasting messages about their own standing in the larger society quite different from the sense they might gain as indiscriminate victims of a calamity of nature. Americans' sense of the national culture and their role within it grew from complex and varied factors. Encounters with life's disruptions, however, were no doubt highly important among them.

NOTES

1. Quoted in Michael E. Parrish, *Anxious Decades: America in Prosperity and Depression, 1920–1941* (New York: W. W. Norton, 1992), 214.

2. John M. Barry, *Rising Tide: The Great Mississippi Flood of 1927 and How It Changed America* (New York: Simon & Schuster, 1997), 204.

3. R. Douglas Hurt, *The Dust Bowl: An Agricultural and Social History* (Chicago: Nelson-Hall, 1981), 34.

4. Ibid., 37.

9

Culture for the Masses: The Standardizing of Daily Life

The conventions of day-to-day and year-to-year existence, together with the new technologies of automobiles, electricity, radio, and cinema, combined to shape the American people's way of life in the years after World War I. In the 1920s, this manner of living rapidly became more standardized throughout the nation. Neither regional nor class differences entirely disappeared from customary practices, popular aspirations, or the public's sense of what was proper or tasteful. Increased frequency and variety of communication, however, contributed to a growing uniformity in American culture.

NEW CULTURAL ERA

If we regard culture as the sum of tastes, behaviors, and values that a society embraces in carrying out its daily life, then the period following World War I appears to have been a new cultural era for the United States. An unprecedented ease of communication and travel worked together to stimulate desire for experiences and possessions previously out of sight and generally unknown, if existing at all. Enhanced awareness of what other Americans were actually doing in their daily lives, or at least appeared to be doing, stirred desires to do likewise. Evidence cropped up repeatedly that American activities and aspirations were becoming increasingly similar across the country. Regional and class differences did not disappear, but they began to fade in significance. In their place, more and more signs of a national culture emerged.

The culture of a country as populous and sprawling as the United States had become by 1920 cannot be described in simple terms. Indeed, this entire book can be read as an attempt to identify merely the most common elements of that culture. Nevertheless, the effort to characterize any period of American life ought to include a discussion of what ideas, values, and tastes were articulated and advanced throughout the society. Addressing the issue of how culture is transmitted helps illuminate its strength and essential nature.

ACCESSIBLE GRATIFICATION

Considering the manner in which American culture was defined and communicated in the 1920s makes evident that at its core was a widespread belief in accessible gratification. Americans in their daily lives came to believe that they enjoyed access to a broad range of opportunities and commodities that would satisfy individual needs and desires. Acceptance of the social, economic, and material limitations of the immediate family and community environment in which one lived became less commonplace than in earlier eras. Americans were encouraged to believe that bounties lay at hand to be consumed and enjoyed. Participation in a culture of consumption was not only possible but proper, and, in fact, what others were happily enjoying. Only personal flaw or failure kept consumption and its enjoyment out of reach.

Encouragements to think that personal satisfaction was within reach were constantly being placed before most Americans as they pursued their daily lives. Such reminders served as a goad to the accumulation of material possessions during the 1920s. Access to gratification, or at least the image of its possibility, worked to justify the notable economic and political complacency of the broad sector of the population that considered itself middle class. Not even the large segment of the populace that was relatively poor remained immune to the idea that it could gain access to life's pleasures. Ironically, the notion of accessible gratification would later become a reason for many Americans to blame their individual failings rather than flaws in the fundamental organization of American society when economic disaster struck in the 1930s.

ADVERTISING THE AMERICAN WAY

New Ad Style A prime reason for the developing faith in accessible gratification as well as one of the most striking features of American life in the 1920s was the rapid expansion of a new style of commercial advertising. Artful description of products did more than render them appealing; it characterized commodities as within reach of everyone as well as essential to their good and fulfilled life. Visually alluring ads with compelling and subtle messages were relatively recent arrivals on the American scene. Their very newness gave them an impact greater than might have been possible with later generations more familiar with mass advertising, saturated with product claims, and accustomed to ad-makers' subtle techniques for stirring personal anxieties and appetites.

Unadorned matter-of-fact announcements of the availability of goods and services for sale had long been a feature of American commerce but tended to be restrained by the realities of limited output and distribution as well as by a sense of dignified business practice. Flamboyant ads for patent medicines and carnival sideshows helped foster a mid-nineteenth-century view that advertising essentially involved trickery and fraud. As the late-nineteenth-century growth of mass production began creating a capacity to manufacture an unlimited supply of goods and improved transportation made possible their wide distribution, advertisements became necessary if businesses were to gain the attention of a sufficient audience of potential customers. For instance, clever advertising swiftly propelled cereal makers C. W. Post and William H. Kellogg to success, reshaping the nation's breakfast habits. The processed food industry helped lead the rapid early-twentieth-century expansion of consumer goods advertising.

By 1920, over $2.9 billion was spent annually on commercial advertising. This represented more than double the amount spent only five years earlier and nearly six times the turn of the century total. By 1929, an additional half-billion dollars of spending on ads raised the total to $3.4 billion. For purposes of comparison, the sum expended by business that year to encourage and instruct consumers amounted to 148 percent of the $2.3 billion total being spent nationally on K–12 education.

Advertising appeared in a variety of forms. Some of the new technologies that benefited from being advertised themselves provided new opportunities for conveying commercial messages. For instance, the rising flood of automobiles moved business to try catching the eye of passengers with distinctive roadside structures, signs, and billboards. At the same time, radio broadcasting came to be funded and defined by the advertisements it carried. Meanwhile, mail-order catalogues and other direct mail appeals retained the significant, if relatively subdued role they had achieved before World War I. Print advertising, however, captured by far the largest share of the ad market during the 1920s and 1930s.

Newspaper and magazine reading was a widespread activity in a era when it remained the best means to obtain **Print** low-cost, detailed, up-to-date information about what was **Advertising** happening in the world beyond a person's immediate reach. Cheap, mass-distribution newspapers appeared in the late nineteenth century, and by the 1920s, the ratio of daily papers printed to total population stood at one to three. The advent of newspaper syndicates and wire services meant that, other than on local matters, the identical Associated Press, Hearst, Scripps Howard, or similar report would routinely appear in newspapers across the country. While more than 2,000 daily and 6,000 weekly newspapers, each with its own editorial posture, were being published throughout the period, the bulk of the news came from relatively few sources. Much the same could be said of a significant portion of the advertisements carried by newspapers. What Americans read became increasingly standardized.

Magazines were just as available as newspapers to a wide public. Nearly 4,500 periodicals were published each year by 1925 and circulated a combined 180 million copies per issue. Advertising revenue provided a substantial portion of the income of newspapers and magazines that ran ads, allowing them to reduce subscription and newsstand prices. This in turn permitted ad-supported magazines such as *Saturday Evening Post*, *Good Housekeeping*, and *Ladies Home Journal* to reach much larger audiences than older magazines such as *Harpers* and *Atlantic Monthly* that declined to carry advertising. New advertising-laden magazines continued to appear, among them *Time* (1923), *Better Homes and Gardens* (1924), *The New Yorker* (1925), *Fortune* (1930), *Newsweek* (1933), *Life* (1936), and *Look* (1937). The latter two in particular relied on striking photographs even more than text to gain large audiences. The more attractive the magazine and the greater its readership, the more ads it could draw and the more it could charge for them; in turn advertisers gained ever more incentive to create effective ads. No wonder one advertising agency executive asserted, "A magazine is simply a device to induce people to read advertising."

Brand Names In an environment where countless ads competed for the attention of readers who were presumably looking for something else to begin with, advertising needed to be attention getting and easy to digest, "attractive" in the strictest sense. "Interesting the Slapdash Hasty Newspaper Reader" was the advertiser's task, an industry trade journal proclaimed. Thus, companies that produced diverse products increasingly devoted attention to the promotion of a trademark or brand name that would be instantly recognized and trusted regardless of the specific product to which it was attached. Campbell, Kraft, Heinz, Borden, Sealtest, Kellogg, and Post were among the large food processors who made this tactic work, while RCA, Westinghouse, and the "Generals,"—Mills, Motors, Foods and Electric—as well as many other firms applied the same strategy to marketing their own goods.

Closely associated with brand names were memorable names for individual new products to distinguish them from similar fare that competitors might produce and to condition consumers to think that important differences existed. Among the items introduced in the 1920s according to this strategy were Milky Way candy bars, Rice Krispies, Wheaties, Popsicles, and Scotch Tape. Advertisements also promoted company symbols such as Betty Crocker and the Jolly Green Giant. Betty Crocker, a cleverly constructed fictional housewife, gave a down-to-earth human touch to the food products of a giant corporation. She provided advice on menus and recipes via radio, newspaper, and magazine ads as well as cookbooks that were themselves subtle pitches for products by General Mills.

Advertisements could have a powerful effect on the perception and mass use of a product. A photo of Old Joe, a Barnum and Bailey circus camel, became the symbol for a just-developed R. J. Reynolds cigarette in 1914. (Yes, there really was a Joe Camel!) The American Tobacco Company responded with its own new brand in 1916, promoting Lucky Strike with the phrase "It's Toasted" to help fix it in the public's mind, though all tobacco was similarly processed with drying heat. Liggett & Myers took a more subdued, though like approach, offering its faintly British-sounding brand, Chesterfield, with the claim, "They Satisfy." Together the three brands did extremely well, dominating a rapidly expanding market as tobacco use swelled and shifted to cigarettes from less convenient, more obtrusive pipes, cigars, and plugs of chewing tobacco.

Cigarette Ads

Cigarette manufacturers devised ad campaigns to keep their brands in the public's mind and to sustain the surge in cigarette use spurred by World War I military service and the disappearance of legal alcohol. "I'd Walk a Mile for a Camel" ads began appearing in 1921 and helped raise sales to 40 percent of the entire market. Women's smoking, formerly regarded as a sign of dubious character, was encouraged as a symbol of newly achieved equality. A young woman in a Chesterfield ad asked that her male companion "Blow Some My Way." Ads depicted smokers as invariably attractive, fashionable, and healthy. The growing interest of both men and women in maintaining a slender profile led to ads advising, "Reach for a Lucky instead of a Sweet." Such health tips along with universal claims of "mildness" and more specific reassurances such as "Not a Cough in a Carton" helped per capita cigarette consumption double during the 1920s.

The large advertising expenditures of tobacco makers drowned out antismoking proponents including Henry Ford, Thomas Edison, Samuel Gompers, Booker T. Washington, and baseball player Ty Cobb. In the 1920s, R. J. Reynolds alone spent the enormous sum for the time of $10 million a year on advertising its product. Well-advertised cigarettes continued to increase their sales throughout the 1930s, perhaps because they were a relatively inexpensive pleasure, perhaps because they were ad-dictive, but certainly because consumers continued to be bombarded with ads portraying smoking as a widespread and admirable custom.

Chain Stores

Advertising took many forms. The drive to gain consumer recognition and confidence spurred the rise of the chain store. The creation of chains of identically named and sim-ilarly operated retail businesses represented more than the efforts of en-terprising corporations to expand market control, increase price leverage through consolidated wholesale purchasing, and maximize the benefits of advertising expenditures, though all of these considerations were in-volved. The growth of chains constituted an awareness that consumers were becoming more mobile and would recognize a name encountered elsewhere. Chain stores also acknowledged that it was becoming feasible to appeal to standard tastes more than local identities. Woolworth's and Kresge's "five and dime" variety stores, A & P grocery markets, Wal-green drug stores, and White Castle and White Tower hamburger stands pioneered the chain store concept. Small local businesses quickly rec-ognized the threat posed by chain stores and in a number of states sought to erect legal obstacles to their intrusion. Success in barring chains proved limited and temporary, though the onset of the depression and World War II delayed the explosion of chain store and franchise retailing until the 1950s.

Personal Anxiety

Advertising creators understood that an effective way to cap-ture an audience was to exploit personal anxiety and insecu-rity about appearance, achievement, popularity, and other measures of social acceptance. Concerns about personal infe-riority, one advertising agency executive acknowledged in 1930, were "a valuable thing in advertising." Efforts to exploit feelings of inadequacy led naturally and easily to messages that the products being offered would generate admiration, success, and pleasure. Rather than merely describe a product's characteristics, ads increasingly focused on a mes-sage of opportunity to share in a satisfying life.

No better example exists of the nature and power of advertising in the 1920s than the success of the Lambert Pharmaceutical Company. Its an-tiseptic mouthwash attracted few buyers until Lambert ad writers started warning readers of the dangers of halitosis, a Latin-derived word for bad breath they discovered in a 1922 British medical journal. Cleverly crafted ads titled "They Say It behind Your Back," "He Never Knew Why," and "Often a Bridesmaid but Never a Bride" warned that halitosis could ruin social and business relationships and undermine one's chance for romance and happiness. Fortunately for those afflicted with such a dreadful condition, halitosis could be banished by Listerine. Not only did sales of Listerine soar, but the hitherto unheard-of ideal of odorless breath entered the list of personal characteristics about which people thought they had to be concerned.

What worked for one advertiser would be imitated by others. Sunkist orange and lemon ads warned that eating too much acid-forming cereal, bread, fish, eggs, and meat without a balance of alkaline-producing fruits, vegetables, and milk could produce acidosis. Lethargic, under-achieving individuals could be rescued from acidosis and set on the road to success by eating citrus fruit. Fleischmann's Yeast jumped on the balanced diet bandwagon to compensate for a decline in it sales for home bread baking. A daily dose of three or four of its yeast cakes, "the richest known source of water-soluble vitamin," would help people build up their bodies and rid them of "poisonous waste matter." Sales of citrus fruit and yeast cakes soared.

Ads did more than skillfully mold existing knowledge, play on anxieties, and appeal to inherent desires. They even sought to encourage dissatisfaction with not-long-ago acquired products by trumpeting "new" and "improved" (if only slightly and superficially changed) versions. Combined with manufacturers' growing willingness to make frequent cosmetic design changes, the "new and improved" ads stirred consumers to replace cars, clothing, and other items well before they were worn out. The advertising copywriter's own need for something fresh to tout in turn stimulated constant efforts to alter design, fashion, and taste. **"New and Improved"**

The advertising industry came, with reason, to see itself as an essential component of the economic process as it motivated people to consume more. As it widened the sphere of what people considered necessities of daily life, advertising stimulated ever-higher levels of consumption. By the 1920s, advertising spokesmen claimed to have solved the problem of over-production by finding ways to continually expand demand. Author and ad agency executive Bruce Barton ghost wrote a speech for Calvin Coolidge in which the U.S. president praised advertisers for teaching people to use prosperity. Advertising, Coolidge read, "is the most potent influence in adopting and changing the habits and modes of life, affecting what we eat, what we wear, and the work and play of the whole nation." **Advertising for Progress**

Ad creators were themselves often detached from the mass public whose buying habits they sought to influence. A 1936 survey of the giant J. Walter Thompson agency found that not one of its writers or executives belonged to a lodge or civic club, only one in five attended church, half never went to public amusements, and the rest rarely did so. Although females made most retail purchases, the ad industry employed nearly all males; only 126 women appeared among the 5,000 individuals listed in **Ad Men above the Masses** the 1931 *Who's Who in Advertising*. Moreover, half of the ad men had never lived within the national average income. Two-thirds of them employed servants at a time when doing so had become exceedingly rare. These people seeking to shape the perceptions and spending practices of the masses were themselves extraordinarily affluent and often lacked meaningful contact with those who were not. The detachment of these molders of culture was captured in 1926 by one who admitted, "To be a really good copywriter requires passion for converting the other fellow, even if it is to something you don't believe in yourself."[1]

Opinion Poll　　Decisions on how to craft advertisements were based increasingly on market research and statistical profiles of the American public. Public opinion polling developed in the 1920s to serve the advertising industry's growing need for information about the tastes, preferences, and reactions of the largest portion of potential consumers. Political polling came along later in the mid-1930s as a means for poll takers to demonstrate their ability to measure the public accurately. An election offered the one opportunity to see how the choice of the general population compared with that of a small sample taken earlier. Again, the needs of advertisers helped shape the evolving culture.

Power of Suggestion　　As ad designers' intuitive judgment began to be replaced by market research, industry leaders talked about how they merely followed consumer choices. That was true in the sense that they delivered messages that their products could bring about what people wanted as opposed to trying to persuade them to desire what they detested. The architects of advertising, however, operated on the assumption that the public could be moved to take action on subconscious desires through the power of psychological suggestion. Women could be reached by messages about how to be more attractive to men or take better care of their families. Men's appetites could be stirred by draping a pretty female on the fender of an automobile. The masses could not be moved to take notice, or much less, action, by mere straightforward product descriptions. Instead they needed to be aroused from the torpor of routine life by strong appeals to their anxieties and aspirations. As one successful ad writer explained, "You do not sell a man the tea, but the magical spell which is brewed nowhere else but in a tea-pot."[2] Through their strenuous efforts to encourage the mass of Americans to want the things they were trying to sell, advertisers not only generated business profits but caused the culture to share a more common vision of how life should be lived.

Ads Define Modern Life　　Ordinary people naturally incorporated the messages of advertisements as they tried to cope with daily life, figure out what traditional practices to hang onto, and determine what new approaches to adopt. Ads gave a sense of the standards of a world beyond personal experience. For instance, far more than information about the taste and nutritional benefits of Post Bran Flakes was conveyed in ad copy that began, "We Americans, what a hurly-burly race we are! Getting up by the alarm clock; racing through our meals; hurrying from this appointment to that as though our lives depended on it." Not only did the ad suggest that eating Bran Flakes would help one's digestion in the midst of a hectic life, but it also declared what was normal in modern everyday life.

LITERATURE FOR THE MASSES

America had long been a nation high in basic literacy. The 1920 census reported only 2 percent of native whites, 13 percent of nonnative whites, and 23 percent of nonwhites to be illiterate. Those figures reflected educational patterns throughout the nation. As schooling improved, illiteracy fell by nearly half over the next two decades.

Americans not only could read; they did read in this era. Newspapers, magazines, and advertisements constituted a significant portion but scarcely all of what was being read. From five to nine thousand new books were published each year throughout the two decades. These included everything from hardbound works aimed at scholars and a sophisticated elite, to pulp fiction and old standards in inexpensive editions for a mass audience, to, by the end of the period, the first cheap paperback books and magazine-format illustrated short stories soon called comic books. Meanwhile, public libraries grew in numbers, size of collections, and rate of use. What was read both shaped and reflected the dominant culture of the era.

A Nation of Readers

A notable example of advertising's influence on American culture in the 1920s and 1930s was the development of the Book-of-the-Month Club. Getting large numbers of middle-class Americans across the nation to read the same few books each year did a great deal to standardize the culture. The Book-of-the-Month Club (BOMC) was created in 1926 by advertising executive and entrepreneur Harry Scherman, who had earlier successfully sold inexpensive editions of longtime literary classics through the mail. BOMC represented something quite different, an active arbiter of culture rather than a supplier of literature of proven popularity. The club solicited subscribers by promising to mail them an outstanding new book each month, unless a cancellation request was promptly returned when an initial notice of the choice was received. The automatic system was presented as sparing club members the disappointment of missing a book they should read, and for BOMC it assured steady sales. A five-member panel of distinguished book critics would screen hundreds of books, assuring BOMC members that they would be reading the one deemed most

Book Clubs

Irwin, Iowa, ladies library club. Photo courtesy of the National Archives.

worthwhile. The idea was so successful that by 1929, BOMC had over 110,000 members as well as a rival, the Literary Guild, that operated in a similar fashion.

As for-profit businesses, BOMC and the Literary Guild quickly discovered how ruinous an unpopular selection that was rejected or returned for refund could be. Therefore, they tended to stick to safe, conventional books, original enough to be appealing but not so shocking as to be rejected. By virtue of their clever distribution system, BOMC and the Literary Guild greatly increased the sales of selected books. Subscribers across the country, whether too busy, insecure, or distant from a bookstore to make their own reading choices, did in fact become a club in the sense that they shared the experience of reading a common text.

Some of the BOMC selections have enduring reputations as noteworthy publications of the era. Sinclair Lewis's *Elmer Gantry* took a serious look at American social, business, and religious practices. O. E. Rolvaag's *Giants in the Earth* realistically examined the hard life of Scandinavian immigrants to the northern Great Plains. Novels by German war veteran Erich Maria Remarque, *All Quiet on the Western Front*, Norwegian Nobel Prize winner Sigrid Undset, *Kristen Lavransdatter*, and American missionary in China, Pearl Buck, *The Good Earth*, provided international per-spectives. Books such as Charles and Mary Beard's *America at Midpassage*, Walter Lippmann's *A Preface to Morals*, and Will Durant's *The Story of Philosophy* presented serious discussions of history and ideas in a manner accessible to a wide readership. Most BOMC selections were less re-markable, and some were truly dreadful. The list was filled with undis-tinguished page turners such as Edna Ferber's *Showboat* and Clarence Day's *Life with Father*. The March 1929 selection, Joan Lowell's supposed autobiography, *Cradle of the Deep*, was later exposed as a literary hoax.

Like the BOMC, the Literary Guild presented a mixed list aimed at "middlebrow" readers, those sufficiently motivated to devote time to books but not interested in the most sophisticated fare. In addition to romance novels and mystery stories, the Literary Guild sent out histories of Reconstruction and the recent past written by journalists with a better sense of what was colorful and attention-getting than what might be the most balanced and realistic accounts. Claude Bowers' *The Tragic Era: The Revolution after Lincoln* and Frederick Lewis Allen's *Only Yesterday: An Informal History of the 1920s* both enjoyed excellent sales, leading one reviewer to write, "It is certain that hundreds of American readers will get their impression of the period from these graphic pages . . . to one who will derive it from the biographies of the professional doctors of philosophy."[3]

The BOMC selection committee passed over eventual Nobel Prize win-ners William Faulkner, Ernest Hemingway, Eugene O'Neill, and John Steinbeck. It also rejected authors who would later be widely regarded as among the most significant writers of the era: Theodore Dreiser, John Dos Passos, F. Scott Fitzgerald, James Joyce, D. H. Lawrence, and Tho-mas Wolfe. These and other important writers did not escape notice al-together. Many of their books received attention in the book-review sections of newspapers such as the *New York Times* and magazines such as *American Mercury* and *The New Yorker* and ended up selling well. They thus achieved standing with a sophisticated readership if not the broad audience being served by the book clubs.

Another force in standardizing middle-class reading was a magazine founded in 1922. *Reader's Digest* was a **Reader's Digest** compilation of articles taken from other magazines and rewritten so that they could easily be read in a few minutes, one a day throughout the month. *Reader's Digest* specialized in cheerful social ob-servations, upbeat patriotic messages, inspiring dramas of triumph over adversity, and practical advice about successful living, all from an ethi-cally and politically conservative perspective. It also included numerous one- or two-line jokes, one-paragraph humorous stories, and self-improvement vocabulary exercises. Printed in a smaller format than most magazines and thus convenient to keep in the bathroom or at the bedside, *Reader's Digest* became standard fare for a large readership who may have thought they were getting a convenient version of a wide sweep of American journalism, but in fact were receiving a carefully selected and constricted view of the world around them.

Etiquette and Influence   Americans proved eager for straightforward advice about how to they ought to live their lives. One of the best-selling books of the 1920s was Emily Post's *Etiquette in Society, in Business, in Politics and at Home*. Scarcely the first advice book on good manners, it became an unusually powerful force in standardizing ideas of how to behave in public because of its wide distribution. Perhaps even more influential was a 1936 book by Dale Carnegie, *How to Win Friends and Influence People*. Carnegie advocated courteous conduct, sensitivity to other people, and awareness of the impression one was creating, not because it was good etiquette or even decent human behavior but because "making people like you" and "handling people" were crucial to personal success. In the midst of the depression, American culture reflected public anxieties and guided the manner of response.

THE MUSIC OF A DIVERSE CULTURE

Centralized Distribution   An elite group of advertisers, broadcasters, film and record producers, and publishers operated from a few centers of creativity and commerce: New York, in particular, but also Chicago and Los Angeles, and to a lesser degree Boston, Philadelphia, and San Francisco. From there they exerted a powerful influence on the evolving culture. The writers, musicians, artists, actors, and other visible figures in that culture also tended to cluster in those places. Some of the most celebrated authors, the so-called "lost generation," angry and disillusioned after World War I, chose to live abroad. But their work went back to New York for publication, distribution, and critical acceptance. The sources of American music were even more scattered, but again centralized production and distribution networks contributed to the growth of a more standardized culture.

Some of the most widely read and well-regarded literature of the era was conceived far from the influence of New York if ultimately published there. Margaret Mitchell wrote *Gone with the Wind*, the best-selling novel of the 1930s, in Atlanta. Fine writing came out of Oxford, Mississippi (where William Faulkner wrote *The Sound and the Fury* and many other novels about nearby, if fictional, Yoknapatawpha County), rural Vermont (where Robert Frost wrote poetry), and Salinas, California (where John Steinbeck wrote novels such as *Cannery Row*, *Of Mice and Men*, and *The Grapes of Wrath*). Other elements of American culture had likewise disparate points of origin. Diversity remained a notable feature of American culture.

Music underwent a notable evolution during this era. Largely because of the phonograph and radio, special- **Classical** ized forms of music entered the cultural mainstream. **Meets** Classical music acquired a much expanded audience, **Contemporary** though because of its well-established repertoire it was less influenced than other musical genres by the new technologies. A few new concert music composers did emerge, including Americans Aaron Copland, George Gershwin, and Roy Harris, and Russian émigré Sergei Rachmaninoff. Only short pieces or excerpts could be presented uninterrupted on 78 rpm records, but radio networks allowed full-length performances of symphonic music and opera to reach audiences far beyond the urban centers to which they had previously been largely confined. When Saturday afternoon broadcasts of the Metropolitan Opera of New York allowed a small-town Iowa homemaker to indulge a taste for opera along with a wealthy Manhattan matron, a national high-art culture was indeed emerging.

The music of various ethnic groups served as a cultural bond for groups that were themselves scattering geographically. In some cases the music also introduced that culture into the mainstream. Phonograph recordings of the music of recent European immigrant groups emerged first. Such music became a staple of the recording industry early in the twentieth century, but sales of "foreign" music, already dwindling as immigration restriction and cultural assimilation took effect, declined sharply when the Great Depression arrived.

Some record companies became interested in African American music in the early 1920s. Reflecting the social seg- **African** regation of the era, companies such as Okeh, Paramount, **American** Brunswick, and Columbia began producing separate lines of **Music** "race records." African American musicians found themselves confined to recording blues, jazz, and gospel music but nevertheless made available a great deal of both traditional and innovative African American music. Over 5,000 blues and 1,000 gospel records by 1,200 artists appeared during the 1920s and 1930s. Generally excluded from the radio, African American music thrived with the phonograph. The music served to connect the majority of African Americans who remained in the South and the increasing number who migrated north. A 1927 survey of African American homes in two Georgia counties found that none owned a radio but nearly one in five possessed a phonograph. Nationally, 5 to 6 million "race records" were sold annually by mid-decade.

Phonograph records helped spread the sounds of African American

South Side Chicago, like New York's Harlem, contained an entertainment district into which middle-class whites ventured in pursuit of black music and nightlife. Here, a racially mixed audience enjoys a black nightclub stage show. Photo courtesy of the Library of Congress.

jazz, which music broadcasters at first considered inappropriate for radio. White youth such as Jimmy McPartland of suburban Chicago and Leon "Bix" Beiderbecke of Davenport, Iowa, listened excitedly and repeatedly to blues and jazz recorded by African American musicians. Because the 78 rpm records of the day could hold only one or two tunes per side, they would play the same record over and over until every note and phrase became familiar. They learned to play jazz by imitation and soon began performing at school dances. While few young men (and fewer women) would follow McPartland and Beiderbecke into careers as jazz musicians, many more would collect, play, and dance to the new sounds of jazz.

Southern Country Music   The music of rural white southerners developed quite separately, not intertwining substantially with black music until the post–World War II era merger of "rhythm and blues" (the new recording industry label for what had previously been called race music) and "hillbilly" music. Radio broadcasts of the *Grand Ole Opry* and the *National Barn Dance* did a great deal to popularize southern white folk music. At the same time, efforts by early entrepreneurs such as the Carter family and Jimmie Rogers to collect, record, and copyright their own versions of traditional tunes helped establish a more common approach to "country music," modifying the highly localized original styles. Even a culture based on tradition underwent standardization.

When the depression reduced markets for ethnic, country, and race records to a trickle, hard-pressed record companies took the lead in stimulating the development of a more homogenized popular music. Creative producers such as Jack Kapp of Decca Records and John Hammond of Columbia Records used newly developed recording technologies to improve sound quality. Kapp also opted for a smaller inventory of highly promoted releases and reduced the price of a record by half to 35 cents. Such business strategies helped create music widely embraced by the public. **Popular Music Producers**

Kapp worked to develop hit records by blending elements of various musical genres. He encouraged the orchestras of Guy Lombardo and Tommy Dorsey to emphasize clear simple melodies as well as light, steady rhythms that would be good for dancing. He also promoted singers with soft, pleasant voices such as Bing Crosby and the four Mills Brothers. Decca's generally upbeat style of music appealed to many Americans in the depression decade, and its more affordable prices helped shape a popular mass-market music business that would explode within a few years.

John Hammond, Kapp's main rival, likewise produced records that softened the styles of jazz and blues. He played an important role in creating new dance music that by the mid-1930s was beginning to be called "swing." Hammond helped clarinetist Benny Goodman increase his band's already considerable appeal by adding flamboyant drummer Gene Kruppa and rhythmically steady piano player Jess Stacy. Hammond also brought African American musicians such as band leader Count Basie and singer Billie Holliday to national attention. He was far more aggressive than Kapp in bringing African American music and artists into the cultural mainstream, a step that foreshadowed and helped prepare the way for subsequent social and political developments.

The early 1930s creation of the coin-operated automatic phonograph placed popular music in restaurants, dance halls, night clubs, soda fountains, and the taverns opening up after the repeal of prohibition. The 150,00 machines produced between 1933 and 1937, soon to be labeled jukeboxes, each held 50 records. Not only did the jukebox help revive the record business, but it focused industry and audience attention on music of the greatest popularity. Jukebox owners naturally wanted them filled with the records most **The Jukebox** likely to attract customers' nickels. By 1939, with 60 percent of all records sold going into Wurlitzer, Seeburg, and other jukeboxes, a once quite diversified music industry was moving itself and the nation's culture toward greater uniformity.

The jukebox boosted the popularity of dancing, an already notable element of mass American culture. Various forms of dancing had long been a part of American life, of course, but the rise of the phonograph expanded opportunities for many, especially young working- and middle-class people, to engage in social dancing. Throughout the United States, in small communities as well as urban centers, dancing became highly popular. As a phonograph industry trade journal pointed out, "Not everyone can have a five-piece band waiting to play for them."[4]

Social Dancing The dances in which people engaged evolved from the rigid postures of the nineteenth-century waltz (itself once thought scandalous because the couple actually held onto each other, although maintaining a safe and rigid distance between themselves). By the 1910s more informal and physically intimate social dancing was being transformed from a morally questionable activity restricted to lower-class urban dance halls and saloons into such a popular pastime for all social classes that it was frequently referred to as a "dance craze."

By World War I, new dances were constantly being introduced. The fox-trot, tango, and dozens of briefly popular dances such as the turkey trot, the cakewalk, and the kangaroo dip involved exuberant body as well as foot movement. Many brought black dance forms into middle-class white society. The most common label for young women in the early 1920s came from such a dance. The "flapper" was not just a modern girl, she was a dancer engaged in birdlike flapping of her arms as she did the Charleston. The flapper's fashion choices, abandoning corsets, cutting her hair short, and adopting shorter, less restrictive clothing, likewise reflected the dance culture.

Dancing retained its popularity throughout the 1920s. It flourished further as inexpensive recreation in the 1930s. The rise of "swing" in the second half of the 1930s responded to the demand of a younger high school- and college-age audience for new, more exuberant dance music. Blending jazz styles with big band orchestration and danceable rhythms, "swing" became a successful commercial musical formula.

Time magazine reported that between 1925 and 1941 swing accounted for 25 percent of all record releases. Popular "hit parade" records claimed another 35 percent. The balance, except for a small category of children's records, was divided roughly evenly among classical, country, and race music. While a great deal of standardization had taken place, cultural diversity persisted.

Saturday night community dance in Irwin, Iowa. (On such occasions, it was not uncommon for two women to dance together.) Photo courtesy of the National Archives.

Other forms of American artistry evolved in the 1920s as well, though not in a fashion that had the widespread impact **Other Art** of innovations in literature and music. Painters developing **Forms** new techniques and distinctive styles ranged from Grant Wood, best known today for his portrait of a farm couple, *American Gothic*, to Georgia O'Keeffe, who experimented with vivid expressionistic images of desert life. Martha Graham brought a dramatic modernism to art dance choreography. Playwright Eugene O'Neill created a series of dramas exploring some of the grim realities of modern life. As influential as each of these artists was in his/her own field, none reached a mass audience.

One concentrated community of artists proved particu- larly important even though much of its output only grad- **Harlem** ually reached a national audience. This was the Harlem **Renaissance** Renaissance, the flourishing of various arts in the African American ghetto of New York City. Dozens of writers led by poets Lang- ston Hughes and Countee Cullen and novelists Claude McKay and Zora Neale Hurston created an impressive body of new literature dealing with the African American experience and perspective. Philosopher and editor Alain Locke gathered some of the best African American writing into a 1928 book, *The New Negro*. Two years later in *Black Manhattan*, James Weldon Johnson underscored the progress African American intellectuals were making. At the same time as white middle-class New Yorkers were venturing into Harlem to hear Duke Ellington, Ethel Waters, Bessie Smith, and other jazz musicians, they began to encounter additional facets of a vibrant black cultural life. The Harlem Renaissance served to solidify and enhance the African American intellectual community's own identity. It also began to bring expressions of the African American experience and viewpoint into the larger culture.

American culture was far from completely standardized by the end of the 1920s. Nevertheless, the shared sense of taste and values communicated by radio, phonograph, cinema, and print as well as the aggressive messages of advertising moved America in that direction. The sudden and unexpected jolt of economic collapse that hit the United States as the decade expired served to create another shared experience, this one extraordinary in nature. In its own fashion, the Great Depression became a powerful engine for the further development of a common national culture.

Shared Sense of Values

NOTES

1. Roland Marchand, *Advertising the American Dream: Making Way for Modernity, 1920–1940* (Berkeley: University of California Press, 1985), 32–38.

2. Jackson Lears, *Fables of Abundance: A Cultural History of Advertising in America* (New York: Basic Books, 1994), 226.

3. Quoted in David S. Muzzey review of Claude Bowers, *The Tragic Era*, *Current History* 31 (1928), 212.

4. Quoted in William Howland Kenney, *Recorded Music in American Life: The Phonograph and Popular Memory, 1890–1945* (New York: Oxford University Press, 1999), 102.

10

Crisis: The Impact of the Great Depression

THE SHADOW OF HARD TIMES

The American people did not share evenly in the prosperity of the 1920s. Nor would all undergo the same distress when the economy crumbled in the 1930s. But just as most people in the 1920s felt an impact on their daily life of economic growth brought about by technological and culture developments, so, too, in the following decade did they experience in some way the severe economic depression. By 1932, an estimated 28 percent of the nation's households, containing 34 million people, did not have a single employed wage earner. Most Americans continued to be supported by their own or a family member's earned income, but even when jobs did not disappear altogether, working hours and wages were often reduced. By 1933, Americans overall had 54 percent as much income as in 1929. Furthermore, almost everyone knew of someone who had been rendered completely destitute. The immensity of the Great Depression caused virtually every American to feel personally vulnerable. Daily life went on, in many respects much like the previous decade, but the reality of hard times cast a shadow few could escape.

Because it was so unexpected, the economic collapse at the end of the 1920s left almost all Americans feeling insecure. The feeling would last a lifetime for many and shape their attitude toward saving or spending money decades later. The experience of living through a depression affected people differently. Some were always persuaded to save as much as possible for the rainy day that was sure to come, others to spend money as soon as they got it since there was no telling when the opportunity would once again disappear.

Nearly a decade of general prosperity and repeated assurances from business and government leaders that such conditions had become permanent had created widespread confidence that bordered on complacency. When a General Motors executive wrote in the *Ladies Home Journal* that "everybody ought to be rich!" and the winning 1928 presidential candidate pledged, "A chicken in every pot, two cars in every garage!" optimism about the future understandably ran high, even among those who had yet to share in the affluence being proclaimed. When instead prosperity shriveled and leaders revealed themselves to be helpless, bewildered, and even inept, no wonder that the confidence of ordinary citizens dissolved and they came to understand the precarious nature of their economic well-being.

UNEVEN GROWTH AND INCOME

Their economic experience through the 1920s did not prepare the American people for what lay ahead in the 1930s. An overall pattern of growth characterized the 1920s, its magnitude heightened by the postwar difficulties of 1919–1921. The economy grew substantially but not evenly. Agriculture remained depressed after the collapse of the wartime boom. Mining and lumbering failed to share in the general nonagricultural expansion. And the rewards of growth were not enjoyed equally. Factory workers' wages rose by 9 percent during the 1920s, not a bad increase by the standard of previous decades but quite modest in comparison to the 63 percent growth in corporate profits.

At the end of the 1920s, household income was unevenly distributed. The nation's 36,000 families having incomes over $75,000 in 1929 received as much altogether as the 12 million families with incomes below $1,500, regarded by the federal government at the time as the poverty line for a family of four, the minimum income required for a decent standard of living. (These figures need to be multiplied by ten to obtain their rough equivalent in beginning-of-twenty-first-century money.) If America's 27.5 million families were divided into five equal groups, the bottom fifth would have annual incomes below $1,000, the next group $1,000 to $1,500, the third $1,500 to $2,000, the fourth $2,000 to $3,000, and the top 20 percent all those over $3,000. In nearly one-third of families, income was produced by more than one person. For the most part, older children supplemented a father's income, but three million wives and nearly two million widows or divorced women worked outside the home as well.

Income was also distributed unevenly between urban and rural dwellers and among regions of the country. In 1929, the highest income, about

$1,000 per person, went to nonfarm workers in the northeastern area anchored by New York and Boston. The income of the farm population in the northeastern region was just over one-third as much, or $366. The comparable figures for the Midwest were $854 and $262, the Far West $953 and $818, the interior Northwest $703 and $426, and the interior Southwest $683 and $366. In the nation's poorest section, the Southeast, the nonfarm population's per capita income was $535 while the farm population averaged $183. The most striking disparities in income stood out between the Northeast and the Southeast and between nonfarm and farm income almost everywhere.

POVERTY COMMON

Thus, even at the end of the economic surge of the 1920s, poverty was the usual situation for at least two-fifths of the American population. The Brookings Institution of Washington, setting a higher standard than the government, regarded a $2,000 annual income as needed to provide the "basic necessities" of a comfortable life and thus estimated that 60 percent of the nation's families lived on a substandard income. The poor labored to pay for food and shelter, rarely could afford to buy clothing much less the new consumer goods, and certainly did not take part in the stock market boom. The 1930s depression would intensify their struggle, but otherwise represent nothing new in terms of their daily lives. The highest income groups were well enough off to escape the worst of the suffering, though many did confront reduced circumstances. Those who experienced the most severe setbacks were middle-income people whose living conditions had recently improved and whose expectations had grown perhaps even more rapidly.

CONSUMER GOODS PRODUCTION

The economic deficiencies of the 1920s were not so much unknown as unacknowledged. Poverty had always been a reality for most rural dwellers, especially those living in the South, as well as for most unskilled urban workers and recent immigrants. Thus, the existence of considerable poverty seemed nothing out of the ordinary. What was extraordinary, and thus the focus of both contemporary attention and later historical talk about the "Roaring Twenties," was the appearance of astonishing growth in the economy during the decade. This growth rested on the availability of consumer products such as automobiles, radios, home appliances, processed food, and cosmetics. A mass market for these and other goods was stimulated by advertising and further enhanced by newly available consumer credit. For middle-income Americans, even those whose own circumstances were not much improved, and the fortunate few with high incomes, visible signs of prosperity were all around. A new barometer of prosperity, the stock market, came to be regarded as a measure of how the national economy was performing, no matter how an individual was doing.

THE STOCK MARKET BOOM AND BUST

Large Enterprises Built by Shares
Shared ownership in large enterprises had become common business practice during the great expansion of American economy during the middle and late nineteenth century. Huge undertakings, such as railroads, required far more capital than even the wealthiest individual possessed. Furthermore, the risks and liabilities of business ownership could only be limited when an investor held shares of stock in a legally independent corporation as opposed to owning an enterprise directly or in partnership. At first, corporate ownership was generally only divided into a few shares, but by the early twentieth century, entrepreneurs, seeking to raise capital, realized that splitting stock into smaller shares would allow them to retain control with proportionally less capital investment while at the same time attracting a broader range of people to put funds into the enterprise. The marketplaces in which new stocks were offered and older ones were exchanged came to be centered in New York. By the 1920s, the largest of these markets, the New York Stock Exchange, located on Wall Street in lower Manhattan, would become the focus of unprecedented national attention.

Common Stocks Increase
On a typical day in 1920, about three-quarters of a million shares of stock were traded on the New York Stock Exchange, only a tiny fraction of the several hundred million shares changing hands on a normal day by the end of the century. The long-standing inclination of pre–World War I investors to buy so-called preferred stocks that paid a set six to eight percent return each year was beginning to fade. The war had increased the popularity of what were termed common stocks, which carried no guaranteed return but would pay dividends that closely reflected a business's growth and profit. Stock buyers increasingly chose to speculate that common stocks would bring them greater rewards than a more conservative investment in preferred stocks. As sales and prices of common stock rose, companies began dividing their stock into smaller and smaller shares, to keep the purchase price generally in the $10 to $250 range, and put stock ownership within the reach of ever larger numbers of potential buyers.

Bond Sales
In addition to common stock, investors also bought corporate bonds, promissory notes backed by no more than the business's good reputation as a guarantee that they would

be paid off with interest. Bonds were considered a safe, conservative investment with a predictable rate of return, assured unless the issuer of the bond went bankrupt, something that rarely happened. The borrowed money generated by bond sales allowed companies to expand their operations and increase the profit paid the owners of each share of stock. As long as profits exceeded the interest paid by the borrower, bond sales helped companies expand and made their stock more attractive.

Borrowing money and using the loan to leverage an investment had long been a strategy employed by businesses themselves, but in the 1920s, thanks in part to low 3 to 5 percent prime interest rates, it became a device widely employed by **Buying on Margin** stock market investors. Instead of purchasing a stock outright, for say $10, an investor could give his broker the money as security on a loan of up to 90 percent of the price, thus allowing him to acquire $100 of stock for his $10. Buying stock on margin, as this practice was termed, permitted this investor to reap ten times as much profit from stock dividend payments and price increases. Instead of a 5 percent dividend on $10 producing 50 cents, the $100 margin account would generate $5, and if the price of the stock doubled, the profit on selling the original $10 investment would not be merely $10, it would be $190 (minus broker fees and the interest charged on the loan). If the stock price fell, the investor would be asked by his broker in a so-called "margin call" to put up more money as collateral; otherwise the broker would sell the stock to recoup the loan. As long as stock prices kept going up, margin calls were no problem. More and more investors bought on margin to maximize their gains from the soaring market. Broker loans went from a total of about $1 billion in 1921 to $2.5 billion by 1926 and an astonishing $8.5 billion by October 1929, while the overall number of shares bought and sold increased from less than 250 million in 1921 to 1.1 billion in 1929.

The rise in the price of stock in the Radio Corporation of America (RCA or simply Radio as it was called) helps **Stock Values Soar** explain the attraction of the stock market in the 1920s. RCA was organized in 1919 to exploit the opportunities of a new technology. Its sales of radio equipment expanded as broadcasting developed. In 1921, RCA stock sold for $1.50 a share. By 1923, it reached a high of $4.75. The next year the price tripled after the corporation reorganized and gave shareholders one new share for five of the old. The new stock peaked that year at $66.87. RCA share prices fluctuated within a narrow range for the next two years, then surged after the company established the National Broadcasting Company (NBC) and began network broadcasts in late 1926. Radio climbed to $101 in 1927 and to a breathtaking $420 in 1928. In 1929, the stock split five for one and hit a high of $114.75. At that point, a share purchased in 1921 was worth nearly 400 times its original cost!

Americans were dazzled by such increases in the valuations of common stocks. Radio was a noteworthy but not unique case. Over the same period, General Electric, producer of electric generators, motors, home appliances, and light bulbs, went from $109.50 to $403.00; General Motors, the leading automobile manufacturer, went from a 1921 low of $9.62 to a 1928 high of $229.00, then reorganized its stock and watched its climb continue; and the Dow Jones average of thirty major industrial stocks went from $63.90 to $381.17. As new commodities became a part of daily life, no special knowledge or inside information seemed to be needed to identify companies in which an investment would return a handsome profit.

Even at the market's peak in 1929 only a relatively small number of people, no more than three million or 2.5 percent of a population slightly over 120 million, actually had the combination of interest and financial resources to own stocks. Talk of the stock market, however, was pervasive. Newspapers gave their millions of readers substantial reports on the market every day, cab drivers in New York talked to their passengers with the confidence of insiders about the latest stock surge, and radio audiences heard market reports—on Radio (RCA) among other stocks—as news routinely broadcast along with the time and weather forecast. During the late 1920s, as stock prices spiraled higher and higher, the average person could hardly escape knowing what the market was doing, getting caught up in the excitement, and overlooking the fact that the economy, on which stock values were presumably based, was slowing down.

The Economy Slows Down Then, as now, the formula for making money on the stock market was "buy low, sell high." Dwindling growth, if not decline in many industries, made most investors aware that stocks were overvalued in terms of the dividends then being paid. Even President-elect Herbert Hoover said after the 1928 election, "Our whole business system would break down in a day if there was not a high sense of moral responsibility in our business world." Hoover failed to acknowledge, if he understood it, that business decisions reflected individual self-interest, not any sense of moral responsibility to society. By mid-1929 a few big investors such as Bernard Baruch of New York and Joseph P. Kennedy of Boston quietly sold every stock they held and reaped enormous profits. Most investors, however, saw prices continuing to climb and, especially those with highly leveraged portfolios, believed that much money still could be made. They chose to wait to sell until the market reached its peak.

Financial Panic In September and October 1929, stock prices wobbled, falling sharply several times only to recover and inch higher. Suddenly on Monday, October 28, a horde of investors decided the time had come to sell and the large New York banks and brokerage houses that had stemmed a frightening price drop only five days earlier proved helpless to stop the slide. With an excess of sellers to buyers, prices dropped steeply. Brokers asked for more margin, requiring investors, in order to meet the call, to sell some shares immediately, even at a loss. But as prices plummeted by more than the percentage originally paid, it cost the margin buyer less simply to let the broker have the shares than to put up additional cash. Brokers soon found themselves awash in stocks of sinking value. Of more immediate concern, they found themselves without the assets to cover the loans they had themselves arranged with banks to finance their margin accounts. The rush to sell stocks while some value could still be recouped rapidly turned into a financial panic spreading outward from Wall Street to banks across the country and, in turn, into every aspect of national economic life.

When the stock market collapsed, President Hoover tried to calm public concern by saying that "the fundamental business of the country—that is, the production and distribution of goods and services—is on a sound and prosperous basis." He was, of course, correct. Factories, offices, shops, and farms still stood ready to produce. Workers and farmers retained their skills, not to mention their desire and need for employment. People's appetite for food, shelter, clothing, automobiles, electrical appliances, entertainment, and myriad other possibilities had not evaporated. The financial system might be in trouble, but otherwise the economy appeared fully capable of functioning.

Hoover's claim, however, resembled those of analysts who asserted that the stock market was still sound, pointing out that some stocks had held their price and others had been overvalued. Such observations failed to acknowledge that **Economic Collapse** economic conditions were deeply influenced by national mood, the psychology of ordinary people as well as business leaders. The growth of the 1920s had been conditioned, at least in part, on optimism that times would continue to be good; that stock prices would rise; that wages would be paid; and that money borrowed to buy consumer goods or stock could be repaid. More important, when the mood changed, the expectation of difficult times ahead not only caused stock prices to fall, but led potential buyers of products or services to defer purchases. As increasing numbers of people followed suit, suppliers gradually cut back and laid off workers. Layoffs rendered more people unable to pay their bills, much less purchase new goods and services. This led in turn to more cutbacks, larger layoffs, and ever more unsold goods and services. The downward spiral fed on itself and, as conditions worsened, the national mood grew more and more pessimistic. One sign of how the economic collapse affected daily life was that by the beginning of 1933, over 40 percent of the nation's home mortgages

What made the Great Depression so difficult to comprehend as well as discouraging to many Americans was that it devastated an economy that had been producing an unprecedented flood of technologically advanced goods and had the resources and facilities to manufacture many more. Photo courtesy of the Library of Congress.

were in default. The only reason relatively few foreclosures occurred was that banks knew they could neither rent, sell, nor afford to maintain all these residences.

BANK FAILURES

America's banks proved to be the first line of fiscal defense against hard times to fail people in their daily lives. The U.S. banking system was loose, diffuse, and characterized by many relatively small local banks rather than a few large national institutions, as was the European pattern. The Federal Reserve System, since its establishment in 1913, had knit together and supervised most larger banks, but thousands of state chartered banks, savings associations, and other financial institutions operated outside the national bank system with little or no regulation. In the 1920s, bank failures, arising out of bad investments and defaulted loans and leading to the loss of all or a portion of depositors' funds, were common, ranging from 367 in 1922 to 976 in 1926. These failures, however, occurred mainly among small rural banks. While the closings hurt their customers, they did not have wide impact. When bigger banks

Many, although not all banks that were ruined in the early 1930s were small-town and rural institutions with limited financial reserves. This failed bank was located in Haverhill, Iowa. Photo courtesy of the Library of Congress.

that had financed broker loans were caught up in the stock market collapse, however, far more people felt the blow. In 1929, 659 banks with $250 million in deposits failed, but in 1930, 1,352 banks with $853 million in deposits did so. In 1931, 2,294 banks with $1.7 billion in deposits closed their doors.

Depositors, hearing rumors that their bank might be in trouble, would rush to withdraw their funds, often standing **A Run on** in lines that would themselves attract notice and cause other **the Banks** people to hurry to join the line. No bank could turn a profit or pay interest on deposited funds without having most of its assets loaned out and earning interest. Even the soundest bank could not instantly borrow large sums or call in all its loans and mortgages at once to satisfy large and unanticipated depositor demands. A bank suffering stock market losses or many defaulted loans and mortgages was in even greater difficulty. When rumors, either true or false, spread that a bank was overextended and a run on the bank began, the institution could not meet withdrawal demands and thus had to close its doors. Sometimes after accounts were settled depositors would receive all or a portion of their funds, but on other occasions they would lose everything, and in any case, accounts would long be frozen. No wonder that depositors would panic at the first hint of trouble.

Scrip

Not only individuals but churches, charities, businesses, and local governments could lose their resources in a bank failure. Whole communities could suddenly find themselves without the capacity to pay wages, make purchases, or extend charity. With their money supply frozen, communities would turn to barter or resort to a substitute currency, often called scrip. For instance, Goodyear Tire and Rubber Company of Akron, Ohio, paid its workers in its own self-produced scrip, pledging to exchange it for U.S. currency when that became possible. Grocery stores agreed to accept the scrip as currency, and the community persevered. But the scrip was not recognized outside of the immediate area and could not be used to pay taxes People had little choice but to use the scrip to the extent possible even though they knew it was a temporary and inadequate solution.

Bank Holidays

With bank failures still continuing in early 1933, the governor of Michigan, William Comstock, suddenly declared a statewide "bank holiday." With reason to fear that Detroit's largest bank was about to fail, Comstock thought it best to suspend all banking in the state to provide the shaky institution time to secure new financing and avoid the possibility of a panic that might pull down the state's entire banking system. The one-week bank holiday, freezing the accounts of 900,000 depositors, proved insufficient and so Comstock extended the closure. Other governors followed suit. By March 3, when New York and Illinois forced the country's two greatest financial centers to suspend operations, banks in 38 states had taken a holiday. The other ten states imposed strict limits on withdrawals. The bank holiday had come to affect practically every American. The banking system was completely immobilized.

LIVING IN HARD TIMES

For most Americans, unusually hard times did not instantaneously follow the stock market crash. Business expansion did quickly cease. Worker layoffs, however, increased more gradually. Employment did not hit rock bottom for more than three years. But potential producers and consumers, each fearing a prolonged period of economic difficulty, gradually decided not to make or buy more goods (even if they could do so on credit). Construction, factory production, and other economic activities slowed, and employment began to shrink. News of such developments caused business people and consumers to become even more defensive and the economic decline accelerated. Even advertisers trying to sell products promoted them as useful to people seeking to economize, thus reinforcing the image of a culture experiencing hard times. By the end of 1932 national income totaled only 54 percent of its 1929 level.

Unemployment in October 1929 registered a low 1.5 million or 3 percent of a labor force estimated at 50 million. The jobless number rose to 3 million during the next six months and 4 million after a year, still only 8 percent of the work force. Then joblessness began to accelerate. It stood at 7 million in October 1931 and 11 million in October 1932. By early 1933, an estimated 12 to 14 million people were out of work, between 25 and 30 percent of the American work force. (None of these figures are entirely reliable and are most likely underestimates since the federal government's capacity to collect labor information was imperfect and overwhelmed by the circumstances.)

Unemployment

Young, old, and minority workers suffered disproportionate layoffs. A 1931 survey found that while overall unemployment had reached 15 percent, already about 35 percent of young workers, those between sixteen and twenty-five years old, and older ones, those over 60, had been dismissed while another 14 percent worked only part time. African Americans suffered even more. In Memphis, they comprised 38 percent of the population and 75 percent of those out of work. In Chicago, African Americans made up only 4 percent of the population but 16 percent of the jobless. African American women, most frequently employed as domestic servants and thought expendable by pinched middle-class families, were the first to lose their jobs. Already by January 1931, African American female unemployment had reached 75 percent in Detroit, 58 percent in Chicago, and 51 percent in Pittsburgh. All of these patterns persisted as employment continued to decline.

The urban workforce was, not surprisingly, disproportionately affected by the industrial collapse. Those in the largest cities were hit the hardest. For example, in Ohio, a large state with an economy divided between industry and agriculture, unemployment figures told the tale. In 1937, after some recovery had been achieved, a survey reported that joblessness in rural and small town Ohio stood at around 12 percent. In cities of 10,000 to 100,000 it was 13.5 percent, but in the eight major cities it averaged 20.5 percent. Big city unemployment ranged from 14.7 percent in relatively small Dayton to 23.7 percent in the largest urban center, Cleveland.[1] The 1930s depression should be remembered as being most severe in America's great cities.

Urban Workforce Hardest Hit

Even at its worst, complete joblessness faced only a minority of the overall American workforce. Most American workers held onto their positions. But they, too, were affected. Rather than dismiss workers with experience and skills, many businesses tried to keep them at reduced hours and wages. The rubber industry experimented with six-hour daily shifts and thirty-hour weeks as a substitute for the eight-hour shift and forty-hour workweek. Rubber workers held onto their jobs, but with no hourly wage increase, paychecks shrunk by 25 percent. Steel foundries went to a four-day workweek, then three days, then less. By 1932, the average for all U.S. factory workers who could claim to have jobs was less than thirty-five hours per week at a time when most still considered normal a five-and-a-half-day workweek of 44 hours. Coal miners in 1932 averaged only twenty-seven hours a week.

Rural Crisis In previous periods of industrial distress in the United States, some workers had returned to the countryside while farmers, knowing that they could at least feed themselves, stayed put. By the 1930s, however, far fewer urban residents had rural roots to which they could return, and farmers were facing a severe crisis of their own. The post–World War I agricultural depression continued throughout the 1920s and into the next decade. The mechanization of farming with tractors and other equipment reduced the need for hired labor and put small farmers out of business. Another blow was the drought beginning in 1930 that made growing crops or feeding livestock extremely difficult. Seventeen million farm people, half the nation's total, from Maryland and Virginia to Missouri and Arkansas, from the Dakotas to Montana, and the states of the southern Great Plains, were affected by drought conditions.

The agricultural areas to be hit the hardest and longest were the southern plains of Kansas, Colorado, New Mexico, Oklahoma, and Texas, which turned into what was called the Dust Bowl. Extreme heat accompanied by the lack of rain throughout much of the decade caused dry soil literally to blow away in great dust storms. Most farmers struggled on through a bleak decade, but especially in the Dust Bowl many left, unable to pay even the interest on their mortgaged land or forced to give up unproductive tenant farming. An estimated 3.5 million people left their farms during the 1930s, many of them taking along only what could be packed into the Model T, farm truck, or pushcart. They headed west to California where agricultural jobs were rumored still to be available.

Community Self-Help Overwhelmed In the 1920s, temporarily unemployed workers could usually obtain assistance from community institutions, churches, mutual aid societies, philanthropic agencies, and local government. As urban unemployment and agricultural displacement mounted in the early 1930s, these resources were soon overmatched. One civic-minded Ohio Fraternal Order of Eagles lodge opened a free lunchroom for the needy in February 1930. At first it served 200 people a day, but ten months later the number had doubled, and by early 1931, the Eagles were serving 130 gallons of

Chicago soup kitchen line, 1931. Photo courtesy of the National Archives.

soup, 200 loaves of bread, 100 gallons of milk, and 175 pounds of cheese to 600 or 700 people each day. By April, the Eagles, along with other groups such as Parents and Teachers Associations, the Salvation Army, and Volunteers of America who also tried to feed the hungry, had exhausted their resources. The city of Akron, which had provided small relief checks, could not take up the slack. Its debt had already passed the legal limit; it had been forced to slash the number of municipal workers and the salaries of those who remained, and it was facing a 25 percent decline in tax receipts. The dimensions of the depression stretched city as well as private generosity past the breaking point.

Community self-help, the traditional American response to economic distress, was swamped by the tide of unemployment. Bank failures deprived many people of what little savings they had. Philanthropy did not cease, but its providers found themselves with less to give just as the need was soaring. The magnitude of the depression, together with inherent flaws in a system of private, voluntary, selective, and localized assistance, exhausted the system's capacity to provide relief. By 1932, most private charities were only able to offer food relief, and even that was limited. Soup kitchens, often using past-its-prime surplus produce, and bread lines did not offer the destitute a sufficient or balanced diet, but represented the best that churches and charities could do.

Cities and States Go Bankrupt   Even when banks did not fail, and the vast majority did not, communities found themselves with far too few resources to care for the number of people in need. With tax revenues shrinking, even paying the modest wages of municipal workers and school teachers proved difficult. Public employees who knew that their positions paid less than private sector jobs but thought that they were more secure found themselves laid off. For those fortunate enough to retain their posts, salaries were cut, then cut again. Some government units borrowed in anticipation of tax payments which then did not appear. By 1933, 1,300 cities, towns, counties, and school districts, together with the states of Arkansas, Louisiana, and South Carolina, had defaulted on obligatory payments, in essence, declaring bankruptcy. Maintaining routine services proved hard, especially if they could not be justified as essential. The city of Detroit, deciding it could no longer justify operating its zoo, slaughtered the animals to feed hungry people.

Mexican Americans Deported   In the Southwest, Mexican Americans became targets for local California, Arizona, and Texas authorities concerned about the possibility of having to care for an expanding number of indigents. Living in separate neighborhoods or *colonias*, Mexican Americans were convenient scapegoats in difficult times. With the help of the Federal Bureau of Immigration (after 1933, the Immigration and Naturalization Service), over 80,000 Mexican Americans were rounded up and formally deported. More than 320,000 other *repatriados*, many of them born or naturalized U.S. citizens, followed the deportees across the Mexican border.

Apple Selling   With unemployed urban workers desperately looking for any source of income, Pacific Northwest apple growers, faced with a bumper 1930 crop, found a way to do well by doing good. Distributors sold crates of apples on credit to the jobless. A man could buy a crate for $1.75, stand on a street corner, and sell apples for a nickel apiece. With luck he could sell a crate full of sixty apples within a day, take in $3.00, pay the distributor, and have $1.25 (minus any spoiled and unsalable fruit). The growers advertised, "Buy an apple a day and eat the depression away," and those who could afford to do so bought the fruit out of a sense of responsibility. Apple selling became a common big city activity, indeed, a symbol of coping with the depression. But selling a crate of apples each day of the year would generate less than $500. With thousands of sellers (6,000 in New York City alone) and suppliers soon increasing the price per crate, apple selling provided jobless workers too little income to survive, much less prosper.

Other destitute urban dwellers literally scrambled to get something to eat. By 1931, adults and children **Hungry Families** were digging in St. Louis and New York garbage dumps. Orderly lines formed at some dumps as people waited their turn to hunt for food; elsewhere they rushed frantically to each new pile of refuse. Meanwhile, in Harlan County, Kentucky, families subsisted on dandelions and blackberries. Elsewhere in Appalachian mining communities, some families resorted to eating every other day. Though President Hoover claimed, "Nobody is actually starving," New York City officials recorded 29 deaths due to starvation in 1933, and 110 the following year. The national total of cases of starvation remained unacknowledged as did the larger number of persons who officially succumbed to something else but whose condition was made worse and whose death was hastened by malnutrition.

Those who held onto at least part-time work found ways to scrape by. Many families planted gardens; did home **Scraping By** canning, pickling, and baking; ate less meat and more beans, pancakes, or macaroni and cheese; went back to making their own clothing; and did their own home repairs. Using the telephone for local or long-distance calls came to be regarded as an unaffordable luxury in many homes. The number of telephones in service declined from over 20 million in 1930 to fewer than 17 million by 1933. As many as one-sixth of families doubled up and shared living quarters. Children increasingly took small jobs running errands, mowing lawns, shoveling snow, baby-sitting, or delivering newspapers to supplement the family income. In California, for instance, half of all teenage boys and one-fourth of teenage girls held part-time jobs. "Making do" with hand-me-down clothes, day-old bakery bread, shoes repaired with cardboard, and coats relined with old blankets became common. Socializing with non-family members declined sharply because the cost of going out or entertaining guests was considered prohibitive.

Nearly half of the population remained more or less fully employed and lived much better than those in re- **Reduced** duced circumstances, considering that the price of almost **Consumption** everything fell. Such fortunate people were not without worries that their situation could suddenly fall apart, as had so many others. Patterns of consumption reflected the reduction of income and alteration of outlook. A tape made of transparent cellophane backed with pressure-sensitive adhesive, developed by the Minnesota Mining and Manufacturing Company in the 1920s, became popular during the depression as people chose to repair household items with this Scotch Tape rather than buy new ones. Sales of automobiles and other expensive commodities dropped sharply. In 1929, Americans purchased 4,455,000 new cars, but during the following decade, an average of only 2,142,000 new automobiles were sold per year. Nevertheless, people drove more than ever. Although the number of cars on the road increased by only one-seventh by 1939, gasoline consumption increased by one-fourth. Similarly, while overall food sales declined, cigarette sales shot up sharply, if anything a sign of attempts to calm frazzled nerves or distract an unfulfilled appetite. Once national prohibition ended in 1933, legal sales of beer, wine, and liquor resumed, though throughout the 1930s at well below pre-prohibition rates. Inexpensive mass entertainment, sports, and motion pictures in particular experienced only slight declines. The middle class, the backbone of their audience, continued, insofar as possible, to pursue familiar activities.

Family Life Strained American family life was severely challenged by the depression. Confronted by loss of jobs and income, families struggled to pay mortgages, rents, and bills. Many suffered deprivation and humiliation, and quite a few, under the strain, fell apart. The divorce rate actually declined in the early 1930s, perhaps because of the prohibitive legal costs involved. Divorce grew to unprecedented levels by the middle of the decade, but cost remained an obstacle. Frequently couples just broke apart informally. Desertion of one's family was not inhibited by cost, and so abandonment rates soared. Having lost the ability to support a family, some men simply disappeared. Perhaps they thought that an abandoned family would be more likely to receive assistance, or perhaps they simply could not cope with the pressure to provide when that was proving impossible.

Birthrate Declines An even more evident change in family patterns was the decision by many couples not to start families. Unable to support themselves, they postponed weddings, sometimes for years, and marriage rates plunged. Even more noteworthy, birthrates fell to the lowest point in the nation's history. Primarily as a result of fluctuating birthrate, the U.S. population grew by 16 percent in the 1920s and 15 percent in the 1940s, but during the 1930s, it grew only 7 percent. Nothing better indicated the extent of current personal economic difficulty or pessimism about the future than the decision, repeated in millions of instances, not to bring children into the world. The generation of children born in the 1930s would be the smallest of the century. Throughout their later lives these children would continue to experience the consequences (some of which, such as less competition for college admissions and jobs, would be quite welcome).

Hoovervilles and Hobos Those who lost their jobs often lost their homes as well when they could not afford to pay the mortgage or rent. Some built makeshift shacks on vacant land. As whole communities of cardboard, scrap lumber, and tarpaper shacks arose, they came to be called Hoovervilles, a sneering reference to the president who had predicted growing prosperity. Others among the unemployed left home in search of work. Hitchhiking or hopping trains to ride in or under freight cars became a way of life for tens of thousands of men and a few women. Hobos, as they were called (as opposed to "bums" who traveled but did not seek work, instead subsisting by begging for handouts), seldom found employment at the end of the journey, but at least enjoyed a rough camaraderie with others in the same situation.

The most notable gathering of destitute wanderers occurred in Washington, D.C., in 1932. World War I veterans, who ten years earlier had been promised a government pension beginning in 1945 as a retirement bonus for their **The "Bonus Army"** patriotic service, applied for immediate payment of the bonus in their time of distress. A "bonus army" of nearly 20 thousand veterans and their family members descended on the nation's capital. Camping in parks and unused government buildings, they successfully lobbied Congress for partial payment of the bonus. Almost half of the bonus army decided that partial payment was not enough and stayed on, enjoying the convivial encampment more than what they could look forward to at home or elsewhere. The Hoover administration grew fearful of the bonus marchers, launched an unsuccessful effort to have them removed by District of Columbia police, and finally sent in the U.S. Army. Soldiers commanded by General Douglas MacArthur and supported by tanks drove the bonus army away, destroying and burning their camps. The image of an unsympathetic Republican government and a heartless Hoover was frozen in place.

Herbert Hoover may have received far too much blame from the public for the depression and his failure to lead the country out of it. Vast and complex economic problems were deeply embedded in the nation's institutions and culture. **Hoover's Cautious Response** Hoover, as secretary of commerce during the two previous administrations and then as president, worked diligently to improve the economy and foster cooperative self-help within its various sectors. When the collapse nevertheless occurred, he sought to provide as much government aid to recovery as he thought was appropriate without fostering what he thought would be an unhealthy future reliance on government support in times of difficulty. By 1932, he had secured congressional approval for a Reconstruction Finance Corporation, the biggest federal economy recovery effort ever to that time, a $2 billion program of low-cost loans to banks and other financial institutions to help them meet emergency needs and reinvigorate the economy. Hoover had shown during World War I that he was a man of deep humanitarian concern and generosity. At the same time, he was a shy man, unwilling to reveal his emotions and unable to stir an audience. Consequently, he came across to the public as cold and uncaring. Hoover's own limitations handicapped him in dealing with the crisis, but at the same time it was a catastrophe of such magnitude that his very failure may have been necessary to demonstrate to the American people and their other political leaders that cautious and conventional responses, even the relatively progressive ones that Hoover employed, were inadequate and that radical steps had become essential.

"At the End of Our String" By the end of President Hoover's term in office on March 4, 1933, the daily life of virtually all Americans had been disrupted by the economic collapse and reduced employment of the previous three years. The spreading bank holiday during the final weeks of his term brought what remained of the nation's financial system to a grinding halt. Daily life for the American people had been reduced to barter, subsistence, and worry. When Hoover told the press on March 3, "We are at the end of our string," he may have been speaking of his administration's efforts to cope with the depression, but he might as well have been referring to the mood of the nation. The American people awaited the swearing in of a new president, not so much because he inspired confidence but because he represented an alternative to Herbert Hoover, the leader so closely linked in the public's mind with indifference to the shocking economic and social catastrophe of recent years.

NOTE

1. U.S. Bureau of the Census, *Census of Partial Employment, Unemployment, and Occupations: 1937*, vol. 3 (Washington, D.C.: GPO, 1938), 71–97.

11

Creating the New Deal: A Larger Role for Government in Daily Life

A DISTANT FEDERAL GOVERNMENT

Before the onset of what 1932 Democratic presidential candidate Franklin D. Roosevelt pledged would be "a new deal for the American people," most residents of the country seldom encountered the U.S. government in their daily lives. In the nineteenth century, the only federal service directly reaching people was the U.S. mail. Even in that instance, prior to the establishment of rural free delivery in the 1890s, contact with a federal postal worker required a trip to the post office, something not on most daily schedules. Noncitizens entering the country, inventors registering a patent, and currency counterfeiters were the only ones almost certain to confront federal officials. Except during and just after the Civil War, the federal government imposed no direct taxes on individuals until 1913; thereafter it only levied a small graduated income tax on the wealthiest 10 percent of the population. Only times of war and military service created extensive contact with a federal government that was much expanded in the emergency situation. Every other year national elections raised issues for debate and drew a high percentage of adult white males to the polls, but election results seldom produced changes discernible at the grass roots. The addition of women to the electorate in 1920 and the simultaneous implementation of national alcohol prohibition increased the awareness and reality of the federal presence, but otherwise the U.S. government remained distant from their lives as people struggled with depression conditions.

EMERGENCY BANKING ACT

Beginning in Roosevelt's first week in office, the New Deal altered the role of the U.S. government in the daily affairs of the American people. On the day after he was sworn in, Roosevelt declared the already widespread bank holiday to be a national one, shut the few remaining banks, and summoned a special session of Congress to deal with the nation's financial crisis. When it met four days later, the House of Representatives took only a couple of hours to pass emergency banking legislation that most congressmen never even read but accepted because it was what the president said he wanted. The Senate acted just as rapidly, and the bill was on Roosevelt's desk for signature by the president's dinnertime. The Emergency Banking Act called for immediate federal inspection of all national banks (and state banks prepared to join the system), the reopening with federal endorsement of those banks determined to be sound, and new rules of operation to prohibit lending practices that had brought on the crisis. Within two weeks, 90 percent of banks were reopened and popular confidence in them was greater than ever before. If federal inspectors found them to be sound, what need was there to worry? In many cases, despite having gone more than a month without access to their accounts, people generally put more money back into the banks than they withdrew to pay bills. Some of the money that flowed into the banks had been hidden at home under floorboards and mattresses for fear that it would be lost if placed in a bank.

BANKING LEGISLATION RESTORES CONFIDENCE

Within the next three months, further banking legislation followed, enhancing confidence in the financial system and further protecting both lenders and debtors. Congressional Democrats insisted that the bank accounts of small depositors should be safeguarded by the government, whatever big investors and speculators might do. The Federal Deposit Insurance Corporation (FDIC), funded by a small tax on bank deposits, was created to insure accounts up to $500. The FDIC brought panicked runs on banks virtually to an end and proved to be one of the New Deal's most highly regarded and long-lasting achievements. The Home Owner's Loan Act helped banks by allowing them to exchange defaulted mortgages for government bonds. At the same time, home owners were able to save their dwellings by means of mortgages on more favorable terms. By 7:00 A.M. on the day that the Home Owner's Loan Corporation (HOLC) opened for business in Akron, Ohio, a double line of applicants stretched three blocks down Main Street. Eventually, the HOLC refinanced one out of every five home mortgages in America. Indirectly it strengthened the private mortgage market as well. In its prompt actions to deal with the banking crisis, Roosevelt's New Deal had directly affected millions of lives.

GOVERNMENT ECONOMIZES AND BREWERIES REOPEN

Following the reopening of the banks, Congress immediately took two additional steps. It passed a government economy act, cutting federal spending and salaries by 15 percent. Modern economists appreciate that such a reduction slows instead of stimulates the economy, but in March 1933, the act sent a message of a prudent government willing to share the pain being felt by its citizens. Then Congress quickly turned its attention to national prohibition. A constitutional amendment to repeal the widely despised Eighteenth Amendment had been approved near the end of the Congress that expired with the Hoover administration. The new amendment, however, would take many months to be ratified by three-fourths of the states. So, at Roosevelt's urging, Congress revised the definition of intoxicating beverages in order to remove the ban on drinks containing no more than 3.2 percent alcohol. By April 7, Americans again could drink beer legally. Celebrations erupted in many cities, none more enthusiastic than in the great beer brewing cities of St. Louis and Milwaukee. Being able to drink a legal glass of beer, even if it was fairly weak beer, or go to work in a brewery, gave millions of people a further sense, as the banking and economy acts had already done, that the new government was taking prompt and direct steps to improve their lives.

THE HUNDRED DAYS CONGRESS

Over the next several weeks the special session of Congress, which lasted exactly 100 days, adopted a series of other measures at the president's request or on its own initiative. Legislation provided relief to farmers, promoted industrial as well as financial recovery, and made available temporary jobs in a variety of federal projects. By the adjournment of the Hundred Days Congress, as it was known thereafter, a powerful sense had formed that the country and its economy were starting to move again and that the federal government was helping the American people in their daily struggles to cope with the depression.

THE NEW DEAL

In the years following the remarkable first phase of the Roosevelt administration, or the New Deal, as journalists and the public soon came to call it, further steps were taken by the federal government to deal with the causes and consequences of the depression. Some of these steps, such as the Securities Exchange Act of 1934, which established federal government oversight of stock markets, were important additions to the initiatives of 1933. Others were refinements of early legislation or substitute measures when initial efforts were found to have practical deficiencies or legal problems. Until late in the decade when attention began shifting to rising international problems and threats of war, the federal government continued its effort to deal with the ongoing depression. Throughout the 1930s, the New Deal stirred enthusiastic support, bitter opposition, and endless controversy. Matters of national politics and public policy came to concern people throughout the country because the impact on their own lives was so evident.

A PERSONALIZED PRESIDENCY

Franklin Roosevelt made use of radio far more than his predecessors, Harding, Coolidge, and Hoover, to whom it had been available. Roosevelt successfully employed radio in an attempt to connect with and gain the support of ordinary citizens. Not only were his formal presidential speeches broadcast (as had been the case with Coolidge and Hoover), but Roosevelt also conducted an unprecedented series of "fireside chats." These radio talks from a well-equipped White House studio were designed to create the impression of an informal living room conversation between FDR and his listeners. The president would explain calmly and in straightforward terms the legislation he was proposing and the steps he was taking to deal with the depression. The fireside chats attracted audiences estimated to be as large as 60 million and created, as never before, a sense of direct and personal connection between the president and the ordinary citizen.

Roosevelt possessed an extraordinary ability to convey a sense that he understood the circumstances of the average person, even though in fact he shared little in the way of life experiences with most of them. Indeed, FDR had led an unusually privileged life. The only child of wealthy aristocratic parents who lived on a comfortable estate overlooking the Hudson River, Roosevelt was graduated from Groton, a private school, and Harvard College, moved into New York and then national politics at an early age, and suffered only one serious setback on his climb to the presidency at the age of fifty, the 1921 polio attack that left him wheelchair dependent. Nevertheless, his radio messages, along with his presidential actions, forged a remarkable link between the president and the people.

A POLITICAL REVOLUTION

During his presidency Roosevelt managed to persuade many ordinary Americans, especially workers, immigrants, and minorities, to abandon the Republican party or to begin voting. He was so successful that the Democratic Party retained a near-constant national political majority from the time Roosevelt took office in 1932 until the late 1960s, nearly 25 years after his death in 1945. The political revolution he brought about at the grass roots went even further. Before Roosevelt, a reference to "the government" might mean either the city, county, state, or federal government. During the New Deal, the very language changed so that, unless they specified otherwise, people throughout the United States were speaking and thinking of FDR and the federal institutions centered in Washington, D.C., when they referred to "the government."

AID TO AGRICULTURE

Among the first issues the New Deal addressed was the agricultural depression that had gripped the nation since the early 1920s and was being made worse in the 1930s by drought conditions. During the 1920s, over 6 million people **Agricultural Depression** abandoned farm country; although births exceeded deaths, America's rural population had fallen by 1.2 million. Various solutions to the farm problem had been put forth, but no plan for government intervention could be agreed upon, and no proposal for private action enlisted sustained voluntary compliance. With American farmers able to produce more crops, livestock, and dairy products than the market could absorb, inadequate prices for farm commodities were a central problem. Farmers often found they could not even recover their costs, much less gain a sufficient profit to be able to earn a living. By 1930, over a quarter of U.S. farms, home to over 7.5 million people, produced less than $600 of farm products a year. Schemes to use government facilities or private cooperative programs to hold farm commodities off the market in order to obtain higher prices failed repeatedly. By 1933, some groups of angry farmers in Iowa and elsewhere resorted to crop burning and milk dumping to achieve the same result, but with no more success. With their mortgaged land and equipment in jeopardy of foreclosure, a mob of desperate farmers in LaMars, Iowa, even threatened to lynch their local banker.

The New Deal responded with the Agricultural Adjustment Act (AAA), the first of many programs that would come to be known by its initials. Adopted by the Hundred Days Congress in May 1933, the AAA set up a federal administration, also called the AAA, to pay farmers who **Agricultural Adjustment Act** agreed to plant one-third fewer acres or raise one-third fewer animals so that they would suffer no decline in income when they cut production. The funds for the payments came from a tax on processed food. In essence, consumers would pay a small tax on their food to provide a subsidy to farmers for not producing a surplus and weakening the overall farm economy.

**Planned
Inflation Angers
the Wealthy**

Another provision of the AAA, insisted on by farm state senators, sought to inflate the U.S. currency. Roosevelt had already taken a step in this direction weeks earlier by taking the United States off the gold standard, refusing to pledge, as in the past, to freely exchange dollars for a set amount of gold. The inflationary provision of the AAA moved the process much further. Inflated dollars would make it easier for debtors to repay mortgages and loans; thus, this measure benefited many indebted farmers, home owners, and small businesses. At the same time, however, planned inflation outraged lenders who blamed Roosevelt for cheating them out of what was legitimately theirs. Hatred of Roosevelt and charges that he was a dangerous radical spread quickly among the wealthy.

**Crop and
Livestock
Reduction**

While the AAA was a sensible enough plan to raise commodity prices, allow farmers to earn a decent living, and insure a dependable national food supply, it was not without problems. The division it widened between the rich and the rest of the people was only the first of them. The AAA was approved by Congress after southern farmers had just planted their cotton and after spring litters of hogs had been born. To receive their AAA payments in 1933, farmers had to plow up ten million acres of cotton fields and destroy six million baby pigs. At a time when hunger was a widespread problem, the "slaughter of little pigs," as critics called it, was hard for many Americans to understand.

The crop and pig destruction took place only in 1933; advance planning avoided the need to repeat the process thereafter. Still, in the same year, some moviegoers discerned a negative political message in Walt Disney's cartoon *The Three Little Pigs*. They equated the New Deal with the "Big Bad Wolf" who destroyed helpless creatures. The cartoon itself was ambiguous. Others viewed the wolf as a symbol of the depression; the wise little pig who planned ahead, worked hard, and built a solid house as a role model; and the musical accompaniment, "Who's Afraid of the Big Bad Wolf?" as an upbeat New Deal anthem. In any interpretation of Disney's cartoon or popular understanding of the AAA, however, little pigs remained a central theme.

**Tenant Farmers
Become Migrants**

By paying landowners to take cotton fields out of production, the AAA unintentionally undermined many southern tenant farmers by eliminating their opportunity to produce a crop, earn a meager living, and remain on the land. In 1935, the New Deal set up a new agency, the Resettlement Administration, to help tenant farmers relocate, but fewer than 5,000 farm families actually benefited. In 1937, another new agency, the Farm Security Administration (FSA), started helping more tenant farmers to buy land. But neither of these programs was adequately funded or successful. A stream of former tenant farmers from Arkansas and Oklahoma continued to head for the vegetable fields and citrus groves of California. By the end of the decade, a million migrants made the trek west. Perhaps the FSA's greatest achievement was the slight improvement it was able to bring about in the cleanliness, order, and health conditions of migrant labor camps. Otherwise, the landless rural southern poor remained, at the end of the 1930s, the most wretched group of Americans.

In 1936, the Supreme Court ruled that the AAA was unconstitutional. The food-processing tax used to fund the program, a conservative-dominated Court decided, was not a legitimate use of federal power to levy taxes. Farm commodity prices immediately began to fall. The administration responded quickly by devising a new law, the Soil Conservation and Domestic Allotment Act, which paid farmers to plant soil-enriching grasses and legumes instead of soil-depleting crops such as cotton or corn. The basic plan of subsidizing farmers to restrict production and boost farm prices did not change, though the funding now came from the federal government's general budget rather than a special tax, and so the program was widely referred to as the Second AAA. Farm production, income, and life did not suffer a lasting setback from the Court's ruling, but it was not until World War II that the long agricultural depression was fully over. **Getting around the Supreme Court**

The New Deal altered rural agricultural life significantly by bringing affordable electricity to many of the nine-out-of-ten farms that lacked it. One of the important acts of the Hundred Days Congress was the establishment of the Tennessee Valley Authority (TVA). The TVA assumed control of hydroelectric dams and munitions factories built along the Tennessee River during World War I. These facilities were turned into providers of low-cost electricity and fertilizer for the river's watershed. By providing electricity at the cost of production, Roosevelt explained, the TVA would provide a "yardstick" to measure what power should cost as opposed to the four times higher per kilowatt hour price that private utility companies were charging at his rural, Warm Springs, Georgia, cottage compared with the price charged at his Hyde Park, New York, home. The TVA boosted the economically backward eight-state Tennessee Valley region's agricultural productivity as well as gave its rural residents access to electric power. In so doing, the TVA established a model for regional power and economic development that the New Deal soon tried to copy along the Colorado, upper Missouri, Columbia, and other rivers. **Tennessee Valley Authority**

Electrifying
Rural America
The creation, in May 1935, of the Rural Electrification Administration (REA) made government loans available to assist power companies and nonprofit cooperatives in erecting electric transmission lines in rural areas. Previously, that had not been commercially feasible because rural America had too few electric customers spread too far apart. Thus, many rural dwellers continued to make do with wood, coal, kerosene, and candles for heat and light. Some farmers used a gasoline-powered generator or an extra automobile battery to obtain a little electricity, while others did without. The isolation and sense of backwardness resulting from lack of access to the electricity that powered urban America evaporated as soon as the REA brought electric lines into the countryside. By 1940, a third of American farms had acquired electricity, and ten years later, 90 percent had done so. The ability to switch on electric lights, motors, and appliances transformed rural life both technologically and psychologically.

SUPPORT FOR THE EMPLOYED

Putting People
Back to Work
Putting people back to work and reviving American business was another of Roosevelt's prime objectives at the outset of the New Deal. Before the administration could put forth a plan to accomplish this, senators talked about adopting a law reducing the workweek to five six-hour days. The thirty-hour plan assumed that the American economy had reached a point where it could efficiently produce more goods and services than could be consumed. Thus, for everyone wanting a job to be able to have one, the available work needed to be spread out. Alabama Democratic Senator Hugo Black, the thirty-hour plan's chief sponsor, did not think incomes would shrink as much as working hours, but even if they did, the overall situation would be improved. Incomes might be smaller, but at least a significantly greater number of people could support themselves. Society and government then would not have to contend with a substantial portion of the population constantly out of work and a burden on others.

National
Industrial
Recovery Act
Rather than accept such an assessment, Roosevelt sought to stimulate a business rehabilitation that would link economic growth, job creation, and better treatment of workers. The National Industrial Recovery Act of June 1933 sought to modify traditional free enterprise cutthroat competition, ruinous price-cutting, and harsh treatment of workers by allowing companies in the same industry to cooperate without being accused of monopolistic practices. Under the supervision of the government's National Recovery Administration (NRA), competing companies

would agree on (1) minimum prices for their goods and services; (2) minimum wages and maximum hours for employees; and (3) fair working conditions and a reasonable code of business conduct. Companies participating in the NRA would also be obliged to bargain collectively with workers who chose to form labor unions. As he had done with banking reform, Roosevelt was striving with the NRA to rescue the private enterprise system by eliminating its worst excesses and requiring it to function under the supervision of government agencies that would seek to protect the public interest.

As the NRA started to function in the summer of 1933, many businesses hurried to agree on codes of fair competition. This allowed them to display the symbol of compliance, the NRA Blue Eagle, and gain the customer support that followed. Everywhere newspapers ads and store windows featured the NRA Blue Eagle and the slogan, "We Do Our Part." In New York, a Fifth Avenue parade to demonstrate support for the NRA drew a quarter million marchers.

By October 1933, the ten largest industries had all agreed to NRA codes, and many smaller industries soon followed suit. In return for their concessions (higher wages, acceptance of the principle of collective bargaining, and abolition of child labor in the cotton textile industry), the NRA allowed industries to set higher prices and limits on production. Not every business accepted its industry's code. Henry Ford, for instance, charged that the automobile code was a plot of his competitors to limit his success and refused to sign. Most business, however, went along with the NRA, and signs of renewed business confidence and recovery started to appear. The downward economic spiral ceased, wages and hours stabilized, and nearly two million jobs were created.

Criticism of the NRA did not take long to appear. Consumers soon complained about rising prices, businesses objected to government regulation and paperwork, and workers found that collective bargaining pledges went unfulfilled by business and unenforced by the government. The greatest complaint was that the NRA codes let the big companies in an industry set the competitive rules and put their smaller rivals at a disadvantage. Before long enthusiasm for the NRA was fading. By the time that the Supreme Court in 1935 found it to represent an unconstitutionally broad delegation of legislative power to an administrative agency, the NRA had already lost its effectiveness, done in by its reliance on voluntary cooperation with guidelines that the federal government helped to set but then did not enforce.

Abandoning efforts to secure business cooperation, in 1935 the New Deal moved in the direction of strengthening workers' ability to bargain collectively and effectively, presuming that this would lead to fair wages,   **National Labor Relations Act** hours, and working conditions. Competition, together with fair treatment of workers, would keep business functioning properly in an open market. The National Labor Relations Act, proposed by New York Senator Robert Wagner and endorsed by FDR once it passed the Senate, had a dramatic effect on many workers. The Wagner Act, as it was frequently called, compelled employers to deal with the labor unions that employees—in elections supervised by the National Labor Relations Board (NLRB)—chose to represent them. The act also prohibited unfair labor practices such as discharging workers for union membership, favoring an employer-dominated company union, or refusing to negotiate in good faith with a union. All of these practices had long been common before the National Industrial Recovery Act and continued after its adoption. But now, with an independent federal agency overseeing labor relations, the weight of the federal government stood behind organized workers in their efforts to negotiate better terms of employment.

Two years later, the Supreme Court upheld the constitutionality of the Wagner Act, confirming a fundamental change in the relationship between no longer all-powerful employers and no longer helpless employees. From the adoption of the Wagner Act in 1935 until the Supreme Court's approval of it in 1937, the NLRB was asked to conduct 76 elections in which workers could choose whether or not to be represented by a union; from that point to the end of 1940, the NLRB supervised 3,310 such elections. The American Federation of Labor (AFL) or the Congress of Industrial Organizations (CIO) won over three-quarters of all such elections, labor unions became a workplace reality for over a third of American workers, and even nonunionized workers began to share in improved wages and working conditions.

Unionization Efforts

Workers in some industries where treatment had been particularly brutal or compensation especially low moved most quickly to take advantage of the Wagner Act. The great manufacturing industries—automobiles, steel, and rubber—were among the first to undergo unionization campaigns. Employers found it hard to avoid NLRB elections to establish unions, but found that as long as they agreed to keep talking to union representatives and appeared to be negotiating, they could easily resist agreeing to a contract. Such tactics frustrated workers in the rubber and auto industries who turned to sit-down strikes in which they simply took over a factory, refusing either to work or to leave, knowing it unlikely that employers would remove them forcibly for fear of damage to valuable machinery. Workers in these and other industries formed picket lines to block companies that refused to settle with unions from doing business. Violence erupted on numerous occasions between security forces hired by stubborn employers and workers frustrated by failure to gain a satisfactory contract.

In 1938, the New Deal acknowledged that unions alone
could not do everything for their members, much less   **Fair Labor**
those workers who remained unorganized. FDR obtained   **Standards Act**
congressional approval of its last major measure for
workers, the Fair Labor Standards Act. Adoption of this act, which set
minimum wages and maximum working hours, was one mark of the
relaxation, after 1937, of the Supreme Court's opposition to federal regulation of interstate commerce. The Fair Labor Standards Act granted
many exceptions to its coverage, but nevertheless established a $.40 min-
imum wage and a higher rate for work in excess of forty hours per week.
These provisions improved wages and shortened the normal work week
for those who worked in the most depressed and labor-unfriendly industries.

The Fair Labor Standards Act, in effect, created the modern American weekend. The standard six-day workweek of   **A Two-Day**
nine, ten, twelve, or even more hours per day in   **Weekend**
nineteenth-century industry had gradually given way in
some sectors of the economy during the early twentieth century to a five-
and-a-half-day week with a half holiday on Saturday and a full day of
rest on Sunday. The reduction in hours for so many workers during the
1930s moved the nation toward acceptance of a shorter work week. The
Fair Labor Standards Act made a workweek with two full days free from
obligatory labor the standard pattern even when the economy revived.
Farm life was more difficult to change, given the daily needs of livestock
and the pressures of the planting and harvest seasons, but as in other
respects, what became conventional in urban, industrial practice set the
standard for the rest of the nation.

WORK FOR THE UNEMPLOYED

While trying to restore the industrial economy consti-
tuted a long-term goal of the New Deal, providing relief   **Government**
to people in distress was an immediate concern. Encour-   **Relief Work**
aging reeployment of workers by the private sector was
a prime objective of the National Industrial Recovery Act. But from the
first weeks of the Hundred Days Congress, another major focus of the
New Deal was creating temporary government-sponsored jobs until
the private sector could once again provide positions. "Make-work
jobs" turned out to be one of the things for which the New Deal became best known.

Government relief jobs, especially those that did not lead to any worthwhile accomplishment or the larger number that did not appear to require great exertion, caused some who held such jobs and others who
observed them to view federal employment in a negative light. The New

Deal, however, took the position that it was important not to simply hand out relief checks. Instead, the New Deal sought to put people into positions where they would do something in return for public support, regain a measure of self-esteem, and receive a paycheck sufficient to allow them to spend money to stimulate the economy. Some taxpayers, lacking this vision of the economic and social objectives of work-relief programs, understandably resented what they saw as wasteful spending on unnecessary projects and unproductive workers.

The New Deal embraced the widespread notion that a distinction could and should be drawn between the "worthy poor," whose impoverished situation was no fault of their own, and "lazy and shiftless people," who chose their lot and did not deserve assistance. Screening people to determine whether they were truly destitute or merely shamming was justified on these grounds. This approach limited relief to people who had exhausted their assets and led some to resist seeking government relief jobs because it required them to admit that they were destitute. Consequently, unemployment relief did not reach all of those who faced unemployment and poverty because of the depression.

Civilian Conservation Corps
Roosevelt himself devised the first New Deal work-relief program, the Civilian Conservation Corps (CCC), to put young men to work planting trees, building national park facilities, fighting fires, and doing other worthwhile tasks to improve public land. CCC workers were required to be between seventeen and twenty-five and from families already on relief. They lived in camps run by the U.S. Army, and, in addition to room, board, and medical care, were paid $30 per month, three-quarters of which was sent home to their families. Within three months nearly a quarter million young men had enlisted. Eligibility requirements were later eased and enrollment peaked at 500,000 in 1935. During the program's nine-year existence some 2.5 million men served in the CCC, including 200,000 African Americans in segregated camps.

Federal Emergency Relief Act
The Federal Emergency Relief Act of May 1933 provided $500 million in grants to the states. Every federal dollar was to be matched by three city or state dollars for work-relief projects. The Federal Emergency Relief Administration (FERA), understanding that city and state officials would reserve their funds for their own residents, also set up a special program to help transient or migrant workers. Another program was designed to help move farm families from submarginal acreage to more fertile land. At one time or another, FERA employed 2.5 million workers and aided thousands of farmers. It gained a reputation as wasteful, in part because some state officials tried to manipulate it for their own political advan-

tage and also because some of its projects seemed to have little purpose other than putting a relief check in the hands of those in need.

The National Industrial Recovery Act, adopted a month after FERA, contained a provision establishing **Public Works** the Public Works Administration (PWA) with a first- **Administration** year $1.3 billion budget to construct highways, bridges, tunnels, dams, federal buildings, and other projects. The PWA would also pay 30 percent of the cost of state and local school, water, and sewage facility construction. In the course of the decade, the PWA, working with states and municipalities, spent $6 billion on public works construction, employed an average of 140,000 workers a year, and was responsible for the creation of another 600,000 jobs. Among other things, it funded half of all school-building construction during the 1930s.

Since its projects were complex and often took some time to plan, the PWA did not put as many people to **Civil Works** work as quickly as the New Deal had hoped. In No- **Administration** vember 1933, FDR took $400 million from the PWA budget to create the Civil Works Administration (CWA), an entirely federal program that employed workers on public projects ranging from paving 265,000 miles of streets and roads to constructing 40,000 schools and 469 airports to less-substantial projects that would put as many people to work as possible. Within a month, nearly 4 million previously unemployed people went to work for the CWA. Although it only lasted a few months, the CWA helped many people get through the harsh winter of 1933–1934 and stimulated some economic recovery. But concerned about the costs of an ongoing federal work-relief program and believing that the economy was rebounding, FDR allowed the CWA to expire in April 1934.

A year later, the depression persisted and Roosevelt committed the New Deal to a far larger federal work- **Works Progress** relief program than the CWA. The Works Progress Ad- **Administration** ministration (WPA) was established in May 1935 with a $5 billion budget, the largest single appropriation in U.S. history up to that time. The WPA replaced the FERA, left relief of the aged, the handicapped, and the unemployable to the new Social Security Administration and the states, and focused on providing public jobs for the otherwise unemployed. By the time it ended in the midst of World War II, the WPA (reduced and renamed in 1939 as the Works Projects Administration but retaining the same initials) spent over $11 billion and employed as many as 3.3 million people at a time. WPA workers built thousands of hospitals, schools, airports, highways, sidewalks, utility plants, parks, and recreation facilities. The WPA even put some 40,000 unemployed artists and intellectuals to work on a variety of cultural projects.

New Deal relief programs provided a variety of opportunities for workers with different skills and needs. At this Michigan work site in 1939, WPA construction workers built curbs and sidewalks as a WPA artist sketched them at work. Photo courtesy of the National Archives.

In addition to reconstructing the American landscape in an unprecedented fashion, the WPA put perhaps one-third of all unemployed Americans to work at an average monthly income of $50. This gave millions of hard-pressed people not only an income, but a daily activity and renewed self-respect. The WPA, in turn, stimulated economic recovery and similar social effects in the private sector. Still, in many eyes, the WPA was not a complete success. Since people had to be certified by local authorities as unemployed and eligible for a work assignment, some individuals who desired work were turned away. Women and minorities in particular faced discrimination. Critics viewed some of the projects as fraudulent and workers as "boondogglers."

National Youth Administration   A final important work-relief program of the New Deal, the National Youth Administration (NYA), was aimed specifically at helping unemployed young people. Overall it involved nearly twice as many persons as the CCC. Established in June 1935, the NYA was not simply a "junior WPA." Instead it sought to combine education and work. The NYA funded part-time jobs, often on campuses, for 1.5 million high school students and over 600,000 college students struggling to afford to stay in school.

It also provided skills and citizenship education along with full-time employment for nearly 2.7 million out-of-school youth working in NYA projects. Altogether nearly 5 million NYA participants received the lasting benefits of further education as well as the immediate benefits of work and income during the depression.

Some Americans felt embarrassed by having to take a New Deal work-relief job in the 1930s, whether **Mixed Feelings** through the CCC, FERA, PWA, CWA, WPA, or NYA. They found it demeaning and a mark of personal failure. Others regarded such a job as a godsend, an escape from unmanageable circumstances, a means of supporting their family, a chance to practice their craft, learn new skills, and make new friends in the workplace. Some people had mixed feelings, but ultimately it appears that most saw these jobs as opportunities to do meaningful work that they could point to with pride. Whether they helped build a school, sports or entertainment facility, airport, federal building, paved road, or other public facility, they believed that they had participated in a worthwhile improvement of their community and at the same time had personally triumphed over the depression.

AID FOR THE AGED AND OTHERS

Helping those people who were able to work to secure employment in the midst of the depression challenged **Traditional** the New Deal. Helping those unable to work because of **Social Welfare** age, disability, or other circumstances proved even more difficult. Above all, federal action in this respect ran counter to the American tradition that attending to the social welfare of those unable to provide for themselves was the responsibility of families first, then private charities, and, finally, communities and states. Families had always been the primary caregivers, taking in aged parents and relatives, providing for the physically or mentally unfit, and assisting victims of misfortune. Private charities through churches and other community-based institutions had been able to deal with most of the exceptions, and, as a last resort, local and state governments usually took action. The depression of the 1930s tested traditional social welfare arrangements and found them wanting. The huge number of people who found themselves destitute or nearly so became vocal advocates of change.

Louisiana Senator Huey Long claimed that 9 million people spread across every state had joined Share Our **New Tax Plans** Wealth Clubs inspired by his plan to tax heavily large incomes, property holdings, and inheritances in order to provide every family with an adequate annual income. Long's movement still appeared to be gathering force in September 1935, when he was assassinated in

Alternatives to the New Deal were constantly presented to the American people. The Townsend Plan proposed a monthly grant to all citizens over age sixty in which they would be required to spend it all and thereby stimulate the economy. Photo courtesy of the Library of Congress.

the Louisiana State Capitol in Baton Rouge. Without its charismatic leader, the movement faltered, despite the strenuous efforts of Long's assistant, Gerald L. K. Smith, to keep it alive. Nevertheless, the New Deal's Wealth Tax Act of 1935, an increased and graduated tax on estates, gifts, and capital gains to help fund government relief and social welfare efforts, represented, in part, an attempt to address the grassroots discontent Long had stirred.

Between 1933 and 1935, at least 10 million people signed petitions endorsing another radical formula to redistribute income, the Townsend Plan. Dr. Francis Townsend of Long Beach, California, urged that every American citizen above age sixty (noncitizens need not apply) be given $200 per month provided they gave up paying jobs (which would provide work for younger people), had no criminal record or other income (they thus belonged to the "worthy" poor), and spent it all within the month (which would stimulate economic activity). Dr. Townsend became wildly popular among people age sixty or older, four-fifths of whom he estimated would be eligible for benefits. Many, especially in the West, joined Townsend Clubs to agitate for the plan's adoption. The superficially plausible design had fundamental flaws. It proposed to finance the payments with a 2 percent tax on business transactions. Journalist Walter Lippmann calculated that, given the current $30 billion per year in total annual business sales and the $20 to $24 billion cost of the Townsend benefits, a sales tax to fund its costs fully would need to be set at 70 percent. Furthermore, enforcing the requirement to spend all the money every month would be impossible without creating a vast federal inspection force. Finally, the plan would directly benefit only the one-in-eleven Americans who had passed their sixtieth birthday.

As imperfect as Share Our Wealth, the Townsend Plan, or other schemes advocated by farm leader Milo Reno and Catholic radio broadcaster Father Charles Coughlin may have been, they all spoke to a serious national problem: how should American society care for those who, even when the economy functioned normally, were unable to care for themselves? With the average person living longer, the number of Americans age sixty-five or older had grown 59 percent just since 1920, from 4.9 to 7.8 million. The number over sixty had climbed to more than 12 million. An unknown but significant number of persons were blind or otherwise permanently disabled. Tens of thousands of children had a single parent, or none at all, to care for them. Finally, of course, there were the unemployed and destitute who, for one reason or another, were not participating in a work-relief program. Not to provide for the welfare of the needy was increasingly seen as uncivilized by Americans who were learning in the depression decade that they themselves might suddenly be among those in need.

The Social Security Act of 1935 established a system whereby the federal government oversaw a program of social welfare for retirees and, with state administration and matching funds, aid for the unemployed, aged indigents, the blind or otherwise disabled, and dependent children of single mothers. The system was far from comprehensive. In its unemployment insurance and retirement pension program, the federal government, understanding itself to be restricted by the Constitution, only sought to deal with workers involved in interstate commerce. Thus, the system excluded, among others, farm laborers and domestic servants, two of the poorest and most needy categories of workers. Those included were expected to pay for its benefits through a tax on every paycheck until they retired at age sixty-five. Amendments to the law in 1939 provided benefits to the surviving spouse of a participant in the system.

Levying a Social Security payroll tax on both employers and employees placed responsibility on working individuals to contribute to their own retirement. Pension benefits would eventually be paid in proportion to the length and volume of contributions, much like private pension systems set up earlier by some employers. In this respect the system stood in marked contrast to European state welfare systems for which

Social Security

all citizens were eligible and that paid a standard unemployment or pension benefit out of general tax revenues. The comparatively conservative U.S. system was not only less sweeping in its coverage and less generous with its benefits, but, by taxing every paycheck, it took money out of the pockets of people who otherwise would spend it to help revive the economy. Roosevelt justified the approach as necessary to win political approval and thereafter guarantee that Social Security could not be dismantled. The employee contributions, the numbered identification card that every participant was given to carry in his or her billfold or purse, and thus a large public sense of entitlement would make it impossible, FDR thought, for any politician to argue successfully for a reduction or end to Social Security benefits.

Social Security funds began to be used immediately to provide unemployment compensation together with a limited amount of disability relief and aid for dependent children. The last two categories were so small as to be largely invisible during the 1930s. Under the terms of its legislation, it was not until 1940 that Social Security began paying pension benefits averaging $22.60 per month to those retirees who had been paying into the system. Anyone who retired between 1937 and 1940 received only a small lump sum settlement; those who retired before 1937 got nothing.

Entitlements and "Doles" Only when Social Security began delivering pension benefits to those who could be said to have earned them, did the program come to be regarded as an entitlement, a deserved repayment for contributions to the system. Until that time, many Americans continued to think of the New Deal social welfare system as a "dole" to the improvident and irresponsible. Public attitudes wavered between the view that individuals should take responsibility for themselves and the belief that society had a duty to aid the unfortunate. Despite abundant evidence during the depression that people in need of help were usually victims of circumstances beyond their control, the attitude lingered—and was reinforced by the design of the U.S. social welfare system—that those who did not earn their benefits were welfare "spongers" and "chiselers," if not downright "cheats." The distinction born in the 1930s between earned entitlement to social welfare and unearned (and somehow undeserved) access would long persist in the minds of the American people.

A DEMOCRATIC CULTURE

A New Culture While the New Deal focused on the renewal and reform of American economic life, and in so doing altered social and political arrangements, it also reshaped cultural life for millions of Americans. The high culture of literature, music, theater, and visual arts that had been largely the preserve of an elite came to be shared with a far more diverse population. At the same time, the culture of cinema, popular music, and photography aimed at a mass audience was sustained in a time of high demand for inexpensive entertainment. Large-scale government support for culture was unprecedented in the United States, but Franklin Roosevelt and those around him understood that exposure to the arts enriched life. Therefore, by design, the New Deal helped fashion a new culture aimed at and ultimately supported by the general public.

One of the noteworthy features of the New Deal's relief and recovery program was its recognition that the depression had struck hard at not only the patrons of high culture but also its creators. Artists, writers, composers, and performers found themselves unemployed at least as often as any other jobless group, and, because what they produced was considered a luxury, more so than most. In a series of special programs the New Deal put these creative individuals to work at tasks that would bring their art to a broader audience than they had ever before reached.

Initial public works programs in 1933 under the FERA and CWA included the arts in their plans for government buildings. At first, unemployed artists were put to work painting murals in 1,200 post offices and other federal facilities. **Art for Public Buildings** These murals were intended to depict the landscape, history, and everyday life of the community and region in which they were located. Painting the murals required artists to look at situations around them, and the completed projects gave viewers a sense that art could relate to daily life. The early successes of public building art projects, many of which still survive, helped lead the WPA to include artists in its relief work planning.

The WPA established four special programs that eventually employed about 40,000 out-of-work artists in endeavors that reached an enormous audience. The **Special Programs** Federal Writers Project (FWP) sponsored over 6,000 writers to write articles, pamphlets, and books concerning all aspects of American life from history and folklore to nature and African American studies. In its most noted project, the FWP set teams of gifted writers to the task of producing a guidebook for every state. These guidebooks, initially sold for about $2.50, gave residents, travelers, and other readers vivid descriptions of a state's landscape, history, culture, government, and people. Many of the FWP guides remained in print a half century later, unsurpassed as descriptions of the states. The Federal Art Project (FAP) yielded over 2,500 murals, 17,000 sculptures, 100,000 paintings, and 11,000 graphic designs for the public to view in high schools, community centers, hospitals, and government offices. The Federal Theatre Project (FTP) sent actors and crews to present plays ranging from Shakespeare to George Bernard Shaw and Eugene O'Neill to contemporary American playwrights in communities across the land, 60 percent of which had never experienced a live professional theater performance. The Federal Music Project (FMP) followed suit, putting professional musicians, unusually hard hit by the depression, to work as teachers and conductors of amateur groups and as performers. By 1940, FMP teachers had conducted 1.5 million classes involving nearly 18 million vocal and instrumental students, while FMP performers gave 250,000 orchestra, band, and ensemble concerts heard by 150 million people, not counting the radio audience for 14,000 broadcast concerts. The FMP brought professional musicians and performances to audiences large and small in urban settings and out-of-the-way places. Altogether the WPA arts projects introduced millions of Americans to the excitement of first-hand contact with creative artistry. Reactions varied, but audiences and artists felt the effects of this unprecedented mass distribution of high culture.

Other New Deal programs employed artistry in different ways that ended up reaching large audiences. Most notable was the Farm Security Administration (FSA) project to have skilled photographers create a documentary record of contemporary America. Employing a handful of exceptionally talented still photographers to travel throughout the nation between 1935 and 1941 taking pictures of ordinary people in their everyday lives, the FSA photography project eventually produced a collection of images that one admirer called "endless fractions of reality."[1] Concentrating on agriculture, from farm work to food processing, but covering a wide variety of urban as well as rural topics, the FSA project captured a quarter million images, made them available through newspapers, magazines, and other forums, and shaped the public's understanding of what the depression was like beyond their own experience. Bleak black-and-white images of the rural South and displaced "Okies" migrating to California proved particularly memorable and permanently molded public understanding and memory of the era. The worn and weary face of a migrant woman photographed by Dorothea Lange became perhaps the best-known image of the 1930s after the smiling face of Franklin Roosevelt, though neither could be said to be typical of the era.

Influence of New Deal Art   New Deal programs involving the arts soon made their mark on privately created mass culture. For instance, when filmmaker John Ford made a movie of *The Grapes of Wrath*, John Steinbeck's novel of the Okie migrant experience, he mimicked the FSA photography style in order to persuade his audience that his was an honest and authentic portrayal of real lives. Similarly, a new large-format weekly magazine called *Life* sought and achieved instant and unparalleled popularity when it began appearing in 1936 with its principal content of black-and-white documentary photographs, a few borrowed from FSA, others taken by the same photographers or their imitators. At a time when most news of the world beyond their personal view reached people in either printed form or from radio, the vivid, carefully composed FSA photos shaped their sense of what was going on and whetted their appetite for more products of this new culture.

The documentary style reached into other aspects of American culture during the 1930s as well. Government **Documentaries** agencies made documentary films to demonstrate the need for flood control and soil conservation. *The River* and *The Plow That Broke the Plains* were powerfully effective and widely seen. Among the Federal Theatre Project's most frequently repeated presentations were a series of plays about contemporary real-life events. With titles such as *Power, Steel,* and *Living Newspapers* and with sympathetic characterizations of workers, labor unions, immigrants, and minorities, these plays expressed viewpoints that were often more starkly critical of social and economic conditions as well as more reformist than the New Deal itself. Conservative cries that these documentary-style plays were "subversive" and "communistic" eventually undermined political support for the FTP.

By its various documentary efforts as well as its other attempts to measure the extent and impact of the de- **Federal Help** pression, the New Deal made the lives of ordinary peo- **Now Expected** ple more visible to the federal government. At the same time, the great variety of federal relief and recovery efforts that directly touched people at the grass roots made the nation's central government more immediately visible and meaningful to these same people. The specific actions of the New Deal to respond to the depression were unquestionably important in the 1930s. However, what may have been more profound and what was certainly more long lasting was the cultural shift produced by the New Deal. Franklin Roosevelt's administration altered popular expectations so that for the first time in U.S. history, the federal government's response to the needs of ordinary individuals, not members of special groups such as veterans, slaves, immigrants, or elites, became the normal political expectation. In other words, the American political culture became more genuinely democratic than ever before.

NOTE

1. Alfred Kazin, *On Native Ground* (New York: Reynal & Hitchcock, 1942), 496.

12

Continuity and Change: America at the End of the 1930s

By the end of the 1930s, the worst of the Great Depression lay in the past. That, of course, was less evident to people at the time than to those with historical perspective who know that just ahead lay World War II with all its social upheaval and economic revitalization. At the end of the depression decade some people were paying increasing attention to events abroad and worrying about the marching armies of Japan, Germany, and Italy, but most Americans believed that such distant occurrences bore little relevance to their own situation. Life in the United States, they expected, would continue to unfold much the same as it had recently.

Americans could look back two decades to the Great War without having a hint that such a pivotal event would soon be relabeled World War I. Round two of the great conflict would take place between similarly aligned forces but on an even more immense scale. World War II would, like its predecessor, have a significant impact on the United States, transforming its economy and society, elevating the status of its women and people of color, advancing its technology, and propelling it into a position of international leadership. In so doing, the Second World War would alter the course of American daily life and set the 1940s and after distinctly apart from the previous decades.

The two decades following World War I produced notable technological advances, cultural shifts, economic ups and downs, and political changes. By the end of the 1930s, conditions seemed to those at the grass roots to have reached something of an equilibrium. Many of the advances in day-to-day living conditions had been absorbed into people's daily routine. The highs and lows of the economy had been succeeded by a situation somewhere in between where few appeared to be getting rich but most were getting by. Having achieved a measure of perceived stability for the moment, it was no wonder that most people anticipated a future much like the present.

Assessing American life on the eve of the tremendous changes wrought by World War II is certainly appropriate. Such stocktaking is necessary in order to appreciate the impact of events soon to occur. Of equal importance, the appraisal permits a consideration of what American life had become before the intrusion of the Second World War. Historians tend to evaluate situations in light of developments they know will follow. While such an approach often produces insight, it tends to focus on matters that will later assume importance rather than on those that at the time were seen to possess significance. Taking stock of a moment can also be useful simply to survey the circumstances on their own terms. English historian C. V. Wedgwood once observed, "We know the end of the story before we know the beginning, and we can never fully recapture what it was like to be present at the creation."[1] Looking at the United States at the end of the 1930s, we cannot today remain entirely oblivious to the war that lay just ahead, but we can seek to better understand on its own terms American life on the eve of World War II.

THE AMERICAN PEOPLE BY DECADE'S END

1940 Census   As it does at the conclusion of every decade, the Census Bureau provided a statistical picture of the United States at the end of the 1930s. The bureau collected data on the situation of the nation and its residents in April 1940. When compared with data from the January 1920 census, the 1940 results offer evidence of the alterations that had taken place over two decades. The comparison also indicates many conditions that did not undergo significant change. The new data provide as well measures of the impact of the depression and the extent of the recovery. Individual variations in circumstances and experiences are lost in numerical compilations, but the statistical profile is nonetheless worthwhile.

Increased Life Expectancy   In twenty years the nation's population had grown 24 percent from 106.5 million to 132.1 million. Two-thirds of the increase occurred in the 1920s before depression conditions led to a sharp drop in births. Life expectancy had lengthened from 56.3 to 62.8 years for males and from 58.5 to 67.3 years for females. Combined with far fewer births, longer life expectancy produced a notably older population than had been the case two decades earlier. Children under the age of fifteen now represented only 25 percent of the population instead of the 31.6 percent of 1920. The percentage of Americans over the age of sixty had expanded from 7.4 to 10.4, and those over sixty-five now accounted for 6.8 percent instead of just 4.6 percent. The population's median age had risen from 25.3 to 29 years.[2]

Marital arrangements remained outwardly stable during these decades. Sixty-three percent of males and 61 percent of **Families** females over fourteen told the 1940 census takers that they were married. Thirty-one percent of males and 24 percent of females said that they were single. Five percent of males and 13 percent of females reported that they were widowed. About 1.3 percent of males and 1.7 percent of females acknowledged that they were divorced. The longer life expectancy of women accounted for most of the gender differences in the totals. The figures conceal the number of abandonments without divorce and likewise the number of families that stayed together only because of economic necessity. While those instances were, by other indications, more frequent in the 1930s than before, they had not been altogether absent earlier. Therefore, the most valid conclusion to be drawn may be that the overall profile of American marital relationships changed only modestly during the period.

Likewise, the ethnic balance remained stable. Whites constituted 89.7 percent of the population, blacks 9.8 percent, Na- **Ethnicity** tive Americans 0.25 percent, and Asians 0.19 percent. The number of foreign-born individuals within the population had declined significantly as a result of the immigration restriction laws of the early 1920s. Whereas just prior to World War I, one million immigrants entered the United States each year, the number dropped to 300,000 per year during the war and rebounded to only 400,000 during the 1920s. In the depression decade, immigration fell to 50,000 per year, and when the economy was at its worst in 1933, more aliens departed the United States than entered. Among those listed in the 1940 census as white, 11.2 percent of males and 10.1 percent of females were foreign born, while another 21.6 percent of males and 21.7 percent of females had one or more foreign-born parents. In twenty years the percentage of white residents who either had come to the United States or were children of those who had done so dropped from almost 45 percent to slightly over 32 percent. This decline, which would continue, reduced outside influences on life in the United States and contributed to a less culturally diverse society.

The movement of the American people into urban areas had accelerated in the 1920s, but then slackened in **Urban Growth** the 1930s. Between 1920 and 1930, the percentage of people living in urban places (as defined by the modest standards of the Census Bureau) increased from 50.8 percent to 56 percent. By 1940, no doubt as a result of the depression and the difficulties of city life, the urban population rose only to 56.3 percent. Overall, however, this meant that 20 million more people, 74.4 million in 1940 compared to 54.1 million in 1920, resided in urban places. During the same period of time the rural population also grew, but only from 51.6 to 57.2 million.

The largest cities encompassed much of the era's urban growth, particularly during the 1920s. Cities with more than 500,000 residents swelled from twelve with 16.4 million people in 1920 to thirteen with 20.8 million in 1930 to fourteen with 22.4 million by 1940. Cities of 100,000 to 500,000 increased over the same twenty-year period from 56 to 78 in number and from 11.1 million to 15.6 million in population. In the 1930s, communities of 10,000 to 100,000 grew the most and at the end of the decade totaled 984 with 24.7 million residents, in contrast to 684 with 16.3 million people in 1920 and 889 with 22 million in 1930. Over the same twenty-year span, towns of 2,500 to 10,000 enlarged in number from 1,970 to 2,387 with combined population growth from 9.4 million to 11.7 million. Villages under 2,500 expanded from 12,855 with 6 million residents to 13,288 with 9.3 million. Rural dwellers completely outside of settled communities had aggregated 42.6 million in 1920, and by 1940 totaled 47.9 million. Thus, while the 24 percent population growth of the era was concentrated in urban areas, it was distributed across the country.

Northeast Most Populated

As had been the case twenty years earlier, almost exactly half of the nation's 1940 residents lived north of the Potomac and Ohio Rivers and east of the Mississippi. Growth meant that this quadrant's population density rose significantly to an average of more than 172 people per square mile by 1940. (For comparative 1920 regional and density figures, see Chapter 1.) The states of the old Confederacy, while retaining about a quarter of the population, experienced only a slight rise in density to forty-six people per square mile. The states of Missouri, California, and Texas still contained the largest populations outside the northeast quadrant, but they only grew to 55, 44, and 24 people per square mile, respectively, a sharp contrast to the most urban northeastern states, Rhode Island, New Jersey, and Massachusetts, which reached statewide densities of 680, 553, and 551 residents per square mile. New York, Pennsylvania, Ohio, and Illinois, industrialized states with large expanses of farmland, saw their statewide densities increase to 282, 220, 169, and 142 people per square mile. The states of the mountain west and the northern Great Plains remained the most thinly settled. The Dakotas had a per square mile population density of about 9, Idaho and Utah less than 7, Montana under 4, Wyoming 2.6, and Nevada only 1.

Neither the prosperity of the 1920s nor the depression of the 1930s made isolated rural life appear any more attractive, economically or otherwise, to most Americans. During these decades Americans moved **Movement Away from Rural Areas** away from the already least-populated regions of the country. Those who changed their place of residence tended to go to warm climates and already moderately populated areas. The prospect of work also motivated state-to-state migration, especially in the 1930s. Florida and California saw their populations double within these twenty years, and Texas grew by 37 percent. Elsewhere growth patterns closely paralleled the overall national population increase, suggesting that most people preferred to stay close to home rather than migrate to another state or region.

A CLOSER LOOK AT SIX COMMUNITIES

Looking at individual American communities allows one to probe beneath the statistical picture provided by the U.S. Census Bureau. A handful of case studies cannot portray the full range of the American experience, but they do suggest, in ways that numbers do not, the varied character of daily existence. Robert and Helen Lynd's examination of the life of Muncie, Indiana, had been highly unusual in the early 1920s. In the middle of the following decade, the Lynds took another look at "Middletown" as its people confronted the depression. Shortly thereafter, other investigators undertook their own detailed community studies, with academics examining various urban and industrial communities and U.S. Department of Agriculture economists and sociologists surveying a number of small rural communities. Thanks to government documentary photography projects, a visual record of daily life at the grass roots accompanied some of these studies and have been used to illustrate this book. Both texts and photographs provide a means of assessing the daily life of ordinary people across the United States by the end of the 1930s.

The middle-sized industrial city of Muncie, Indiana, the Lynds discovered on their return in the midst of the depression, had grown considerably. **Middletown (Muncie, Indiana)** From the early 1920s to the mid-1930s, according to *Middletown in Transition*, the city's population had increased from 35,000 to 47,000. Residential patterns had also grown more segregated. The upper class increasingly resided on the city's northwest side where the college, hospital, and golf course were located. This area was set off from the rest of the city by a large park, a cemetery, the retail district, and railroad tracks. The white working-class majority occupied the south side closer to the city's factories, and the small African American population lived in the northeast.[3]

Eroding Sense of Community   Middletown's earlier sense of community cohesion perceptibly eroded as the city grew in the 1920s and struggled during the 1930s. People were identified by where they lived, how they earned a living, and what they owned. Tensions increased between the well to do and the less fortunate, the business class and the working class, those who continued to have employment and those who did not. The further one moved down the social scale, the Lynds observed, the less likely that people felt they "belonged" to the community or had any influence within it. In the years between the Lynds' two visits, Middletown paralleled the national pattern of prosperity followed by economic collapse and then gradual, incomplete revival. The closing of a General Motors transmission plant in 1932 had marked the low point in Middletown's fortunes.

Employment Patterns   High unemployment, especially among young people, and the willingness of impoverished workers to take low-wage jobs, thus lowering the overall wage scale, left marks on the community. Young people, forced to chose between education and idleness, most often stayed in school longer, finishing high school and attending the local state college in larger numbers. Older workers found themselves more likely to be employed regularly, if not constantly, at lower wages than what prevailed in the 1920s. Since Social Security retirement benefits would not begin to be paid until 1942, few were prepared to stop working before required to do so by infirmity or death. Voluntary retirement became, if anything, more uncommon.

Nearly 2,000 people, mainly older workers, the Lynds observed, had moved from urban residences to farms in the county but, along with others living on the land, found at least part-time employment away from the farm. The Lynds observed that 80 percent of the county's farmers worked elsewhere for pay at least fifty days a year, 57 percent at least 150 days, and 29 percent 250 days. At least close to an industrial center, the distinction between urban and rural work patterns appeared to be evaporating.

The numbers of women working outside the home doubled in the 1920s to 21 percent of all jobholders. The number of married women, especially older women, working for wages grew faster than the number of young single women doing so. Women were concentrated in low-wage and low-status occupations: clerical jobs as well as teaching and nursing. During the depression, however, the number of female jobholders fell sharply, in part because the drop in men's wages eliminated much of the attraction to employers of lower-paid women. More important, the Lynds reported, was that giving preference to men, especially married men, when jobs became available, was perceived as a means to reduce the relief burden on local charities and taxpayers. Once male heads of households had been taken care of, married women with family responsibilities would be given preference over single women.

Overall, after years of depression, the people of Middletown had come to assume that there would continue to be too few job opportunities for the number of persons who wanted to work. Furthermore, the prospect of climbing the employment ladder to become a foreman, manager, or "boss," the assumed reward for being a good worker in America, appeared increasingly remote. Therefore the gap between Middletown's three-out-of-ten residents who identified with the upper class and its seven out of ten who saw themselves as workers grew wider than ever and less likely to be bridged.

Gap between Upper Class and Workers

The class of business owners and managers, particularly its small elite, ran Middletown, the Lynds found, through the banks, law firms, industries, and retail establishments. This class controlled the educational system, civic institutions, churches, government, and local newspaper. For the most part, parents passed on membership in the business class to their children. The business class provided the bulk of the charitable funds and later the local tax revenues with which Middletown at first tried to provide relief from the depression.

In 1925, Middletown had organized most of its charitable giving into a community fund. Contributions to the fund became an accepted responsibility for those with jobs and property. Local businesses encouraged and facilitated participation through paycheck deductions. In the prosperous late 1920s, two-thirds of Middletown households

Depression Overwhelms Community Funds

contributed, and many businesses bragged that 100 percent of their employees participated. Middletown thought of this system, which in 1929 dealt with seven-eighths of the community's small relief burden as private voluntary charity, even if in reality it functioned much like a system of taxation.

The well to do accepted as traditional their responsibility to care for destitute women, children, and disabled residents but tended to think of economic hardship as a reflection of an individual's flaws. They found it harder to justify granting relief to able-bodied males even when temporary government make-work jobs could only be found for half of the unemployed, and they simply refused aid to transients. The burden of need mounted much faster than resources in the early 1930s, overwhelming the community fund. By 1932, three-fourths of relief came from public funds and indeed was paid for by borrowing against future tax revenues. Even so, the size of individual relief allotments shrank from an initial level of $2.00 per week for two persons to a lower level of $1.00 for the first person and 50 cents for each additional member of the household and finally, by 1935, to the further reduced level of 85 cents for the first person in the household, 50 cents for the second, 45 cents for the third, 35 cents for the fourth, and 30 cents each for others. Those Middletowners in difficulty through no fault of their own found it more and more difficult to cope, while the more fortunate proved helpless to correct a situation beyond their means and comprehension.

Mixed Reaction to New Deal The appearance of federal work programs in 1933 eased the economic situation, but did not entirely satisfy the community. The local business class remained distrustful of government relief beyond its own control; some denigrated the New Deal as "socialism." Those dependent on various federal programs, while they welcomed the assistance, at the same time often resented the low incomes as well as the stigma attached to such employment. The Lynds sensed that class divisions had widened. Meanwhile, the city welcomed and benefited from a variety of public-works projects, a sewage plant, roads, sidewalks, bridges, parks, a swimming pool, airport improvements, and college buildings among others, that it would not or could not finance on its own. In all, the depression required adjustments in Middletown life that were viewed as both beneficial and negative but were certainly difficult for all concerned.

Families Economize By the time the Lynds' second visit to Middletown concluded in 1935, the percentage of its residents over the age of twenty desiring employment who were working at either public or private jobs was very close to what it was a decade earlier. Skilled male workers averaged 45 cents an hour, unskilled workers 43 cents; women less. This represented a sharp decline for skilled workers, who in 1924 had received 50 cents to $1.00 an hour. Teachers' salaries, which had improved gradually during the 1920s but had been cut by 10 percent, then cut again by 5 percent during the depression, averaged about $1,600 a year. Incomes were stagnant at best. Consequently "belt tightening" was in evidence throughout the community.

Middletowners in the mid-1930s lived for the most part as they had a decade earlier, though they economized wherever they could. Single family homes accommodated 80 percent of the population, semidetached units another 13 percent, and various sorts of apartments 7 percent. People ate their meals at home, with the relatively wealthy abandoning restaurants and instead taking up outdoor grilling in their backyards. Women returned to the pre–World War I practice of making their own clothes. Extravagance was rare, whether from lack of personal resources or from consideration for others in difficult economic circumstances. Insofar as they were able, people struggled to hold onto their automobiles, though sales of new cars fell by half, then by half again between 1929 and 1932. Middletowners drove older cars, but gasoline sales held steady.

The people of Middletown occupied their leisure time with inexpensive pursuits, most notably gardening (which also cut the food bill), reading, and listening to the radio. **Inexpensive Leisure** Movies remained a widely enjoyed entertainment. Dancing was widespread among those under 30, and card games common among older people. Especially among the working class, engaging in sports at school or in newly built parks and other facilities became popular. Some other forms of socializing declined. The Lynds observed that, because of the anticipated costs of providing food or drink, Middletowners were less likely to invite nonfamily members into their homes. The upper class combined entertainment with business at meals or at the golf course, while working-class people became more isolated and less connected to the community.

The churches of Middletown, important community institutions that had grown in the 1920s and in several cases erected expensive new buildings, suffered in the **Church Support Declines** 1930s. Their traditional charitable efforts were quickly overwhelmed by the depression, and they showed little imagination in adapting to new realities. The Lynds noticed that the congregations were older than they had been a decade earlier. For whatever reason, young people were less in evidence in the churches.

Overall, Middletown was less secure and more divided, in essence, less of a community than it had been **Less Secure, More Divided** in the prior decade. People focused more on their own circumstances and less on being part of a collective enterprise. Aid in situations of difficulty came less from one's neighbors and more from a distant federal government. Some were angry about this shift, others welcomed it, but all were affected. In this middle-sized, midwestern city much remained the same, but the sense that life had changed was pervasive.

By the end of the 1930s, the small farming community of Irwin, located in the rolling prairie of western Iowa sixty **Irwin, Iowa** miles east of Omaha, Nebraska, appeared less traumatized than Middletown by the depression. A cluster of neatly kept houses adjacent to the Chicago and Great Western Railroad (C & GW), the village of 345 residents supported surrounding farms that were home to about another 1,000 people. For this larger community, Irwin was where they bought frequently needed supplies, went to school, church, lodge meetings, movies, and dances, and met the trains of the C & GW. Settlement of the county had begun in the 1850s by people eager to own their own farmland—Danish Lutherans, German Catholics, Norwegians, and by people of various backgrounds relocating from states to the east, especially Ohio, Pennsylvania, Indiana, and New York. Not until the arrival of the railroad in the 1880s, however, did the area acquire much

Irwin, Iowa. Residential street. Photo courtesy of the National Archives.

of a population. After some years of economic uncertainty and difficulty, the county settled into raising corn-fed cattle and hogs and enjoyed
great prosperity throughout the first two decades of the twentieth century.[4]

**Agricultural
Depression
and Drought**
The agricultural depression after 1920 caught Irwin and
the surrounding countryside of Shelby County in its grip.
Those who had incurred debt to purchase land and equipment during the preceding boom found themselves especially hard pressed. Some farmers lost title to their land
to mortgage-holding banks or insurance companies, while others found
themselves unable or unwilling to take the risks of buying land. Shelby
County lay well east of the worst Dust Bowl conditions, but the drought
hit the area hard in 1934 and 1936. By 1940, although farming continued,
52 percent of the county's farm operators were tenants on rented land.

The national industrial collapse of the early 1930s made difficult conditions noticeably worse. Shelby County farmers, who had joined the
Farmers Alliance in the 1880s to protest an earlier period of agricultural
difficulty, now enlisted in the Farmers Holiday Association (FHA) led
by Milo Reno from nearby Oskaloosa, Iowa. The Farmers Holiday move-

Irwin, Iowa. Main street. Photo courtesy of the National Archives.

ment advocated the withholding of farm products from the market in order to drive up prices and focus attention on the farmers' plight. In some cases FHA members dumped milk and destroyed the crops of those who refused to cooperate. Irwin area farmers did not take such radical steps, but many sympathized with them.

The New Deal agricultural relief programs proved highly popular in Shelby County and, together with increased **Agriculture** rainfall and the introduction of higher-yield hybrid seed **Assistance** corn, accounted for Irwin's steady economic improvement **Welcomed** after mid-decade. Still facing a burden of debt, the community praised the Farm Security Administration credit assistance program and the retirement pensions of Social Security. The Civilian Conservation Corps (CCC), National Youth Alliance (NYA), and Rural Electrification Administration (REA) were also extremely popular, though the Works Projects Administration (WPA) provoked some complaints that the program made it harder for farmers to hire short-term, part-time help at low wages. Irwin people still believed that success was always possible through hard work and thrift, saying, "Sure we can solve our problems if we can get cooperation."[5] Government assistance to agriculture, long sought but only recently obtained, was accepted as a reasonable means of dealing with perennial problems of farm finance, market instability, drought, and soil erosion. In 1939, over 90 percent of Irwin area farmers participated in the second Agricultural Adjustment Act (AAA) and were generally pleased with it, especially its emphasis on soil conservation.

Farming Remains Central   Farming remained central to Irwin and Shelby County life. No less than 98.8 percent of the land in the county was used for agriculture, two-thirds in field crops and one-quarter in pasture. Only 2 percent of the county's land was tree covered. Rectangular quarter-section (160 acre) farms, laid out and settled under the terms of the 1862 Homestead Act, remained the predominant pattern, though some farmers rented additional land for cash or a share of the crop. By 1940, some 75,000 hogs and 60,000 beef and dairy cattle were being raised in Shelby County, fed on the corn and oats grown on half the county's acreage. A typical livestock farm nurtured about 48 cows and 56 hogs at a time.

Farming and tending livestock in western Iowa continued to be hard and unrelieved year-round work, especially during planting and harvest seasons. The morning chores of feeding livestock, milking cows, and cleaning stalls usually began at 5 A.M., and, after a full-day's labor, the evening chores were not finished before 7 P.M. Mutual assistance with planting and harvest or in times of illness or other trouble had long been common, and such cooperation appeared to increase in the depression era. During the 1930s, farms in the county with tractors increased from just under 35 percent to slightly over 60 percent; such "power farming," as it was called, eased some of the physical burden as well as the need for hired help. By 1940, thanks to the REA, 35 percent of farms were electrified. Nevertheless, one Irwin area farmer explained, "We can get away for a short time, but unless someone else does our chores for us, we've got to be home at chore time."[6]

Entertainment and Social Life   The routine of farm life was commonly broken by visiting with neighbors. Also, ever since most farmers had acquired automobiles, going into Irwin on Wednesday evenings for the once-a-week movie and Saturday evening for a dance became social rituals. Irwin people occasionally traveled the fourteen miles to the county seat of Harden to shop or, less frequently, fifty or sixty miles to Council Bluffs, Iowa, or Omaha to sell or buy livestock and purchase clothing, furniture, and other household goods. Young people liked to drive to nearby (and sometimes not so nearby) towns for dances, parties, and school sporting events. Council Bluffs and Omaha newspapers and radio stations influenced the community through news reports, broadcast entertainment, and advertising. Nevertheless, Irwin itself continued to be the primary focus of daily life and where most residents, both younger and older, intended to stay.

Families provided the focus for much of daily life. On the farm, every family member was involved in the economic enterprise, with men managing the farm, women taking care of the household and garden, and children—as soon as they were old enough—given smaller responsibilities. Hired help, once common on Shelby County farms, had largely disappeared as tractors and other equipment made it possible to operate with only family labor. As farm families gathered every day at set times for meals, their conversations often centered on their work in the fields, the farmyard, and the home. A strong sense of the family bonds of obligation and protection helped Irwin residents deal with the depression. One explained, "We all had to work together to keep going at all."[7] Family solidarity was reinforced by means of summer picnics and reunions of the extended family in the area as well as through letter writing and, increasingly, telephone conversations.

The Farm Family

Creating a family, always an important life step, was a particular challenge in the depression. Most Irwinites thought that young people should marry as soon as practicable after finishing school. Because of hard economic times, parents were increasingly sharing their homes with young couples who could not otherwise afford to marry. Weddings themselves tended to be small family-only events held in the home. Friends and neighbors young and old, would, however, turn out for a "shivaree" during which ice cream, candy, and tobacco would be served. Thereafter, it was normal to start raising a family as soon as couples felt able to provide for children. Family size, however, was declining. Where once a family of ten or twelve was considered large, now six or seven was thought to be so.

Parents considered educating the young to be their first and foremost responsibility, though one increasingly shared with Irwin's schools and churches. They believed moral education, "teaching right from wrong," and discipline to be their responsibility, not to be shared with school teachers who might have different ideas. At the same time, while Shelby County adults averaged eight years of schooling, an education through high school had become an almost universal expectation for the young. While nine small one-room elementary schools were still in operation, most area children attended the consolidated elementary and high school in Irwin. By bringing farm and village children together in classes, sports, music, and other activities, the consolidated school had broken down barriers between the two groups and become a focus of community life.

Education

Three Protestant churches (Methodist, Church of Christ, and Norwegian Lutheran) were also regarded as important community institutions. While a majority of adult residents rarely or never attended church, they sent their children for religious education and declared the churches highly valu-

Declining Church Attendance

Irwin, Iowa. Students playing baseball in the schoolyard. Photo courtesy of the National Archives.

able to the well-being of Irwin. Sunday morning radio broadcasts of religious services with better speakers and music than the local churches offered appeared to be one reason for declining church attendance.

Strong Community Ties
The people of Irwin were generally aware of the world beyond their community. They read Des Moines, Omaha, and Council Bluffs newspapers and farm magazines such as *Wallace's Farmer*, *Iowa Homestead*, and *Successful Farming*.

They also listened to the radio. The programs of the New Deal had increased their attention to national developments, and the importance of foreign markets for agricultural products led them to give notice to international affairs. Nevertheless, few Irwinites were drawn away from the community. City life, regarded as noisy, crowded, anonymous, and unfriendly, held few attractions for them. A strong sense of attachment to the local community, enhanced by the almost universally shared experience of farming, characterized Irwin and accounted for its general sense of well-being at the end of the 1930s.

Harmony, Georgia
Over 800 miles southeast of Irwin, Iowa, stood Atlanta, Georgia. Some seventy miles further southeast in the midst of rural Putnam County rested the farming community of Harmony, Georgia. Harmony shared a few characteristics

with Irwin, but many of its features were notably dissimilar. Distinctions in agriculture and economic conditions were significant, but most distinguishing were the social contrasts between the community's twenty white families and fifty black families. Ironically, given its name, Harmony was highly segregated, divided by race into two separate societies with little in common except for location and occasional unequal interaction.[8]

Early in the nineteenth century, white settlers and their black slaves rapidly displaced the previous long-time Creek Indian occupants, cut down the hardwood forests, and developed large cotton plantations. By 1830, blacks outnumbered whites almost two to one in Putnam County; the ratio reached nearly three to one by the 1890s. Despite the gradual depletion of the sandy loam and clay soil as well as the decline in both prices and output per acre, cotton remained the agricultural focus until an onslaught of boll weevils devastated local fields in the early 1920s.

The Civil War had abolished slavery but had not ended a strictly two-tier local society. Although large plantations were broken up, generally among multiple heirs, land ownership remained overwhelmingly in the hands of whites, **Two-Tier Society** some local but by the 1930s 60 percent absentee. Within the white community, social status varied with land holding and length of residence in the county, but even the lowliest white enjoyed a standing higher than any black. Former slaves and their descendants, lacking either land, equipment, or other resources, were forced to resort to tenant farming, most often sharecropping. Landlords would provide farmland, seed, mules, tools, housing, and "furnish," food and other necessities for survival until the crops were harvested and sold. In return, landlords would receive half of the cotton and corn produced. Better situated white tenants and blacks with their own mules and tools usually made better rental arrangements, often for cash. None of the tenants, however, earned much as the cotton economy steadily deteriorated. Nevertheless, at its peak in 1920, over four-fifths of the nearly 2,300 farmers in Putnam County (over 70 percent of whom were black) remained tenants.

Boll weevil attacks beginning in 1920 forced sudden and profound changes on Harmony and all of Putnam County. **Boll Weevil** Many farmers went bankrupt, and 20 percent of the rest **Damage** abandoned the effort to produce a cotton crop. Putnam County land planted in cotton fell from 42,000 acres in 1919 to 6,000 acres by 1924. By the 1930 census, the county's population had plummeted by 45 percent and the number of farmers by more than half. Both whites and blacks departed for Atlanta and elsewhere. During the depression decade that followed, the population stagnated.

Shift to Dairy Farming   In a few cases before the 1920s but more often after the boll weevils arrived, white farmers shifted from cotton farming to dairy farming. Dairying involved a very different type of agriculture. While cows had to be milked twice a day every day, much less field work was needed than with cotton. With reduced labor demands, farmers could dispense with sharecropping and "furnishing." Between 1924 and 1939, land devoted to pasture went from 20 percent of the county's total to 63 percent. Feed crops such as hay, oats, corn, wheat, and legumes could be rotated, renewing the soil rather than depleting it from the constant planting of cotton. Milk and butter could be marketed every day year-round; this spared the need for credit and crop sales at the market's low point. By 1929, Harmony and the rest of Putnam County produced over a million gallons of milk per year, and in the next decade output increased another 43 percent. Dairy farmers experienced a significant rise in income, and their farms grew in size by an average of 45 acres. They were most likely to be among the mere 8 percent of local farmers who had shifted from mules to tractors, and their gross income from milk sales by 1939 ranged from $230 to nearly $2,000, all major advances in the poorest region of the nation.

Landless African Americans   A handful of African American farmers owned land (one in Harmony and eighty in the entire county compared with 536 whites), but 95 percent remained landless. Harmony's single African American landowner joined the shift to dairying, but other African Americans in the community lacked the financial resources to escape cotton farming. Furthermore, regarding blacks as ill-suited for dairying, the white community would not help tenants convert. Most dairy farmers did, however, hire African American laborers because of their availability at the lowest local wage rate. One white farmer who initially shared the view that blacks were rough and insensitive to cattle eventually realized that they could milk effectively once their hands, long callused from cotton field work, grew softer and smoother.

African Americans farmed far fewer acres on average than did whites—110 acres in 1939 compared with 279 for whites—and earned much less. Black sharecroppers did least well of all with only seventy acres per farm. Even these small farms were larger than the typical sharecropper's plot in most of the South. A sharecropping family in Harmony could grow its food and have a modest cabin to call home, but normally would only see about $150 a year in cash income. The most impoverished class in the most economically backward section of the nation remained mired in the agricultural activity least likely to improve its lot.

Harmony, Georgia. Men farming with mules. Photo courtesy of the National Archives.

Harmony's economic conditions shaped its daily life. Everyone worked except the very young and elderly. In white families, women did the housework, **Everyone Worked** light outdoor work such as gardening and caring for poultry, and, in an emergency, some milking. In black families, by contrast, women shared in the heavy field work. When cotton-picking time arrived in August and September, the whole family, including young children, normally took part. Males often supplemented their tenant farming income with occasional day labor as well as steady jobs at dairy farms or sawmills. Employers complained that whites had become less willing to do such work because, unlike blacks, they could obtain better wages and hours on nearby WPA projects.

In Harmony, most work was physically strenuous. Mules provided the power on every black farm as well as most white ones. Tractors and trucks were becoming more common on dairy farms, but far less so than automobiles (which could be found on almost half of Putnam County's farms). Electric lines had not yet reached the county. More well-to-do people looked forward eagerly to replacing sooty kerosene lamps with clean-burning electric lights and obtaining other electric-powered devices, but tenant farmers, black and white, said electricity was too expensive for them.

Harmony, Georgia. Main street on a Saturday afternoon. Photo courtesy of the National Archives.

Racial Divide
Cooperation beyond the individual family and farm was limited. Compensated assistance—truck or tractor rental and wage labor—prevailed rather than the unpaid sharing of tools and tasks. Blacks and whites lived nearby one another, but they did not cross racial boundaries to lend each other a hand. White farmers and business people belonged to the Putnam County Farm Board and the Eatonton Cooperative Creamery. African Americans had a Masonic Lodge. No cooperative agency crossed the racial divide.

Limited Socializing and Entertainment
Not only did family members tend to work in isolation, but they also spent their limited leisure time by themselves. Visiting with neighbors, remembered as frequent in decades past, had declined since the boll weevil attacks and the departure of so many residents. Contact with neighbors at the market on Saturday afternoon had largely replaced home visiting. For those with automobiles, a Sunday drive with the family became so popular that one resident complained, "People go riding instead of going to church."[9] Almost every white family spent time listening to the radio, but only one black family even owned one. Commercial amusements were rare. The once-a-week movie

Harmony, Georgia. A group of men talking on a street corner. Photo courtesy of the National Archives.

in Eatonton was a considerable distance away, not to mention expensive for families with very little cash income.

Social contact across racial lines was awkward, to say the least. By long-established southern custom, white adults **Segregation** expected blacks to address them as Mr. or Mrs., or by some title indicating superior status. Failure to observe this ritual was labeled "uppity" and carried penalties. No white would hire or rent land to a person so identified; once denied economic opportunity, such a person would find it difficult even to remain in the community. Equally strict custom barred whites from addressing a black person as Mr. or Mrs. or shaking hands. Mixed race social gatherings were strictly taboo, with the lone exception of attendance at funerals.

Segregated local churches and schools remained the primary local institutions, though much weakened by the loss of population in the 1920s. Most white residents belonged to the Harmony Baptist Church, which could only afford to bring in a trained preacher once a month and then had difficulty finding a family willing to feed him Sunday dinner. Some attributed declining church attendance to theological indifference or disputes, others to the rival attraction of a Sunday automobile drive, and still others to embarrassment over shabby clothing.

Jefferson Baptist Church served the African American community. It also held preaching services once a month, and, like its white counterpart, filled in with weekly prayer meetings and Sunday school. August marked the high point of the church year with a week of prayer meetings followed by a week of preaching; the final Sunday brought former residents back to the community from far and wide. The black church drew near universal attendance, made clear its behavioral guidelines, and censured the few who engaged in conduct of which it disapproved. Thus, it served as a much stronger agent of social cohesion and control within its community than did its white counterpart.

White students attended a one-teacher elementary school and then were bused at county expense to a high school in Eatonton, eight miles distant. Quite a few of these children went on to college and rarely returned to the community thereafter. Harmony's school for its African American students, by contrast, combined elementary and high school subjects. Although it had more students, it lacked the advantages of a consolidated school. Limited educational opportunities for African Americans help explain the overall pattern of schooling for adults in the county: 6.1 years for females, 5.2 years for males.

By the late 1930s, Harmony appeared a bit less isolated. Au-
Isolation tomobiles made it possible for their owners to travel to Ath-
Somewhat ens, Macon, and Atlanta, although they rarely did.
Lessened Newspapers and the radio allowed white residents to establish more regular connections with the outside world. African Americans, on the other hand, had fewer resources to maintain external contacts and did so mainly through letters and visits from family members who had left in earlier years. Those who remained in Harmony—the white dairy farmers who were comparatively prosperous and especially the black tenant farmers who were not—could usually trace their roots in the community back a century or more. Accepting the familiar, they seemed prepared to remain.

Thirteen hundred miles west of Harmony, the small com-
El Cerrito, munity of El Cerrito, New Mexico, lay hidden in a valley
New Mexico near the Pecos River, east of Albuquerque. Surrounded by great expanses of high mesa with little rainfall and poor soil only suited for livestock grazing, this isolated village traced its origins to settlers of vast Mexican land grants in the early nineteenth century. In the 1920s and 1930s, its Hispanic American residents owned small plots of land that they irrigated and farmed for subsistence. The village's meager cash income was earned outside El Cerrito through labor on nearby sheep ranches or, recently, in various New Deal programs. "It isn't that I want to leave," one man explained, "It's a matter of making a living." In a state where overall per capita income was only two-thirds the national average, 51 percent of the rural population earned less than $100 in 1938. El

El Cerrito, New Mexico. Tending sheep near the village. Photo courtesy of the National Archives.

Cerrito typified this meager existence. Attachment to a traditional culture, not an easy or abundant life, kept the community quite stable.[10]

A powerful sense of community prevailed in El Cerrito. Its twenty-five adobe residences were clustered together, all within 250 yards, a number of them attached to each other. Sharing of food and tools was common as was trad- **Strong Community Feeling** ing labor on farming tasks. In times of illness or calamity, the community provided all manner of assistance. Every male partici- pated in the ongoing task of maintaining the irrigation system necessary to sustain the farm plots upon which life depended. A strong sense of obligation to the community meant virtually no dishonesty or failure to carry out responsibilities. Informal visiting in or about each other's homes, often several times a day, was routine for women. Men tended to gather to converse at the end of their workday or after church on Sunday, while children from different families constantly played to- gether once their chores were done.

Families used their small irrigated plots to grow corn, beans, and chili peppers, the staples of their diet. Most also **Small Irrigated Gardens** maintained fruit orchards ranging in size from a few trees to a half acre; they often earned a few dollars taking to market the peaches, apricots, and apples the family did not consume

El Cerrito, New Mexico. A large, three-generation Mexican American family at the dinner table. Photo courtesy of the National Archives.

or preserve. Families typically raised ten to fifteen chickens, mainly for their eggs. A few kept milk cows. Only four families raised hogs and then chiefly for the lard; a rare hog butchering marked one of the few occasions when everyone in the village ate meat.

Self-Contained and Isolated With no electricity or telephones, only two battery-powered radios, and the nearest community twelve miles away over poor roads, El Cerrito was very much a self-contained community. Residents could, when necessary, arrange a ride to Las Vegas thirty miles northeast in one of the hamlet's two aged cars or two old trucks, but they mostly stayed close to home except when pursuing wage labor. Unfamiliar and uncomfortable with the Anglo culture that was increasingly likely to be encountered the further they went, villagers felt little incentive to travel other than for work. Women and small children in particular rarely left El Cerrito more than once or twice a year.

Devotion to the Church The church and school stood at the center of El Cerrito in both geographic and social terms. The Catholic Church to which, without exception, all belonged was the best maintained building in the village. Women were especially devout, and they performed most religious services since the priest, who

El Cerrito, New Mexico. Townspeople leaving church after a Sunday morning service. Photo courtesy of the National Archives.

lived elsewhere, came to conduct mass and hear confessions only once a month. Children received religious instruction from an early age. Their first communion represented a major family and community event, concluding in a parade around the church led by the priest, the parents, and the children. Weddings, the annual two-day festival of the patron saint, and funerals were other occasions that involved the entire community in celebration or sorrow.

The main function of the school was to teach basic English and math. Parents considered an eighth-grade education **Limited** valuable but sufficient for their children. Housed in an old **Education** and dilapidated building, with furnishings, equipment, and lighting to match, the village school could accommodate thirty to fifty students. The teacher, who lived elsewhere and drove to El Cerrito each day, had completed four years of high school and one college summer term; she relied on textbooks that seldom related to her students' lives. School attendance was poor, especially for boys past the age of twelve, and students seldom developed much proficiency in English or any other subject. One young man admitted, "I have learned more during my 3 years in the [CCC] camp than I did in all the years I was in school."[11]

Low-Cost Local Entertainment

The school building was the site of El Cerrito's principal recreation, a weekly Saturday night community dance. Local musicians would play violin, guitar, and accordion as long as the dancers felt like continuing, often quite late into the night. Young and old alike attended. This was the one occasion when adolescent boys and girls were allowed, under parental supervision, to court each other. While young people danced, primarily to fast traditional Spanish folk tunes, their elders sat, kept time with their feet, and talked. Equally low-cost entertainments, consisting of fishing and occasional trips to nearby towns, filled other leisure time.

Impending Change

El Cerrito's young people were becoming increasingly aware of the limitations of their impoverished village's life. Some had gone to work in CCC and NYA camps, earning more wages as well as learning useful skills and better English. They gained confidence in living away from home and acquired tastes for things not available in El Cerrito: sports, different foods, shower baths, and movies. Their stories in turn excited the younger children. As a result, a sense of impending change was gathering in the stable, tradition-bound community of El Cerrito.

Aliquippa, Pennsylvania

Twenty-six miles down the Ohio River from Pittsburgh, Aliquippa, Pennsylvania, a city of 27,000 residents, was dominated by its huge Jones & Laughlin Steel Corporation plant. Built between 1905 and 1912 to augment the company's overextended Pittsburgh facility, the steel mill, with its associated wire, pipe, tube, and tin works, employed over 90 percent of the city's 9,000 workers in the 1920s and 1930s. In fact, Jones & Laughlin, through its subsidiary Woodlawn Land Company, also built most of the housing and offered it for sale to employees. Aliquippa's origins as a company-developed industrial city distinguished it from small agricultural communities such as Irwin, Harmony, and El Cerrito as well as from older cities such as Middletown, which had evolved gradually and developed a diverse industrial economy.[12]

A Company City

Workers and their families had been attracted to Aliquippa in the years before World War I by the prospect of steady work at relatively good wages. The availability of affordable housing, almost all equipped with indoor plumbing and electricity and two-thirds with central heating, added to the appeal. Jones & Laughlin leaders had taken a dim view of workers' living conditions in Pittsburgh. They thought the establishment of a cleaner, more modern, and well-ordered town was both a civic responsibility and a way to curtail labor unrest, which they detested. At the

Aliquippa, Pennsylvania. A working-class neighborhood within sight of the Jones & Laughlin steel mill. Photo courtesy of the Library of Congress.

same time, the company ran the mill continuously, paid low wages to unskilled and semiskilled workers, offered no vacation or disability compensation, and blocked, sometimes brutally, any effort to form a labor union.

The owners of Jones & Laughlin were Welsh and Irish. Their managers and most of the skilled workers **Ethnic Enclaves** were likewise predominately descendants of northwest Europeans. The unskilled and semiskilled steelworkers, on the other hand, came from elsewhere. Large numbers of eastern and southern European immigrants—thirteen identifiable ethnic groups—formed the bulk of the labor force. African Americans from the rural South formed a separate stream of workers. Commonly, laborers, who on arrival found Aliquippa satisfactory, encouraged and assisted family members as well as others from their place of origin to join them; thus, the Aliquippa population contained clusters not merely from similar backgrounds, but from the same distant villages.

Each group established its own community in Aliquippa. Slavs, Serbs, Italians, and Greeks constituted the largest foreign-born populations. The approximately 11 percent of the city's people who, according to the 1940

Aliquippa, Pennsylvania. Men listening to the radio at their Greek ethnic club. Photo courtesy of the Library of Congress.

census, were African American found themselves particularly isolated. Each separate ethnic enclave had its own small businesses, social organizations, mutual benefit societies, and churches. Attending neighborhood schools with others of the same heritage, obtaining jobs in the same department at the steel mill through ethnic connections, and marrying within their own ethnic group, people retained the sense of cultural identity brought by them or their forebears to Aliquippa.

Community Perseverence 	In such an environment and with 40 percent of all housing in Aliquippa owner occupied, the society was extremely stable. Not even the depression, which brought deep cutbacks at the steel mill in the early 1930s and only gradual improvement from 1934 onward, altered the social structure. Economic hardships punished but did not shatter the community. The mill continued operations, though most steelworkers only had employment a few days per week. Savings were used up, insurance policies were abandoned, credit was exhausted, and debt accumulated. Increasing numbers of women sought work outside the home; eventually one-in-five women found jobs. Assistance from within the ethnic community, later on state relief, and eventually New Deal programs helped residents to scrape by.

Some people moved to cheaper quarters; others took in boarders, gaining extra income in exchange for more crowded housing. At decade's end unemployment still stood at nearly 13 percent, while another 3.3 percent continued working for the WPA or NYA. But despite the hard times, few felt compelled to leave the city. The 1940 census reported a population only 93 persons smaller than that of 1930.

Few dramatic shifts in situation or status occurred from one generation to the next. Most upward mobility in- **Little Change** volved merely an elevation from an unskilled to a semi- **for Workers** skilled job, a slightly better wage rate, but not a change as significant as a move into skilled labor or management. Throughout the 1920s and 1930s, only about one-in-four sons achieved a position higher than his father, and daughters rarely outdid their mothers. Immigrants did better in this respect than African Americans. By the end of the 1930s, however, the potential for change appeared to be increasing. Within ten years, the proportion of foreign-born residents, those least likely to burst the bonds of family and community, had slid from one in four to one in five. Whereas about one-third of males over the age of twenty-five had four years of schooling or less and another third only five or six years (with females doing slightly better), 80 percent of Aliquippa's seventeen year olds attended high school, no doubt in part because the depression reduced the opportunities to leave school for a job.

While each ethnic community had its own internal cohesion, practices, and standards, until 1937 overall **Company Control** leadership of the city remained firmly in the hands of Jones & Laughlin. Company managers dominated local government, the school board, the press, and the police force. At first, a number of saloons, gambling houses, and brothels had developed in McDonald Hollow, an area of cheaper housing outside the areas developed by the Woodlawn Land Company, but city leaders and the police, assisted by Jones & Laughlin's own security force, gradually reformed the area. The police also assisted the company in efforts to identify any labor union organizers who arrived in town and warned them away from Aliquippa.

From the outset, Jones & Laughlin management vigor- ously opposed unionization. The company firmly resisted **Unionization** and eventually crushed an industry-wide strike for better **Opposed** wages and working conditions in 1919. When the 1933 National Industrial Recovery Act (NIRA) required all U.S. businesses to permit collective bargaining, Jones & Laughlin established an Employee Representation Plan, a powerless company-controlled substitute for an independent union. When a disabled former steelworker began recruiting members in 1934 for the American Federation of Labor's Amalgamated Association of Iron, Steel, and Tin Workers (AAISTW), he was

Aliquippa, Pennsylvania. The children of a steelworker playing with toys on the porch of their home. Photo courtesy of the Library of Congress.

beaten by local police, then committed to an insane asylum until a Pittsburgh reporter exposed his treatment. The revelation prompted union ranks to swell from 1,000 to 4,000, but the drive stalled when the U.S. Supreme Court declared the NIRA unconstitutional and the American Federation of Labor (AFL) expelled the AAISTW local, Beaver Lodge 200, for indiscriminately recruiting unskilled and semiskilled workers as members.

Workers Win   For a time Aliquippa became center stage in the battle over the new Wagner National Labor Relations Act. Beaver Lodge 200 reorganized itself as part of the Steel Workers Organizing Committee (SWOC), a founding unit of the Congress of Industrial Organizations (CIO). The lodge continued building an industrial rather than a craft union, believing it more effective for bargaining purposes to unite all workers rather than separate them according to skills. Meanwhile, Jones & Laughlin challenged the constitutionality of the Wagner Act, fired pro-union workers over National Labor Relations Board (NLRB) objections, and refused to hold an NLRB-mandated union election. Although rival United States Steel negotiated a contract with

SWOC, Jones & Laughlin continued to resist. However, in April 1937, the Supreme Court upheld the Wagner Act in *NLRB v. Jones & Laughlin*. The next month 20,000 striking workers shut down the firm's Aliquippa and Pittsburgh works. The company at long last came to terms with New Deal labor policy, SWOC, and its own workers. Jones & Laughlin quickly agreed to a contract providing a base wage of $5 for an eight-hour day, a forty-hour work week, grievance and seniority provisions, three annual paid holidays, and one week's annual paid vacation after five year's service.

Following the 1937 strike and settlement, industrial tension quickly faded in Aliquippa. So, too, did company efforts to control the city. Pro-union Democrats won the next local elections, replacing the company's Republican government and its police force. Thereafter, Aliquippa's elite began moving out of the city, so that by the end of the decade control was definitely in the hands of its new leaders. Since they had little experience in achieving cooperation among their various ethnic enclaves, not to mention community leadership, the future of this now decidedly working-class city was less certain than it had been in previous decades.

Future Uncertain

As the nation's second largest city, Chicago was vastly more complex in the 1920s and 1930s than cities the size of Middletown or Aliquippa. It was a focal point for finance and commerce, a national railroad hub, and an immense manufacturing center. Steel mills, meat packing plants, and factories making telephones, farm machines, clothing, and a host of other products dotted the city. Far more than small cities, not to mention rural villages, Chicago reflected the most recent changes in culture as well as material conditions taking place in the United States in the 1920s and 1930s. Indeed, in 1933 and 1934, the city hosted a world's fair forty years after its first, more famous such exposition. The Century of Progress Exposition drew 22 million visitors in its initial season and 16 million in its second to a grand display of technology and culture made somewhat ironic by its setting in a city hard hit by the depression.[13]

Chicago, Illinois

By 1940, Chicago's 3.4 million residents represented growth of 700,000 in the city's population since 1920, though only a modest 20,000 increase since 1930. Like the inhabitants of Aliquippa, Chicagoans came from different ethnic and racial backgrounds and clustered in separate neighborhoods. What made the Windy City extraordinary was the number and size of its disparate cultures, no one of which was dominant.

Ethnic Mix

The foreign-born population had begun to decline as immigration restrictions took effect and the American-born children of immigrants increased in number. Even so, the city held 35,000 British-born individuals;

Chicago, Illinois. A parking lot and the skyline of Chicago, as seen from the lakefront. Photo courtesy of the Library of Congress.

another 35,000 from Ireland; 70,000 Scandinavian immigrants; 83,000 Germans; 119,000 Poles; 76,000 from the old Austro-Hungarian Empire; 67,000 Russians; 26,000 Lithuanians; 13,000 Yugoslavs; 66,000 Italians; 22,000 Canadians; 7,000 Mexicans; and a smattering of people from many other countries. In addition to its 355,000 foreign-born whites, the city contained 277,000 African Americans, most of whom had arrived from the American South during or since World War I.

African Americans Live Apart   The diverse peoples of Chicago, especially newer arrivals, tended to cluster together in neighborhoods, often abutting other ethnic communities. They usually settled in areas close to their prime employment opportunities. There they would establish distinctive ethnic shops, bakeries, butchers, taverns, mortuaries, and social clubs as well as parishes, synagogues, or churches. The notable exception to the general pattern of distinguishable but intermixed ethnic neighborhoods was the Black Belt of the South Side to which 90 percent of the city's African American population was restricted. From this ghetto, second in size only to New York's Harlem, as well as four much smaller residential ghettos, African American workers often had to travel long distances to their jobs in the steel mills, packing plants, and other large factories.

Except for the African American ghettos, the ethnic
clustering throughout Chicago began to break down **Common Urban**
during the 1920s. This trend was encouraged in a time **Experiences**
of prosperity and rapid growth by improved housing
opportunities in the farther reaches of the city and even the suburbs
beyond, an excellent public transit system, a growing number of chain
stores, and an attractive central commercial district. Mass commercial
entertainment including radio, large vaudeville and motion picture theaters, and two professional baseball teams drew people out of their
neighborhoods and into a common urban experience. Hostility to national prohibition, widely shared by the city's ethnic groups, played a
powerful role. Czechs, Germans, Italians, Irish, and others overcame traditional rivalries to fight the liquor ban. Before the end of the decade,
the white ethnic masses had discovered that by allying they could seize
control of the city's political structure, government, and law-enforcement
system.

The onset of the depression, and with it unemployment
reaching as high at 50 percent in the manufacturing sector **Depression**
of a city heavily dependent on industrial wages, served to **Hits Hard**
further erode ethnic differences. During the 1920s, employers had sought to retain worker loyalty by practicing what became
known as welfare capitalism, paying heed to worker complaints and
providing a variety of benefits to reduce employee dissatisfaction and
turnover. Workers learned to expect better treatment from their employers, but the depression served as a reminder not to rely on them once
hard times hit. Traditional sources of aid within the ethnic community
proved insufficient as well, overwhelmed as they were by the magnitude
of the catastrophe. Despite every effort to economize, find other jobs,
and put women and even older children to work, families often found
themselves in desperate situations.

Government, local and especially federal, proved to
be Chicagoans' salvation during the depression. **New Deal Relief**
Hardly a family did not have at least some member
obtain relief, secure a government loan to ward off mortgage foreclosure,
or acquire a government job. African Americans, usually the first to lose
their jobs in the private sector, benefited particularly from the WPA. By
treating people as individuals rather than as members of ethnic groups,
federal programs bridged differences. By 1936, traditional divisions were
being set aside as working-class people voted overwhelmingly for Franklin Roosevelt and the Democratic Party. African Americans in particular
abandoned long-standing loyalty to the party of Lincoln and by 1935,
they cast 81 percent of their ballots for the Democratic candidate for
mayor.

Chicago, Illinois. After prohibition was repealed in 1933, people could once again drink legally in Chicago clubs. Photo courtesy of the Library of Congress.

Unionization
The programs of the New Deal did not solve every problem. Increasingly, working-class Chicagoans, although they remained loyal to the Democratic Party, turned to labor unions as a means of dealing with their employers. Stimulated by the adoption of the National Industrial Recovery Act and spurred especially by the passage of the National Labor Relations Act in 1935 and the rise of the CIO, unionization brought workers of disparate ethnic backgrounds together. A workforce that was increasingly second-generation American, English speaking, and attuned to the industrial environment found it easier to band together in sustained labor action than had their counterparts two decades earlier. In winning union contracts from U.S. Steel, Armour, International Harvester, and many other employers, sometimes after long and bitter struggles, they strengthened bonds that cut across ethnic boundaries. Even defeats—most notably the failed 1937 SWOC strike against the rigidly antiunion Republic Steel Corporation during which Chicago police shot demonstrators, killing ten and wounding nearly a hundred in a "Memorial Day Massacre"— helped build a sense among workers that they deserved better treatment and reward for their labor. Where ethnic divisions continued to

retard worker unity, the AFL's craft-union organizing strategy clashed with the CIO's industry-wide recruiting, and unions became bogged down in leadership struggles and bureaucracies that were insensitive to local circumstances. Industrial workers faltered in their efforts to establish solidarity and gain the power that their numbers seemed to justify.

Strong ties to their churches helped preserve the cultural identities of many Chicagoans. The city was home to the largest Roman Catholic archdiocese in the United States as well as substantial Protestant, Orthodox, and Jewish communities. Neighborhood parishes served daily needs and cemented the traditions of Irish, Italian, and Polish Catholics; Scandinavian and German Lutherans; Greek and Russian Orthodox; German and Eastern European Jews; and a multitude of other denominations. As political alliances, government programs, union movements, commerce, and mass entertainment all acted to standardize urban life, religious observance tended to maintain traditional distinctions, large and small. **Strong Church Ties**

Schools, based in neighborhoods and including many parochial as well as public institutions, would not rapidly alter the local culture. By 1939, the 2.1 million Chicagoans over twenty-five years old typically had a limited education. Four percent had never been to school and another 7.5 percent had attended for fewer **Education**

Chicago, Illinois. The Chicago Art Institute. Photo courtesy of the Library of Congress.

than five years. Sixty percent of all adults had no more than eight years of school, and three out of four had not finished high school. Fewer than one in ten had attended college, and less than one in twenty had graduated. So while the metropolis provided more educational opportunities than most smaller communities, the vast majority of city dwellers had been unable to take advantage of them. The depression decade had changed Chicago's education pattern. At the end of the decade, 78 percent of seventeen year olds were still in school. This was up from 58 percent in 1930, indicating once again the impact of hard times in encouraging teenagers with little prospect of good jobs to stay in school longer.

Employment and Wages Increase
Among the 1,594,000 city dwellers in the labor force as the decade came to a close, 1,328,000 or 85 percent were employed and another 62,000 or 4 percent were involved in WPA and similar government projects. Eleven percent, or 180,000, were seeking work. More than one-in-three workers (34 percent) were involved in manufacturing and another quarter (27 percent) in clerical or sales work. The Chicago economy was not exactly robust, but far more people were working than earlier in the decade, and the combination of union contracts and the Fair Labor Standards Act minimum-wage provisions meant that wages had begun to rise.

Modern Lifestyle
Not only had Chicago weathered the worst of the depression, but its residents almost universally shared elements of modern life that remained less common in places like Aliquippa, Pennsylvania, and Irwin, Iowa, and elusive in remote locations such as Harmony, Georgia, and El Cerrito, New Mexico. For example, Chicagoans had access to a variety of newspapers, ranging from the conservative, isolationist *Chicago Tribune* and the anti-New Deal but more internationally minded *Chicago Daily News* to the labor-backed *Chicago Times*, the African American *Chicago Defender*, and several local ethnic papers. Also, over 99 percent of Chicago households possessed radios. Local newspapers and radio stations provided information about what was happening across the city as well as nationally and internationally. They drew city dwellers into shared experiences and common knowledge that would counteract the limitations of membership in a circumscribed community.

THE IMPACT OF THE 1920s AND 1930s ON DAILY LIFE

No six locales, even ones as varied as those described here, can provide a complete picture of daily life throughout a nation which, by the conservative calculations of the U.S. Census Bureau, contained nearly 17,000 communities. Location, economic situation, ethnic composition, local tradition, and even climate contributed to the individuality of each community and assured that no two would be exactly alike. And yet, certain factors of time and circumstance assured that individuals in all of these various places would have something in common.

The growth of the American population as well as shifts in its composition influenced both pressures and opportunities for individuals. New technology, while not equally accessible to all, had a profound effect on those who possessed it and altered the aspirations of many who did not. For example, radio, virtually unknown in 1920, had become a staple of daily life twenty years later, a means for listeners to become connected to a common national experience. Those who did not have access to radio felt isolated and backward simply because their circumstances had not changed while the culture around them had done so. The spread of automobiles, electricity, motion pictures, and many lesser commodities produced a similar impact. Altered material conditions helped create more of a shared national culture than had ever before existed, despite the growth in population.

New Technology

Finally, the improving economic conditions of the 1920s, the collapse of the 1930s, and the nation's response to both led to enlarged expectations regarding the role of government, especially national government, in the daily lives of the American people. More than ever before, government came to be seen as bearing a responsibility to assist citizens facing difficulties beyond their capacity or control. Bankers, businessmen, and farmers accepted the government's rescue of a private enterprise economy, though many objected to the regulations that accompanied the aid. They also opposed assisting workers who were unemployed, wanted to unionize, or faced old age without pensions. Those workers, many of whom had begun during the 1920s to expect a more stable and comfortable life than had previously been their lot, came to count on the government as an ally in their struggle with exploitive employers as well as a provider of last resort during dire economic times. Not everyone benefited from the New Deal and not everyone accepted its role in American life, but for the time being, attitudes about the purpose and value of government were widely positive.

Larger Role for Government

Anxiety about the future may be a constant human commonplace regardless of time or circumstance. Certainly, the end of the 1930s appeared to be no exception, and understandably so, given the many unexpected changes of the recent past. That anxiety, however, was generalized and nonspecific. While the future was a bit frightening, Americans could no more predict what lay ahead for them in 1939 than at any other time in their history.

Looking toward the Future

As the decade ended newspapers and radio broadcasts in Chicago and elsewhere were reporting that both Europe and Asia had plunged into war. The United States seemed far removed from these conflicts, but in informed circles, apprehensions were beginning to mount. Away from metropolitan centers, less attention appeared to be paid to grim developments beyond the hemisphere. Daily life remained the preoccupation of most Americans wherever they lived and whatever they did. The comparative calm of the moment reflected everyday self-absorption and the sense that, despite the travails of the depression, life was certainly no more painful and in many respects more promising than it had been twenty years earlier. War, accompanied by dramatic upheavals in the day-to-day circumstances of most Americans, seemed unlikely as the 1930s drew to a close and the American people went about the many aspects of their daily lives.

NOTES

1. Quoted in Dean Acheson, *Present at the Creation: My Years in the State Department* (New York: Knopf, 1969), xvii.

2. The figures in this paragraph and those to follow are drawn from the U.S. Census for 1940.

3. Information in this and the succeeding paragraph is found in Robert S. Lynd and Helen Merrill Lynd, *Middletown in Transition: A Study in Cultural Conflicts* (New York: Harcourt, Brace and World), 1937.

4. Information on Irwin, Iowa, found in Edward O. Moe and Carl G. Taylor, *Culture of a Contemporary Rural Community: Irwin, Iowa*, Rural Life Studies: 5 (U.S. Department of Agriculture, Bureau of Agricultural Economics, 1942).

5. Quoted in Ibid., 11.

6. Quoted in Ibid., 42.

7. Quoted in Ibid., 55.

8. Information on Harmony, Georgia, found in Walter Wynne, *Culture of a Contemporary Rural Community: Harmony, Georgia*, Rural Life Studies: 6 (U.S. Department of Agriculture, Bureau of Agricultural Economics, 1943).

9. Quoted in Ibid., 39.

10. The community is described in Olen Leonard and G. P. Loomis, *Culture of a Contemporary Rural Community: El Cerrito, New Mexico*, Rural Life Studies: 1 (U.S. Department of Agriculture, Bureau of Agricultural Economics, 1941), 72.

11. Ibid., 60.

12. David H. Wollman and Donald R. Inman, *Portraits in Steel: An Illustrated History of Jones & Laughlin Steel Corporation* (Kent, Ohio: Kent State University Press, 1999). Contains considerable information on Alliquippa.

13. An excellent description of Chicago in the 1930s can be found in Lizabeth Cohen, *Making a New Deal: Industrial Workers in Chicago, 1919–1939* (New York: Cambridge University Press, 1990).

For Further Reading

Adams, Jane H. *The Transformation of Rural Life: Southern Illinois, 1890–1990.* Chapel Hill: University of North Carolina Press, 1994.

Agee, James, and Walker Evans. *Let Us Now Praise Famous Men.* Boston: Houghton Mifflin, 1941.

Allen, Frederick Lewis. *Only Yesterday: An Informal History of the Nineteen-Twenties.* New York: Harper, 1931.

Anderson, Sherwood. *Hometown.* New York: Alliance, 1940.

Bailey, Beth L. *From Front Porch to Back Seat: Courtship in Twentieth-Century America.* Baltimore: Johns Hopkins University Press, 1989.

Baldwin, Sidney. *Poverty and Politics: The Rise and Decline of the Farm Security Administration.* Chapel Hill: University of North Carolina Press, 1968.

Barnouw, Eric. *A History of Broadcasting in the United States.* Vol. 2. *The Golden Web.* New York: Oxford University Press, 1968.

Barton, Bruce. *The Man Nobody Knows.* Indianapolis: Bobbs-Merrill, c. 1925.

Bayor, Ronald H. *Neighbors in Conflict: The Irish, Germans, Jews, and Italians of New York City, 1929–1941.* Baltimore: Johns Hopkins University Press, 1978.

Bergman, Andrew. *We're in the Money: Depression America and Its Films.* New York: New York University Press, 1971.

Best, Gary Dean. *The Nickel and Dime Decade: American Popular Culture during the 1930s.* Westport, Conn.: Praeger, 1993.

Biles, Roger. *The South and the New Deal.* Lexington: University of Kentucky Press, 1994.

Blair, Karen J. *The Torchbearers: Women and Their Amateur Arts Associations in America, 1890–1930.* Bloomington: Indiana University Press, 1994.

Bodnar, John. *Workers' World: Kinship, Community, and Protest in an Industrial Society, 1900–1940.* Baltimore: Johns Hopkins University Press, 1982.

Brannan, Beverly, and David Horvath. *A Kentucky Album: Farm Security Administration Photographs, 1935–1943.* Lexington: University of Kentucky Press, 1986.

Brinkley, Alan. *The End of Reform: New Deal Liberalism in Recession and War.* New York: Knopf, 1995.

Brody, David. *Steelworkers in America: The Nonunion Era.* Cambridge: Harvard University Press, 1960.

Brumberg, Joan Jacobs. *The Body Project: An Intimate History of American Girls.* New York: Random House, 1997.

Burlingame, Roger. *Henry Ford.* New York: Knopf, 1954.

Burner, David. *The Politics of Provincialism: The Democratic Party in Transition, 1918–1932.* New York: Knopf, 1970.

Bustard, Bruce I. *A New Deal for the Arts.* Washington, D.C.: National Archives and Records Administration in association with the University of Washington Press, Seattle, 1997.

Caldwell, Erskine, and Margaret Bourke-White. *You Have Seen Their Faces.* New York: Viking Press, 1937.

Carr, Carolyn Kinder. *Ohio: A Photographic Portrait, 1935–1941: Farm Security Administration Photographs.* Akron: Akron Art Institute, 1980.

Carter, Paul A. *Another Part of the Twenties.* New York: Columbia University Press, 1977.

Cavan, Ruth S., and Katherine Rauck. *The Family and the Depression: A Study of One Hundred Chicago Families.* New York: Arno, 1938.

Chalmers, David M. *Hooded Americanism: A History of the Ku Klux Klan.* 3rd ed. Durham, N.C.: Duke University Press, 1987.

Cohen, Lizabeth. *Making a New Deal: Industrial Workers in Chicago, 1919–1939.* New York: Cambridge University Press, 1990.

Cohen, Ruth Schwartz. *More Work for Mother: Women and Household Technology.* New York: Oxford University Press, 1977.

Curtis, James. *Mind's Eye, Mind's Truth: FSA Photography Reconsidered.* Philadelphia: Temple University Press, 1989.

Danbom, David B. *Born in the Country: A History of Rural America.* Baltimore: Johns Hopkins University Press, 1995.

Daniel, Pete. *Deep'n As It Come: The 1927 Mississippi River Flood.* New York: Oxford University Press, 1977.

———. *Standing at the Crossroads: Southern Life in the Twentieth Century.* Baltimore: Johns Hopkins University Press, 1986.

Daniel, Pete, Mary A. Foresta, Maren Stange, and Sally Stein. *Official Images: New Deal Photography.* Washington, D.C.: Smithsonian Institution Press, 1987.

Davidson, Cathy N. *Reading in America: Literature and Social History.* Baltimore: Johns Hopkins University Press, 1989.

Dawley, Alan. *Struggle for Justice: Social Responsibility and the Liberal State.* Cambridge: Harvard University Press, 1991.

Debo, Angie. *Prairie City: The Story of an American Community.* New York: Knopf, 1944.

D'Emilio, John, and Estelle B. Freedman. *Intimate Matters: A History of Sexuality in America.* New York: Harper and Row, 1988.

Dollard, John. *Class and Caste in a Southern Town.* New Haven: Yale University Press, 1937.

Douglas, Ann. *Terrible Honesty: Mongrel Manhattan in the 1920s.* New York: Farrar, Straus, and Giroux, 1995.

Douglas, George H. *The Early Days of Radio Broadcasting.* Jefferson, N.C.: McFarland, 1987.

Douglas, Susan J. *Inventing American Broadcasting, 1899–1922.* Baltimore: Johns Hopkins University Press, 1987.

Dumenil, Lynn. *The Modern Temper: American Culture and Society in the 1920s.* New York: Hill and Wang, 1995.

Egerton, John. *Speak Now against the Day: The Generation before the Civil Rights Movement in the South.* Chapel Hill: University of North Carolina Press, 1994.

Ellsworth, Scott. *Death in a Promised Land: The Tulsa Race Riot of 1921.* Baton Rouge: Louisiana State University Press, 1982.

Ely, Melvin. *The Adventures of Amos 'n Andy: A Social History of an American Phenomenon.* New York: Free Press, 1991.

Erenburg, Lewis A. *Steppin' Out: New York Nightlife and the Transformation of American Culture, 1890–1930.* Westport, Conn.: Greenwood, 1981.

Ewen, Stuart. *Captains of Consciousness: Advertising and the Social Roots of the Consumer Culture.* New York: McGraw-Hill, 1976.

Fass, Paula. *The Damned and the Beautiful: American Youth in the 1920's.* New York: Oxford University Press, 1977.

Flamming, Douglas. *Creating the Modern South: Millhands and Managers in Dalton, Georgia, 1884–1984.* Chapel Hill: University of North Carolina Press, 1992.

Fleischauer, Carl, and Beverly Brannan. *Documenting America, 1935–1943.* Berkeley: University of California Press, 1988.

Flink, James J. *The Car Culture.* Cambridge: MIT Press, 1975.

Fuller, Kathryn H. *At the Picture Show: Small-Town Audiences and the Creation of Movie Fan Culture.* Washington, D.C.: Smithsonian Institution Press, 1996.

Galbraith, John Kenneth. *The Great Crash.* Boston: Houghton Mifflin, 1954.

Gordon, Ian. *Comic Strips and Consumer Culture, 1890–1945.* Washington, D.C.: Smithsonian Institution Press, 1998.

Gowans, Alan. *The Comfortable House: North American Suburban Architecture, 1890–1930.* Cambridge: MIT Press, 1986.

Grantham, Dewey W. *The South in Modern America: A Region at Odds.* New York: HarperCollins, 1994.

Green, Harvey. *The Uncertainty of Everyday Life, 1915–1945.* New York: HarperCollins, 1992.

Gregory, James N. *American Exodus: The Dust Bowl Migration and Okie Culture in California.* New York: Oxford University Press, 1989.

Gregory, Ross. *America 1941: A Nation at the Crossroads.* New York: Free Press, 1989.

Grossman, James R. *Land of Hope: Chicago, Black Southerners, and the Great Migration.* Chicago: University of Chicago Press, 1989.

Hallwas, John E. *The Bootlegger: A Story of Small-Town America.* Urbana: University of Illinois Press, 1998.

Homel, Michael W. *Down from Equality: Black Chicagoans and the Public Schools, 1920–41.* Urbana: University of Illinois Press, 1984.

Hoy, Suellen. *Chasing Dirt: The American Pursuit of Cleanliness.* New York: Oxford University Press, 1995.

Huggins, Nathan Irvin. *Harlem Renaissance.* New York: Oxford University Press, 1971.

Hurley, F. Jack. *Portrait of a Decade: Roy Stryker and the Development of Documentary Photography in the 1930s.* Baton Rouge: Louisiana State University Press, 1972.

Hurt, R. Douglas. *The Dust Bowl: An Agricultural and Social History.* Chicago: Nelson-Hall, 1981.

Jackson, Kenneth T. *The Ku Klux Klan in the Cities, 1915–1930.* New York: Oxford University Press, 1967.

Johnson, Brooks. *Mountaineers to Main Streets: The Old Dominion as Seen through the Farm Security Administration Photographs.* Norfolk, Va.: Chrysler Museum, 1985.

——— *Just Before the War: Urban America from 1935 to 1941 as Seen by the Photographers of the Farm Security Administration.* Balboa, Calif.: Newport Harbor Art Museum, 1968.

Kao, Deborah Martin, Laura Katxman, and Jenna Webster. *Ben Shahn's New York: The Photography of Modern Times.* Cambridge: Fogg Art Museum, Harvard University Art Museum, 2000.

Karl, Barry D. *The Uneasy State: The United States from 1915 to 1945.* Chicago: University of Chicago Press, 1983.

Kazin, Alfred. *On Native Ground.* New York: Reynal & Hitchcock, 1942.

Kenney, William Howland. *Recorded Music in American Life: The Phonograph and Popular Memory, 1890–1945.* New York: Oxford University Press, 1999.

Kluger, Richard. *Ashes to Ashes: America's Hundred-Year Cigarette War, the Public Health, and the Unabashed Triumph of Philip Morris.* New York: Knopf, 1996.

Kyvig, David E. *Repealing National Prohibition.* Chicago: University of Chicago Press, 1979. 2nd ed. Kent, Ohio: Kent State University Press, 2000.

Kyvig, David E., and Mary-Ann Blasio, comp. *New Day/New Deal: A Bibliography of the Great American Depression, 1929–1941.* Westport, Conn.: Greenwood, 1988.

Lange, Dorothea, and Paul Schuster Taylor. *An American Exodus: A Record of Human Erosion in the Thirties.* New Haven: Yale University Press, 1969.

Larson, Edward J. *Summer for the Gods: The Scopes Trial and America's Continuing Debate over Science and Religion.* New York: Basic Books, 1997.

Lears, Jackson. *Fables of Abundance: A Cultural History of Advertising in America.* New York: Basic Books, 1994.

Lemons, J. Stanley. *The Woman Citizen: Social Feminism in the 1920s.* Urbana: University of Illinois Press, 1971.

Leonard, Olen, and G. P. Loomis. *Culture of a Contemporary Rural Community: El Cerrito, New Mexico.* Rural Life Studies: 1. Washington, D.C.: U.S. Department of Agriculture, Bureau of Agricultural Economics, 1941.

Leuchtenburg, William. *Franklin D. Roosevelt and the New Deal, 1933–1940.* New York: Harper and Row, 1963.

———. *The Perils of Prosperity, 1914–1932.* Chicago: University of Chicago Press, 1955.

Levenstein, Harvey. *Revolution at the Table: The Transformation of the American Diet.* New York: Oxford University Press, 1988.

———. *Paradox of Plenty: A Social History of Eating in Modern America.* New York: Oxford University Press, 1993.

Lewis, David Levering. *When Harlem Was in Vogue.* New York: Oxford University Press, 1981.

Lewis, Thomas S. W. *Empire of the Air: The Men Who Made Radio.* New York: HarperCollins, 1991.

Lindsay, Ben B., and Wainwright Evans. *Companionate Marriage.* New York: Boni & Liveright, 1927.

Litwack, Leon F. *Trouble in Mind: Black Southerners in the Age of Jim Crow.* New York: Knopf, 1998.

Lowitt, Richard. *The New Deal and the West.* Bloomington: Indiana University Press, 1984.

Lynd, Robert S., and Helen Merrill Lynd. *Middletown: A Study in Modern American Culture.* New York: Harcourt, Brace and World, 1929.

———. *Middletown in Transition: A Study in Cultural Conflicts.* New York: Harcourt, Brace and World, 1937.

Marchand, Roland. *Advertising the American Dream: Making Way for Modernity, 1920–1940.* Berkeley: University of California Press, 1985.

Marsh, Margaret. *Suburban Lives.* New Brunswick: Rutgers University Press, 1990.

Marty, Martin E. *Pilgrims in Their Own Land: 500 Years of Religion in America.* Boston: Little, Brown, 1984.

May, Lary. *Screening Out the Past: The Birth of Mass Culture and the Motion Picture Industry.* New York: Oxford University Press, 1980.

Meikle, Jeffrey L. *Twentieth Century Limited: Industrial Design in America, 1925–1939.* Philadelphia: Temple University Press, 1979.

Mintz, Steven, and Susan Kellogg. *Domestic Revolutions: A Social History of American Family Life.* New York: Free Press, 1988.

Moe, Edward O., and Carl G. Taylor. *Culture of a Contemporary Rural Community: Irwin, Iowa.* Rural Life Studies: 5. Washington, D.C.: U.S. Department of Agriculture, Bureau of Agricultural Economics, 1942.

Moore, Leonard J. *Citizen Klansmen: The Ku Klux Klan in Indiana, 1921–1928.* Chapel Hill: University of North Carolina Press, 1991.

Murchison, Kenneth M. *Federal Criminal Law Doctrines: The Forgotten Influence of National Prohibition.* Durham, N.C.: Duke University Press, 1994.

Murdock, Catherine Gilbert. *Domesticating Drink: Women, Men, and Alcohol, 1880–1940.* Baltimore: Johns Hopkins University Press, 1998.

Nelson, Daniel. *Farm and Factory: Workers in the Midwest, 1880–1990.* Bloomington: Indiana University Press, 1993.

Nelson, Paula M. *The Prairie Winnows Out Its Own: The West River Country of South Dakota in the Years of Depression and Dust.* Iowa City: University of Iowa Press, 1996.

Noggle, Burl. *Into the Twenties: The United States from Armistice to Normalcy.* Urbana: University of Illinois Press, 1974.

Nye, David E. *Electrifying America: Social Meanings of a New Technology, 1880–1940.* Cambridge: MIT Press, 1990.

Ohrn, Karin. *Dorothea Lange and the American Documentary Tradition*. New York: Oxford University Press, 1980.

O'Neal, Hank. *A Vision Shared: A Classic Portrait of America and Its People, 1935–1943*. New York: St. Martin's Press, 1976.

— Palmer, Phyllis. *Domesticity and Dirt: Housewives and Domestic Servants in the United States, 1920–1945*. Philadelphia: Temple University Press, 1989.

Parrish, Michael E. *Anxious Decades: America in Prosperity and Depression, 1920–1941*. New York: W. W. Norton, 1992.

— Riley, Glenda. *Divorce: An American Tradition*. New York: Oxford University Press, 1991.

— Rose, Mark H. *Cities of Light and Heat: Domesticating Gas and Electricity in Urban America*. University Park: Pennsylvania State University Press, 1995.

— Rubin, Joan Shelley. *The Making of Middle-Brow Culture*. Chapel Hill: University of North Carolina Press, 1992.

Schneider, James C. *Should America Go to War? The Debate over Foreign Policy in Chicago, 1939–1941*. Chapel Hill: University of North Carolina Press, 1989.

Schulz, Constance B. *A South Carolina Album, 1936–1948: Documentary Photography in the Palmetto State from the Farm Security Administration, Office of War Information, and Standard Oil of New Jersey*. Columbia: University of South Carolina Press, 1992.

———, ed. *Bust to Boom: Documentary Photography of Kansas, 1936–1949*. Text and commentary by Donald Wooster. Lawrence: University Press of Kansas, 1996.

Sklar, Robert. *Movie-Made America*. Rev. ed. New York: Vintage, 1994.

Sobel, Robert. *The Great Bull Market: Wall Street in the 1920s*. New York: W. W. Norton, 1968.

Spinney, Robert G. *City of Big Shoulders: A History of Chicago*. DeKalb: Northern Illinois University Press, 2000.

Steichen, Edward, ed. *The Bitter Years, 1935–1941: Rural America as Seen by the Photographers of the Farm Security Administration*. New York: Museum of Modern Art, 1962.

Stein, Walter J. *California and the Dust Bowl Migration*. Westport, Conn.: Greenwood, 1973.

Stock, Catherine McNicol. *Main Street in Crisis: The Great Depression and the Old Middle Class on the Northern Plains*. Chapel Hill: University of North Carolina Press, 1992.

Stott, William. *Documentary Expression and Thirties America*. New York: Oxford University Press, 1973.

Stryker, Roy Emerson, and Nancy Wood. *In This Proud Land: America, 1935–1943 as Seen in the FSA Photographs*. Greenwich: New York Graphic Society, 1973.

Tweton, D. Jerome. *The New Deal at the Grass Roots: Programs for the People in Otter Tail County, Minnesota*. St. Paul: Minnesota Historical Society Press, 1988.

Tyack, David, Robert Lowe, and Elisabeth Hansot. *Public Schools in Hard Times: The Great Depression and Recent Years*. Cambridge: Harvard University Press, 1984.

U.S. Bureau of the Census. *Historical Statistics of the United States: Colonial Times to 1957*. Washington, D.C.: GPO, 1960.

Walker, Samuel. *Popular Justice: A History of American Criminal Justice*. 2nd ed. New York: Oxford University Press, 1998.

Waller, Gregory A. *Main Street Amusements: Movies and Commercial Entertainment in a Southern City, 1896–1930*. Washington, D.C.: Smithsonian Institution Press, 1995.

Wandersee, Winifred. *Women's Work and Family Values, 1920–1940*. Cambridge: Harvard University Press, 1981.

Warner, W. Lloyd, and Paul S. Hunt. *The Social Life of a Modern Community*. New Haven: Yale University Press, 1941.

Weiss, Margaret R. *Ben Shahn, Photographer: An Album from the Thirties*. New York: DaCapo Press, 1973.

West, James [Carl Withers]. *Plainville, U.S.A.* New York: Columbia University Press, 1945.

Wollman, David H., and Donald R. Inman. *Portraits in Steel: An Illustrated History of Jones & Laughlin Steel Corporation*. Kent, Ohio: Kent State University Press, 1999.

Woodward, C. Vann. *The Burden of Southern History*. Baton Rouge: Louisiana State University Press, 1960.

Worster, Donald. *Dust Bowl: The Southern Plains in the 1930s*. New York: Oxford University Press, 1979.

Williams, Robert C. *Fordson, Farmall, and Poppin' Johnny: A History of the Farm Tractor and Its Impact on America*. Urbana: University of Illinois Press, 1987.

Wright, Gwendolyn. *Building the Dream: A Social History of Housing in America*. New York: Pantheon, 1981.

Wynne, Waller. *Culture of a Contemporary Rural Community: Harmony, Georgia*. Rural Life Studies: 6. Washington, D.C.: U.S. Department of Agriculture, Bureau of Agricultural Economics, 1943.

Index

About the Author

DAVID E. KYVIG is Presidential Research Professor and Professor of History at Northern Illinois University. He is the author of *Explicit and Authentic Acts: Amending the U.S. Constitution* (winner of the 1997 Bancroft Prize), the editor of *Unintended Consequences of Constitutional Amendment* (2000), *Reagan and the World* (Praeger, 1990) and co-compiler of *New Day/New Deal: A Bibliography of the Great American Depression, 1929–1941* (Greenwood, 1988).